Climate Change and Food Security

Global climatic change has resulted in new and unpredictable patterns of precipitation and temperature, the increased frequency of extreme weather events and rising sea levels. These changes impact all four aspects of food security – availability, accessibility, stability of supply and appropriate nourishment – as well as the entire food system: food production, marketing, processing, distribution and prices.

Climate Change and Food Security focuses on the challenge to food security posed by a changing climate. The book brings together many of the critical global concerns of climate change and food security through local cases based on empirical studies undertaken in Sub-Saharan Africa and the Caribbean. Focusing on risk reduction and the complex nature of vulnerability to climate change, the book includes chapters on the responsiveness of farmers based on traditional knowledge, as well as the critical phenomenon of food insecurity in the urban setting. Other chapters are devoted to efforts made to strengthen resilience through long-term development, with interventions at the regional and national levels of scale. It also examines cross-cutting themes that underlie the strategies employed to achieve food security, including equity, gender, livelihoods and governance.

This edited volume will be of great interest to students and scholars of climate change, food security, environmental management and sustainable development.

Elizabeth Thomas-Hope is Professor Emerita at the University of the West Indies, Jamaica, where she was formerly the first holder of the James Seivright Moss-Solomon (Snr.) Chair of Environmental Management, Director of the Centre for Environmental Management, and Head of the Department of Geography and Geology.

T0384235

Routledge Advances in Climate Change Research

Climate Change and Food Security

Africa and the Caribbean

Edited by Elizabeth Thomas-Hope

Routledge
Taylor & Francis Group

LONDON AND NEW YORK

from Routledge

First published 2017
by Routledge

2 Park Square, Milton Park, Abingdon, Oxfordshire OX14 4RN
52 Vanderbilt Avenue, New York, NY 10017

Routledge is an imprint of the Taylor & Francis Group, an informa business

First issued in paperback 2019

British Library Cataloguing-in-Publication Data
A catalogue record for this book is available from the British Library

Library of Congress Cataloging-in-Publication Data
Names: Thomas-Hope, Elizabeth M., editor, author.
Title: Climate change and food security : Africa and the Caribbean / edited
by Elizabeth Thomas-Hope.
Description: New York : Routledge, 2016.
Identifiers: LCCN 2016030481 | ISBN 9781138204270 (hb) |
ISBN 9781315469737 (ebook)
Subjects: LCSH: Food security--Africa, Sub-Saharan. | Food security--
Caribbean Area. | Food industry and trade--Africa, Sub-Saharan. | Food
industry and trade--Caribbean Area. | Climatic changes--Social aspects--
Africa, Sub-Saharan. | Climatic changes--Social aspects--Caribbean Area.
Classification: LCC HD9017.A357 C55 2016 | DDC 338.1967--dc23
LC record available at https://lccn.loc.gov/2016030481

ISBN: 978-1-138-20427-0 (hbk)
ISBN: 978-0-367-25615-9 (pbk)

Typeset in Goudy
by Saxon Graphics Ltd, Derby

Contents

Illustrations

Figures

Tables

Contributors

Jerram Bateman is a PhD candidate in the Department of Geography, University of Otago, Dunedin, New Zealand. His current research draws on a Sustainable Livelihoods Framework to explore continuity and change in rural livelihoods in Sierra Leone, and his research interests include the role of sport in facilitating development.

Tony Binns is the Ron Lister Professor of Geography at the University of Otago, Dunedin, New Zealand. His research focuses on community-based development among poor communities in Africa. He is a past President of the Commonwealth Geographical Bureau (2009–2016) and the New Zealand Geographical Society (2010–2011).

Anne-Teresa Birthwright holds a BSc degree in Geography from the University of the West Indies, Mona, Jamaica, where she is currently a doctoral candidate. Her research assesses the vulnerability and impacts of climate and economic change on key agricultural sub-sectors in Jamaica, especially the export commodity subsectors.

Mary Caesar is post-doctoral fellow in the Hungry Cities Partnership, Balsillie School of International Affairs, Wilfrid Laurier University, Waterloo, Canada. She has an MA and LLB (University of Cape Town) and PhD (Queen's University, Canada). She researches public health, local governance and race in twentieth-century South Africa.

Ayesha Constable, a doctoral candidate in geography at the University of the West Indies, Mona, Jamaica, is researching climate change and agriculture, with a focus on the vulnerabilities of small farmers, gender, and determinants of adaptation. She is a member of the Jamaica Geographical Society and the Caribbean Youth Environment Network.

Jonathan Crush holds the CIGI Research Chair in Global Migration and Development at the Balsillie School of International Affairs, Wilfrid Laurier University, Waterloo, Canada. He is the founder and Canadian director of the Southern African Migration Programme, the African Food Security Urban Network and the Hungry Cities Partnership.

Anton Eitzinger is a climate change scientist at the Decision and Policy Analysis Research Area, International Center for Tropical Agriculture (CIAT), Cali, Colombia. He focuses on quantifying the impact of climate change on crop systems, the vulnerability of farming communities and monitoring adaptation processes.

Aidan D. Farrell is Lecturer in Plant Physiology in the Department of Life Sciences, The University of the West Indies, St Augustine, Trinidad and Tobago. His research examines the mechanisms used by plants to grow and survive in a changing environment, and he applies this understanding to help improve the sustainability of agricultural systems.

Walter Leal Filho is Professor of Climate Change and Technology at Hamburg University of Applied Sciences, Germany, and he holds the Chair of Environment and Technology at Manchester Metropolitan University, UK.

Gareth Haysom holds a PhD from the University of Cape Town and an MPhil from Stellenbosch University, South Africa. He is currently a researcher in the Urban Food Cluster, the African Centre for Cities, University of Cape Town. His work focuses on urban food governance and food security in the cities of southern Africa.

Halima Abdulkadir Idris holds a BSc degree in geography and an MSc in development (land resources) from Bayero University, Kano, Nigeria. At Bayero, she is currently an assistant lecturer in the Department of Geography and her research focuses on climate change and agriculture, urban change and urban climates.

Linda Johnson-Bhola is a lecturer in the School of Earth and Environmental Sciences, University of Guyana (UG). She holds a CertEd, a BA (Geography) UG, and an MSc (Urban and Regional Planning) the University of the West Indies. She is a Geography Syllabus Review panellist for the Caribbean Secondary Education Certificate.

Jhordanne J. Jones is a research assistant in the Department of Physics at the University of the West Indies, Mona, Jamaica. Her expertise lies in the statistical downscaling of global climate variables to simulate and consequently project the variability in regional climate extremes.

Geoffrey Macharia is a senior lecturer in the Department of Environmental Science at Kenyatta University, Nairobi, Kenya. He is also a researcher and consultant in Ecosystem Services and Management, Environmental Impact Assessment, Sustainable Development, and Land Use Planning and Management.

Cheikh Mbow is a senior scientist at the World Agroforestry Center, focusing on climate change and development issues. He is also Associate Professor at Cheikh Anta Diop University, Dakar, Senegal; Adjunct Associate Professor at Michigan State University; a member of the International Geosphere Biosphere Program (IGBP); and lead author for IPCC WG III.

Haruna Moda Musa is Lecturer in Environmental Health Science at Manchester Metropolitan University, UK. He is a member of the Institute of Environmental Management and Assessment, the UK Indoor Environments Group (UKIEG) and the Higher Education Academy.

Kennedy Muthee is a research fellow at the World Agroforestry Center (ICRAF), Nairobi, Kenya, and a graduate student in Environmental Sciences at Kenyatta University, Nairobi. His research interests are in climate change adaptation and ecosystem services.

Etienne Nel is Professor of Geography at the University of Otago, Dunedin in New Zealand. He was previously lecturer at Rhodes University, South Africa. His research interests are in the areas of community, local and regional development, chiefly in Africa.

Akunne Okoli is a graduate student in the School of Environment, Enterprise and Development at the University of Waterloo, Canada. Her research focuses on biomass metabolism in the context of global and regional biomass production, and trade and interrelationships with land use in food and agricultural systems.

Inês M. Raimundo is Lecturer in Geography at Eduardo Mondlane University, Maputo, Mozambique, and Deputy Dean of Post-Graduate Studies in the Faculty of Arts and Social Sciences since 2012. She co-ordinates the Mozambique components of the Southern African Migration Programme and the Hungry Cities Partnership.

Kevon Rhiney is Assistant Professor of Geography at Rutgers University, New Jersey, USA. He was formerly Lecturer in Geography at the University of the West Indies, Mona, Jamaica, and a member of the Jamaica Civil Society Consulting Group for the Inter-American Development Bank (IADB).

Balfour Spence is a professor in the Applied Disaster and Emergency Studies Department at Brandon University, Manitoba, Canada. He formerly lectured in Geography and Environmental Management at the University of the West Indies, Mona, Jamaica, and the University of Manitoba, Canada.

Tannecia S. Stephenson is Senior Lecturer in Physics at the University of the West Indies, Mona, Jamaica, and is a member of the Climate Studies Group, Mona. Her research interests are in Caribbean climate variability and change, climate extremes, seasonal predictions using statistical models and statistical downscaling.

Adamu Idris Tanko is Professor of Geography and Deputy Vice-Chancellor at Bayero University, Kano, Nigeria. His main areas of research are environment and development, climate change and irrigation management, and he is currently co-ordinating research on energy and water resources in the drylands of West Africa.

Michael A. Taylor is Professor of Physics and Head of Department at the University of the West Indies, Mona, Jamaica, and Director of the Climate Research Group,

Mona. His research includes examining the mechanisms that drive climate variability, investigating the climate change signal, the seasonal prediction of climate and climate data issues in the Caribbean.

Isaac Kow Tetteh is Senior Lecturer in Climate and Environmental Science and the current Head of Department of Theoretical and Applied Biology at the Kwame Nkrumah University of Science and Technology (KNUST), Kumasi, Ghana. He is currently developing products to mitigate greenhouse gas drivers of climates.

Elizabeth Thomas-Hope is Professor Emerita at the University of the West Indies (UWI), Mona, Jamaica. She was formerly the James Seivright Moss-Solomon (Snr.) Chair of Environmental Management and Director of the Centre for Environmental Management at the UWI. She is leader of the Jamaica research team on food security in the Hungry Cities Partnership, and President of the Commonwealth Geographical Bureau (2016–).

Preface

Elizabeth Thomas-Hope

The seeds of the idea for this book were sown at a conference of the Commonwealth Geographical Bureau (CGB) in partnership with the Centre for Environmental Management, The University of the West Indies, Mona, held in Kingston, Jamaica, in April 2015.[1] Most of the chapters that follow are based on papers presented in that forum. As with the conference, so now with this book, the focus is on the effects of global climate change as it impacts food security outcomes. These occur in various direct and indirect ways for those most at risk of food insecurity, namely the rural and urban poor of the Global South. The themes are explored through empirical studies drawn from Africa[2] and the Caribbean.[3]

There is no presumption that Africa and the Caribbean demonstrate the extent of the range of climate change and food security variability of the Global South, but they do demonstrate some of the biophysical and socio-economic diversity that combine to determine levels of vulnerability. Further, the focus is on the adaptive responses which are stimulated to protect food security against the risks associated with a changing, different and unpredictable climate, with few formal risk-management mechanisms. Climate change, in both sub-Saharan Africa and the Caribbean, shows common trends of more intense drought in most parts, the increased occurrence of extreme cyclonic activity resulting in floods, and the effects of rising sea levels in coastal areas. These are critical factors for regions where most rural livelihoods are based on rain-fed, smallholder farming. Further, this book includes chapters dealing with the poorly understood but critical emerging phenomenon of food insecurity in the urban setting. In both regions, the livelihoods of the urban poor are a combination of formal and informal sector activities, with high dependence on the latter. These livelihoods, and the people whose lives they represent, are among the rural and urban poor of the Global South, known to be most vulnerable to the effects of climate change on their food security.

Mitigating climate change through reducing the emission of greenhouse gases is an issue of major global importance and highly relevant within the context of climate change and enhancing food security, but it is not the focus of this volume. Here, the main concern is the responses which are stimulated by climate change. This demonstrates the diversified livelihood strategies employed at the level of rural and urban communities in which households must secure food to cope with the threat of hunger in the short term, or adapt patterns of production and consumption to optimize potential food security and build resilience for the future. The book thus provides insights into the nature of perceptions and awareness of climate change, and the lived experiences that influence remarkably similar human responses to this common global threat, albeit in two very different regions of the world.

Notes

1 The work of the conference was supported by: the Centre for Environmental Management, University of the West Indies, Jamaica; the Commonwealth Geographical Bureau through a grant from the Singapore Journal of Tropical Geography; the Hungry Cities Partnership, Balsillie School of International Affairs, Wilfrid Laurier University, Canada; and the Grace Kennedy Foundation, Jamaica.
2 The focus is on sub-Saharan Africa.
3 The Caribbean is taken to include the islands and mainland countries of the Caribbean Community (CARICOM).

Introduction

The interface of climate change and food security

Elizabeth Thomas-Hope

Background

Mitigating climate change and achieving food security are two of the major world challenges of the twenty-first century. Both are multifaceted issues with interactions that are affected by a wide range of biophysical and socio-economic drivers. There is now a strong indication that there are multiple connections between a globally changing climate and food systems, so that any significant change in one of these will have major implications for the other. As climatic conditions impact food systems in ways that affect food security, so also the effort to improve food security further increases the demands for expanding the production of food crops and livestock, food processing, packaging and distribution with significant increases in greenhouse gas (GHG) emission, thus intensifying the determinants of climate change. Besides, none of the components are static, and the interface between climate and food represents a dynamic set of interactions. The climate is changing, but so also is the global population growing, urbanization increasing and food is in the midst of a major transition. A feature of the food transition is that traditional diets are often being replaced by less nutritionally beneficial options. The trend is towards higher consumption of calories, fats and animal products, as populations become influenced by the globalized marketing strategies of 'big food' which is changing food preferences, including those of the poor.

The global population is estimated to rise from its total of 7.2 billion in 2015 to a projected 9.6 billion by 2050 (FAO 2010; UNDESA 2015). The growth will be almost entirely in the low-income countries of the Global South, with 49 of the least developed countries projected to double in size from around 900 million people in 2013 to 1.8 billion in 2050 (UNDESA 2015). Whereas the urban population accounted for 34 per cent of the global population in 1960, the proportion rose to 54 per cent in 2014 and is predicted to continue at an approximate rate of 1.64 per cent per year between 2015 and 2030 (WHO 2016). Most of the urbanization will also be in low-income countries, where, by 2017, it is estimated that the majority of people will be living in urban areas.

In light of the pattern of population growth, food security is of paramount importance. Although sufficient food is currently produced in the world for all, an estimated billion people go hungry; another billion people overconsume

(Beddington *et al.* 2012). By the 2050s, depending on the sub-region, the proportion of the population undernourished[1] is projected to increase by 25–90 per cent compared to the 2013 figures (World Bank 2013). The state of food security is not uniform, and there has been considerable progress in some countries (FAO 1999). In others, for example, in central, eastern, and southern Africa, more than 40 per cent of the population is undernourished, and the number has risen since the beginning of the present century (Desanker and Magadza *et al.* 2001). The percentage of those undernourished in the population of the Caribbean Community (CARICOM) has been trending downwards since the early 1990s, declining from a high of 27 per cent in 1990–92 to 20 per cent in 2014–16, a reduction of 7 per cent (CARICOM 2014; FAO 2015). But, as in the case of Africa, undernourishment is not evenly distributed across the region and in Haiti, with 60 per cent of CARICOM's population of 17.5 million, 53.4 per cent of the population (5.7 million persons) are undernourished, accounting for approximately 90 per cent of the undernourished persons in the region (ibid.). Furthermore, while the calorie intake in most of the rest of the Caribbean meets the required amount, this is only an average figure and many persons fall below the average. The question of the sustainability of this trend is raised by the food import bill, which is in excess of US$ 4 billion annually, an increase of 50 per cent since 2000, with a projected increase to US $ 8–10 billion by 2020, if food policies continue unchanged. Much of this food consists of processed products, refined carbohydrates, which are calorie-dense, high in fats, sweeteners and sodium (ibid.).

Within the context of the global distribution of population growth, urbanization and the changing value placed on different types of food, there is a major issue of concern. It is that food insecurity, which is already widespread among the poor of the Global South, and negatively impacting human well-being and inhibiting economic growth, is predicted to become more intense as a consequence of ongoing climate change (Nelson *et al.* 2011).

Climate change and food security

The greatest anthropogenic contributors to climate change are the socio-economic systems of the Global North, but the greatest effects of the change are projected to be most acutely felt in the tropics and sub-tropics, thus the countries of the South. As observed in the climate trends of sub-Saharan Africa and the Caribbean, the global climate is changing and countries vary in the patterns occurring in temperature and rainfall regimes, as well as in the intensity of extreme events and in sea level rise. These trends are outlined and expanded upon in Part I of this book and the point is emphasized that climate change is creating unfamiliar 'new' climate regimes (Chapter 2) with unpredictable weather patterns to which people have to adjust, adapt and strengthen resilience to manage the associated risks of future hazards and, despite this, to secure food.

The increasing annual variability in weather patterns intensifies the fragility of food systems by reducing or destroying production, especially that involving rain-fed crops and livestock in environments prone to degradation and desertification, and fish stocks where marine temperatures are affected (Beddington *et al.* 2012). For technologically capable, knowledgeable and economically secure farmers and companies, the adaptation process may be challenging but entirely manageable. In contrast, as studies described in the chapters of Part II show, for small-scale farmers lacking a sophisticated technological and information base, adaptation has to be limited to what they can do to adapt to the new climatic patterns on the basis of their lived experience and perception of the situation. Their capacity to adapt is also conditioned by their available assets to change production techniques and diversify their livelihoods. Besides, the challenge is not only one of food production in rural areas, but there are also important urban dimensions, highlighted in the chapters of Part III of this book. As Frayne *et al.* (2012:1) have argued, 'the current urban transition should be centre-stage in the global relationship between climate change, poverty and food security'.

Urban food insecurity is typically experienced as a problem of food accessibility, determined chiefly by the price of food in different outlets and locations. Climatic conditions affect the cost of food that reaches urban centres, as well as disrupt food supplies within cities, for example, at times of cyclones and floods. As in rural settings, so also in urban, these drivers of food accessibility most acutely impact the food security of the poor. At yet another level, adaptation to the effects of climate change to protect food security should be seen in a broader context than specifically rural or urban challenges. To support the adaptive efforts at rural and urban scales, there needs to be appropriate institutional structures and programmes to bring about sustainable food systems. Part IV of this book looks at this aspect of adaptation, namely strengthening long-term development through interventions at the regional and national levels of scale.

Food security: food systems and food chains

Food security is the outcome of food-related processes throughout the food chain – from the points of production (the sources of the food) to those of consumption (households and individuals) – namely, the overall food system. It is widely expressed in terms of availability (amount and types of food produced and distributed), accessibility (affordability and other aspects of gaining access to the nutritionally necessary and culturally acceptable/preferred food), utilization (nutritional and social value and safety of food) and stability or regularity of the above elements. This framing of food security has recently been expanded to include food adequacy, acceptability and agency (Chapters 10 and 11) as well as food prejudices and preferences (Chapter 12). Nor are all foods that are sought after or preferred necessarily the most nutritious.

A household's food system incorporates all the food chains it participates in to meet its consumption requirements and culturally conditioned dietary preferences. Even in simple food systems, there is need of some items (even sugar and salt) that are produced outside the local area to complement the food produced locally. This shows that it is very unlikely that a household can achieve food security without some cash expenditure, for which an income is required. Virtually all households need livelihoods that include the acquisition of sufficient purchasing power to buy either all or some of the food that they need but cannot or do not produce. Therefore, the circumstances which lead to variations in food security or insecurity for the household are the dynamic interplay of self-sufficiency to produce, and earning capacity to purchase, food from other locations (including other countries). At the level of the state, this translates into there being the need for domestic production and distribution together with food importation. The balance between these two food sources is based on policy decisions determined by the economics of the options and trade-offs between food self-sufficiency and food dependency.

Urban food insecurity has been identified as presenting a different food systems challenge to rural food insecurity; it has a different set of relationships with climate change and requires different governance approaches (Battersby 2012). Access to food in urban areas involves drawing food from a wide range of sources which have complex and diverse supply chains (ibid.). The drivers of vulnerability to urban food security are often long term and function over long distances based on the connection of a series of resource flows, each with their own types of vulnerability and resilience. It is here argued (Chapter 10) that cities of the Global South would be well served by adopting a food mandate that looks beyond production, one that actively seeks to mitigate against food system shocks and volatility – shocks and volatility driven by a fast-changing food system – which are now intensified by the changing climate

Global and local linkages

Because of the complexity of food chains, the impact of climate change at a specific location does not affect the food solely based on the conditions at that place, but also through the relationships with other places. The effects combine all levels of scale from the global to the local, and the rural to the urban. Thus, climatic impacts on food production at a particular global location resonate through a series of flows and linkages to the points of processing and consumption, which can be at places great distances away. At one end of the continuum there are those countries, communities and households that depend on a simple food chain as they subsist almost entirely on the food they produce, gather, catch, process and prepare themselves. At the other end of the continuum are those that depend entirely on the purchase of food which reaches them at the end of a complex food chain comprised of production, processing, packaging and distribution. At whatever point a country, community or household may be on this continuum from total food self-sufficiency to total dependence on other sources of food, the means to produce and/or purchase different components of their diet are the determinants whereby their food needs are met.

In this present age, communities are not totally isolated and are usually part of interconnected systems at various levels of scale – global, regional, national and local – all of which, to a greater or lesser extent, condition the food systems. Therefore, as the Food and Agriculture Organization (FAO) has pointed out:

…it is not enough to limit assessments of the impacts of climate change on domestic production in food-insecure countries. Taking a global picture, one also needs to assess climate change impacts on foreign exchange earnings; determine the ability of food surplus countries to increase their commercial exports or food aid; and analyze how the incomes of the poor will be affected by climate change.

(FAO 2003: 365–366)

Rural and urban linkages

Urban populations, in particular, are highly dependent on the cash economy to secure food produced in rural areas of the same or another country, rather than growing their own. This makes them vulnerable to the effects of climate change across a far broader geographical range than is assumed in rural food security and climate change research. Therefore, it appears that a blend of formal and informal food systems within the city brings about greater food access for poor urban populations (Battersby 2012; Tawodzera *et al.* 2012). This is evident in chapters in this volume on Cape Town (Chapters 10 and 11), and Maputo (Chapter 12). But, it is not only confined to urban food access, as reflected in the livelihood strategies of coffee producers in rural Jamaica (Chapter 4) where households access food by drawing on varying combinations of flows involving food, cash and people through social networks.

The linkages between rural and urban areas are also the basis of informal food systems created by social networks and social capital, through which gifts of food and remittances of cash to purchase food, connect migrant source and destination households. These flows of cash and kind occur in both directions and are also embedded in international networks of migrants crossing borders of both land and sea. These flows complement and supplement the formal system, sometimes providing an alternative food system and a critical safety net in times of severe stress, especially important where formal institutional safety net structures are lacking.

Food systems are dependent on both the formal and informal processing and distribution, pricing mechanisms and economies at all levels of scale – global, national and household. They are also dependent on the overlapping international, national and local governance structures that directly and indirectly determine the existing systems. Climate change can affect any aspect of the system resulting in unpredictable risks. Therefore, how this interfaces with food security outcomes depends on the political, technical, social and economic capacities that condition and enable, or inhibit, the functioning of the food systems under climate-induced stresses and shocks. It is here suggested that this capacity to effectively respond and adapt can be conceptualized and analysed in terms of a vulnerability–resilience nexus.

Vulnerability–resilience nexus

The balance struck between levels of vulnerability versus resilience largely conditions the capacity of people to counter the effects of a changing and unpredictable climate.

This may only be sufficient to cope with the challenge of obtaining enough food to survive in the short term, or it may be to adapt their livelihood and productive mechanisms to the new conditions within which food is secured in the medium to long term. Not surprisingly, therefore, vulnerability has many dimensions.

Vulnerable regions and locations: exposure to risk

Locational vulnerability can be described in terms of the biophysical conditions that expose places to the worst onslaughts of climate change, thus negatively affecting food production and/or consumption. All chapters in Parts II and III reflect the impact of temperature and rainfall changes on food production and/or consumption. Some places are especially at risk, lying as they do below or at sea level, on small islands, coastal plains or deltas exposed to the threat of marine inundation and flooding; other places are directly in the path of cyclones; others in areas of prevailing and persistent drought and drying, or other seasonal disruptions to temperature and rainfall patterns. Examples of exposure to risk of location are coastal Guyana and Maputo (Chapters 6 and 12), or mountain areas as in Jamaica (Chapters 3 and 4) and drylands as in northern Nigeria and Sierra Leone (Chapters 5 and 9). The informal settlements of the urban poor, particularly in coastal cities, are invariably concentrated on floodplains, deltas and along river banks, all at high risk from the effects of local weather extremes, such as cyclones, resulting in flooding and rising sea levels. The high percentage of the land surface covered by concrete and asphalt adds to the risks that city dwellers experience from the additional effect of restricted water runoff at times of floods and affecting housing assets, especially the informal housing of the poor (Dodman and Satterthwaite 2008; IPCC 2012).

The geographic distribution of risk and vulnerability is likely to shift under the impact of persisting climate change. Droughts in sub-Saharan Africa often translate to famine, which leads to acceleration of rural–urban migration flows to cities that are not equipped to absorb the additional poor urban populations (De Lattre 1988). Small island states, as in much of the Caribbean, with settlements, infrastructures and industrial and service activities concentrated along the coast, will continue to experience shifts in the localities most at risk from sea level rise and the storm surge associated with hurricanes. All such factors represent the geographic redistribution of exposure to risk and locational vulnerability of areas not previously regarded to be vulnerable, as climate change continues and accelerates. The consequences have direct and indirect implications which affect food security.

Assets vulnerability

As all the chapters in Parts II and III of this book indicate, assets include physical assets such as infrastructure and household items; financial assets such as stocks of money, savings and pensions; natural assets such as natural resources; social assets, networks and social capital (remittances and cash and kind gifts/remittances) which are based on the cohesiveness of people and societies; and human assets, which depend on education, knowledge and capabilities. The poor have to try to alter their livelihood patterns to come up with strategies that work to sustain their assets and access to food (Moser and Satterthwaite 2008). Prowse and Scott (2008) posited the view that asset adaptation in the context of climate change determines the extent to which the household will be food secure or insecure. That is to say, that the combined assets owned, whether by the rural or urban poor, can facilitate their adaptation to the impacts of extreme weather conditions in the short term, thereby strengthening their resilience over the medium and long term (Simatele 2012).

Livelihood vulnerability and agency

Livelihood can be defined as the combination of assets, abilities and activities that enable a person or household to survive (Stamoulis and Zezza 2003). The capacity to diversify livelihoods is based on assets, especially marketable skills, to provide alternative or additional sources of income as shown in the chapters of this book. Migration is one of these livelihood shifts from rural to urban, either seasonally (Chapter 5) or more permanently (Chapter 12). The role of abilities and activities in conditioning livelihood vulnerability versus resilience is based on agency or the ability and empowerment, psychological capacity and predisposition that resides in people. Therefore, in households and communities, such qualities enable, even propel, people to respond in positive ways to challenges that present themselves through circumstances – biophysical and socio-economic. Although the way in which agency functions to effect action may not be fully understood, nevertheless, what is evident is that the extent and nature of agency facilitates the livelihood diversification which defines levels of livelihood vulnerability versus resilience.

Migration connects the livelihoods of the rural and urban poor in many places. For some, migration is a calculated livelihood shift as part of their food security coping strategy; people move with a view to increasing earning possibilities elsewhere, usually in the towns and cities. Social networks, social capital and remittances link the rural and urban households, and remittances in cash and food are ways of coping with food insecurity in both localities. But migration can be a 'double-edged sword', with people moving from one food-insecure situation to the next. For as the number of poor living in urban informal settlements grows, the availability of both formal employment and informal opportunities decrease, causing a rise in the numbers of vulnerable people who are food insecure.

Vulnerability of minority-status

Additional shocks and stresses on food accessibility brought on by climatic change are likely to increase the risk of food insecurity among those who are victims of pre-existing socio-economic discrimination. Discrimination can cause the nutritional status to deteriorate among marginalized ethnic minorities, women, young children and elderly, ill and disabled people under pressures increased by the impacts of climate change. Evidence shows a strong correlation between gender inequality and food and nutrition insecurity (FAO 2008; BRIDGE 2015);

even though women constitute the majority of small-scale food producers in the world, they are over-represented among the undernourished. To this is added the often limited access to productive resources, education and decision-making opportunities of women. Nevertheless, social roles and economic situations shape the way women respond to climate change impacts (FAO 2015; Beckford 2012) and despite the challenges, women are often the most active agents of change and the drivers of strategies to secure food for their households (Chapter 8).

Additional stressors exacerbating vulnerability

A further challenge in adapting to the impacts of climate change occurs when the economic stresses of fluctuating international markets (as for example, coffee and cocoa in Jamaica and cocoa in Trinidad and Tobago (Chapters 3 and 4) are added to the limitations of assets and livelihoods. Other societal stressors increasing vulnerability to food insecurity in the context of climate change include the burden of disease, political instability and armed conflict. These have been the experience of countries such as Sierra Leone and Mozambique (Chapters 9 and 12) where food systems, and development more generally, have been undermined by years of civil war and disease pandemics.

The temperature and precipitation regimes associated with climate change alter the location of breeding grounds of insect vectors, causing new patterns of pests and diseases to emerge (IPCC 1998). These vector-borne diseases affect plants (including food crops) as indicated in all the small-scale producing communities discussed in this book. The consequences are new risks for ecosystem health, thus reducing the capacity for ecosystem services, food production and food safety.

Additionally, emerging climatic variables increase the spread of water-borne diseases such as malaria and trypanosomiasis, and mosquito-borne viral diseases such as dengue, Nile fever, chikungunya and zika, together with typhoid, cholera and schistosomiasis, and poverty-related diseases such as tuberculosis (Desanker and Magadza 2001; FAO 2008). The health and well-being of people, especially those already struggling to survive in conditions of poverty, add to the stress of climate-driven dislocation of livelihoods. They suffer from the increased difficulty of physically accessing available food, and impaired physiological capacity to absorb nutrients in food consumed and thereby benefiting from its nutrient value (FAO 2008). Additionally, at the national level, disease epidemics as, for example, the HIV/AIDS pandemic and Ebola in parts of Africa, such as Sierra Leone and Mozambique (Chapters 9 and 12), have placed overwhelming strain on the health infrastructure, virtually negating any development and poverty-reduction efforts that had previously been made. Additionally, the increased morbidity and mortality have led to greater national and household economic vulnerability resulting from major losses of productive potential and personal income, intensifying potential vulnerability to the risk of food insecurity.

Governance issues which pervade food systems at global, national and local levels underpin many of the determinants of food insecurity in rural and urban areas. Good governance structures, at all levels, enhance resilience in the face of all exposure to risk, including those related to climate change and food security. Amartya Sen (1981) stressed the importance of governance, institutions and politics for food security (Purdon 2014). The converse is that poor or corrupt governance structures negatively impact food systems, even under conditions of minimal political instability. But where such instability is severe, and armed conflict prevails, adaptation to climate change is left unattended and food production, transportation, marketing, and access to food become totally politicized. As the evidence has shown, civil war has had serious implications for levels of vulnerability, leading to chronic food insecurity at best and the onset of acute lack of food, hunger and starvation at worst.

Sustainable development as long-term strategy for adaptation to climate change

Considering the diversity of environmental and social settings in which food production and consumption take place, solutions for strengthening resilience will differ. But what is evident is that a prerequisite for sustainability in the context of climate change requires that the underlying causes of vulnerability be addressed, including the structural inequalities (IPCC 2012).

Structural frameworks and institutional involvement through knowledge sharing and technical and economic support, are essential for reducing vulnerability and strengthening resilience to manage changes that impact both the production and consumption sides of food security. In addition to institutional involvement, it is also critical that the most vulnerable – namely the poor of the Global South – are central to the discourse, recognizing that systems can only be sustainable if they are culturally grounded and socially coherent. In this scenario of climate change and food security, the resilience of small-scale farming and fishing is critical for bringing about sustainable food production. The traditional knowledge invested in local agricultural communities not only provides practical grounds for their centrality in policy and action but importantly, it empowers, facilitates agency, endorses legitimacy and encourages social inclusivity.

Therefore, it is a moral and pragmatic imperative that the land of smallholders in the countries where this sector dominates domestic food production – including sub-Saharan Africa and the wider Caribbean – involves protection against land grabbing as discussed in this book (Chapter 13). Failure to do so would be to encourage the dispossession of large numbers of small-scale farmers and the significant loss of food production capacity, with its associated security threats. At the same time, such commodification of land for transfer to biofuel production would lead to further acceleration of climate change through the increased GHG emission that would result.

Additionally, the small-scale farmer, for reasons of livelihood and socio-cultural connections to the land, potentially offers better protection of ecosystems, and provides landscape adaptation approaches that can play a vital role in enhancing the ability to promote adaptation and sustainable land management. Besides, small-scale production provides better possibilities for protecting biodiversity and agricultural diversity and consequently of protecting ecosystem services (Brookfield *et al.* 2002; Thomas-Hope and Spence 2002). Biodiversity and ecosystem-based adaptation (EbA), seek to promote societal resilience via ecosystems management and conservation at the landscape level. This approach recognizes the centrality of ecosystems in the adaptation process, and its relevance, in particular to agriculture, is discussed here (Chapter 14) in relation to projects carried out in Burkina Faso and Mali.

Managing risk underlies other adaptive strategies for dealing with the impacts of climate change under current conditions and into the increasingly uncertain future. Among the approaches that could be promoted, one is to support systems designed to share the burden between stakeholders across private and government sectors, which are sustainable over time. Protecting food systems with insurance schemes for small-scale food producers against potential future risks from the effects of climate change offers such an approach to providing a safety net in the event of climate hazards, especially extreme events such as drought and hurricanes. This approach is presented here as a model for risk management policy in the case of the Caribbean Community (Chapter 15).

Conclusion

Beyond the geographies of the rural and the urban, cross-cutting issues are explored in the chapters of this book that reflect the complexities of vulnerability and resilience at the interface of climate change and food security. These are based on the nature of assets, levels of agency, livelihoods dependent on various combinations of formality and informality, as well as combinations of food self-sufficiency and external dependence, reliance on simple production systems, or insertion into national and international commercial trade. A further cross-cutting theme relates to the governance structures. Safeguarding food security in the face of climate change implies avoiding the disruptions or declines in global and local food supplies that could result from shocks from political and economic change.

At the interface between climate change and food security are the locational, political, economic and socio-cultural determinants of the balance between vulnerability and resilience. The extent of the potential negative impacts of climate change on food security will be determined by the vulnerability or resilience of countries, communities and households. This book is intended to increase our insights into the multiple impacts of climate change on the ways in which livelihoods exist, are challenged and changed, and the circumstances under which food security or insecurity is the lived experience, especially of the poor. This increases understanding of the ways in which various vulnerabilities are or could be transformed into different levels of resilience.

Undoubtedly, there are many elements that need to combine to move towards a significant and sustainable reduction in the vulnerability of the poor to the impact of climate change on their food security. Most of these issues are outside the scope of this book. But, suffice it to say, sustainable food systems that will adapt to and endure the current and projected future risks associated with climate change, and will not further exacerbate the drivers of climate change, will depend on national food systems being embedded in an effective interplay of governance, knowledge and action at all levels of scale – from household and community to state and international policies. It is imperative that at every level, the effort be endorsed and action taken to avert the possibility of food insecurity worsening as a consequence of the effects of climate change.

Note

1 FAO defines hunger as being synonymous with undernourishment and it is measured by food deprivation as reflected in the level of intake of dietary energy (FAO 2015).

References

Battersby, J. (2012) 'Urban Food Security and Climate Change: A System of Flows', in B. Frayne, C. Moser and G. Ziervogel (eds.) *Climate Change, Assets and Food Security in Southern African Cities*, Oxford and New York: Routledge, Earthscan, pp. 35–56.

Beckford, C. (2012) 'Issues in Caribbean Food Security: Building Capacity in Local Food Production Systems' in A. Aladjadjiyan (ed.) *Food Production – Approaches, Challenges and Tasks*, InTech. Available at: www.intechopen.com/books/food-production-approaches challenges-and-tasks/issues-in-caribbean-food-security-building-capacity-in-local-food-production-systems.

Beddington, J., Asaduzzaman, M., Clark, M., Fernandez, A., Guillou, M., Jahn, M., Erda, L., Mamo, T., Van Bo, N., Nobre, C. A., Scholes, R., Sharma, R. and Wakhungu, J. (2012) *Achieving Food Security in the Face of Climate Change: Final Report from the Commission on Sustainable Agriculture and Climate Change*. CGIAR Research Program on Climate Change, Agriculture and Food Security (CCAFS). Copenhagen, Denmark. Available at: www.ccafs.cgiar.org/commission.

BRIDGE (2015) 'Gender and Food Security Cutting Edge', Sussex: University of Sussex Institute of Development Studies, Issue number 109. Available at: www.bridge.ids.ac.uk.

Brookfield, H., Padoch, C., Parsons, H. and Stocking, M. (eds.) (2002) *Cultivating Biodiversity: Understanding, Analysing and Using Agricultural Diversity*, London: The United Nations University.

CARICOM (2014) 'Regional Statistics, Caribbean Community, 2014'. Available at: www.caricomstats.org/popdata.htm.

De Lattre, A. (1988) 'What Future for the Sahel?', *OECD Observer*, 153, 19–21.

Desanker, P., Magadza, C., Allali, A., Basalirwa, C., Boko, M., Dieudonne, G., Downing, T. E., Dube, P. O., Githeko, A., Githendu, M., Gonzalez, P., Gwary, D., Jallow, B., Nwafor, J., Scholes, R. Contributing authors: Amani, A., Bationo, A., Butterfield, R., Chafil, R., Feddema, J., Hilmi, K., Mailu, G. M., Midgley, G., Ngara, T., Nicholson, S., Olago, D., Orlando, B., Semazzi, F., Unganai, L., Washington, R. (2001) 'Africa', *Intergovernmental Panel on Climate Change (IPCC) Synthesis Report*, Chapter 10. Available at: http://ipcc.ch/ipccreports/tar/wg2/pdf/wg2TARchap10.pdf.

Dodman, D. and Satterthwaite, D. (2008) 'Institutional Capacity, Climate Change Adaptation and the Urban Poor', *IDS Bulletin* 39 (4): 67–74.

FAO (1999) *The State of Food Insecurity in the World*, Rome: Food and Agriculture Organization of the United Nations.

FAO (2008) *Climate Change and Food Security: A Framework Document*, Rome: Food and Agriculture Organization of the United Nations.

FAO (2010) *The State of Food Insecurity in The World: Addressing Food Insecurity in Protracted Crises*, Rome: Food and Agriculture Organization of the United Nations. www.fao.org/docrep/013/i1683e/i1683e.pdf

FAO (2015) *State of Food Insecurity in the CARICOM Caribbean. Meeting the 2015 Hunger Targets: Taking Stock of Uneven Progress*, Bridgetown, Barbados: FAO Regional Office.

Frayne, B., Moser, C. and Ziervogel, G. (2012) 'Understanding the Terrain: The Climate Change, Assets and Food Security Nexus in Southern African Cities' in B. Frayne, C. Moser and G. Ziervogel (eds.) *Climate Change, Assets and Food Security in Southern African Cities*, Oxford: Routledge, Earthscan.

IPCC (1998) *Special Report on Regional Impacts of Climate Change*, Cambridge: Cambridge University Press.

IPCC (2012) *Managing the Risks of Extreme Events and Disasters to Advance Climate Change Adaptation, Summary for Policymakers*, Cambridge: Cambridge University Press.

Moser, C. and Satterthwaite, D. (2008) *Towards Pro-Poor Adaptation to Climate Change in the Urban Centres of Low- And Middle-Income Countries*, GURC & IIED Discussion Paper Series, Climate Change and Cities 3.

Nelson, G. C, Rosegrant M. W., Palazzo A., Gray I., Ingersoll C., Robertson R., Tokgoz S., Zhu T., Sulser, T. B., Ringler, C., Msangi, S. and You, L. (2011) *Climate Change: Impact on Agriculture and Costs of Adaptation and Food Security, Farming, and Climate Change to 2050*, Washington, DC: International Food Policy Research Institute.

Prowse, M. and Scott, L. (2008) 'Assets and Adaptation: An Emerging Debate', *IDS Bulletin*, 39 (4): 42–52.

Purdon, M. (2014) 'The Comparative Turn in Climate Change Adaptation and Food Security Governance Research', CCAFS Working Paper No. 92. Copenhagen, Denmark: CGIAR Research Program on Climate Change, Agriculture and Food Security (CCAFS). Available at: www.ccafs.cgiar.org.

Sen, A. (1981) *Poverty and Famines: An Essay on Entitlement and Deprivation*, Oxford: Oxford University Press.

Simatele, D. (2012) 'Asset Adaptation and Urban Food Security in a Changing Climate: A case study of Kalingalinga and Linda Compounds in Lusaka-Zambia' in B. Frayne. C. Moser and G. Ziervogel (eds,) *Climate Change, Assets and Food Security in Southern African Cities*, pp. 110–148, New York: Earthscan.

Stamoulis, K. and Zezza, A. (2003) *Conceptual Framework for National, Agricultural, Rural Development, and Food Security Strategies and Policies*, Rome: FAO.

Tawodzera, G., Zanamwe, L. and Crush, J. (2012) 'The State of Food Insecurity in Harare, Zimbabwe', *Urban Food Security Series* No. 13. Kingston, Ontario and Cape Town: Queen's University and the African Food Security Urban Network (AFSUN).

Thomas-Hope, E. and Spence, B. (2002) 'Promoting Agrobiodiversity under Difficulties: The Jamaica-PLEC Experience', *People, Land Management and Environmental Change (PLEC) News and Views*, Vol. 19: 17–24.

United Nations Department of Economic and Social Affairs (UNDESA) Population Division (2015) https://esa.un.org/unpd/wpp.

World Bank (2013) 'Turn Down the Heat: Regional Impacts', Report, June 2013. Available at: www.worldbank.org/en/topic/climatechange/publication/turn-down-the-heat-climate-extremes-regional-impacts-resilience.

World Health Organization (2016) *Urban Population Growth*, WHO Global Health Observatory (GHO). Available at: www.who.int/gho/urban_health/situation_trends/urban_population_growth_text/en.

Part I

Trends in climate change in sub-Saharan Africa and the Caribbean

1 Trends in climate change in Africa

Walter Leal Filho, Isaac Kow Tetteh and Haruna Moda Musa

Introduction

Climate change impacts are known to adversely affect livelihoods in the dry lands of Africa, especially in terms of longer and harsher droughts, shorter and intense precipitation, and floods. The Intergovernmental Panel on Climate Change (IPCC) has documented the scope of this problem in many publications, especially in its latest assessment report, or AR5 (IPCC 2014).

It is widely acknowledged that, even though African countries contribute very little to global CO_2 emissions, Africa is one of the most vulnerable continents to climate change and climate variability. This is so due to a number of reasons. Some of them are:

a) the existence of multiple stressors across Africa, of which land degradation and desertification are examples,
b) declining runoff from water catchments across the continent,
c) high dependence on subsistence agriculture, which in turn increases the impacts of droughts, which negatively interfere with food security,
d) inadequate government mechanisms, and
e) rapid population growth occurring at various levels.

These factors, combined with limited access to financial resources and technologies lead to a limitation on adaptive capacity, which is further exacerbated by factors such as extreme poverty, frequent natural disasters and heavy dependence on rain-fed agriculture.

The likely impacts of climate change are expected to add to these existing stresses and worsen the effects of land degradation. In addition, increased temperature levels are expected to cause damage to agriculture – also leading to additional loss of moisture from the soil, unpredictable and more intense rainfall, and higher frequency and severity of extreme climatic events such as floods and droughts.

These factors are already leading to a loss of biological and economic productivity and putting population in dry lands at risk of short and long-term food insecurity. The Fourth IPCC African Assessment Report estimated that by 2020, between 75 and 250 million people are likely to be exposed to increased water stress and that rain-fed agricultural yields could be reduced by up to 50 per cent in Africa if production practices remained unchanged.

Drought-prone areas are *inter alia* particularly deemed to suffer complex localized impacts of climate variability or change. In the Sahel, for instance, changes in temperature and rainfall patterns have reduced the length of the vegetative period and made it difficult to continue the cultivation of traditional varieties of long and short-cycle millets. Given the social, legislative, market and weather-based sources of vulnerability already prevailing in the region, reduction in agricultural productivity and land area suitable for agriculture, due even to slight climate change, will cause disproportionately large detrimental effects (IPCC 2007).

The communities most vulnerable to the impacts of climate change in Africa are those which inhabit the dry land areas. For instance, the World Health Organization (WHO) states that changes in the patterns in the spread of infectious diseases are likely to be a major consequence of climate change in the dry lands. WHO (2015) indicates that malaria represents a particular and an additional threat in Africa. There are between 300 and 500 million cases of malaria in the world each year, with a very high proportion of those occurring in Africa, largely among the poor. Malaria causes between 1.5 and 2.7 million deaths a year, of which more than 90 per cent are children under five years of age. In addition, malaria slows economic growth in Africa by up to 1.3 per cent each year (UNEP 2005).

Climate change is almost certainly making an already bad situation worse and may already be contributing to the problem of poverty. In one highland area of Rwanda, for instance, malaria incidence increased by 337 per cent in 1987. Some 80 per cent of the increase could be explained by changes in rainfall and rising temperatures. Further, small changes in temperatures and precipitation could trigger malaria epidemics beyond current altitudinal and latitudinal disease limits. Global warming will increase the incidence of floods, warming and drought, all of which are factors in disease transmission. In South Africa, it is estimated that the area suitable for malaria will double and that 7.2 million people will be at risk. Greater climatic variability will introduce the disease to areas previously free of malaria. Populations within these areas lack immunity, which will increase the impact of illness (Zhou *et al.* 2004).

Pastoralist communities are the most vulnerable to climate change. This is because they tend to be located in geographically vulnerable areas such as flood-prone Mozambique, drought-prone Sudan, or cyclone-prone Bangladesh, and in more vulnerable urban locations such as slums and informal settlements, in all cases heavily dependent on natural resources for their livelihoods (Jennings and McGrath 2009).

Vulnerability to climate change is not just a function of geography and dependence on natural resources, it also has social, economic and political dimensions which influence how climate change affects different groups (Leal Filho 2011). Pastoralist communities rarely have insurance to cover loss of property due to drought, storms or cyclones. They cannot pay for the health care required when climate change induced outbreaks of malaria and other diseases occur. They have few alternative livelihood options when their only cow drowns in a flood, or drought kills their maize crop for the year, and they do not have the political clout to ask why their country's early warning system did not warn them of likely flooding. Climate change will also have psychological and cultural effects. For example, beliefs and traditions associated with the seasons being undermined by climate change.

Therefore, climate change interlocks with people's life-worlds differently for different reasons. The geographical location of a community may position it in harm's way when climate change ramifications roll out. The magnitude and impact of the resulting harm may be small or big, depending on where the affected population is located in the politico-economic landscape of the country. This chapter also examines some of the trends on climate change adaptation mechanisms and practice, and their prospects.

Overview of the African Climate Systems

The complexity of the African Climate Systems

The climate systems of Africa, as in other continents, vary from intraseasonal to millennial timescales and beyond. The systems are inherently complex and primarily owe their dynamical existence to competing, interactive processes at the local, regional, and global scales that exert impactful force on the spatio-temporal characteristics of the climates. These processes emanate from eclectic sources, ranging from quasi-stationary orographic forcing (such as Mt. Kilimanjaro in Eastern Africa and the Atlas-Ahaggar Mountain Complex (A-AMC) in Northern Africa), a landmass that houses the world's largest terrestrial desert (the Sahara Desert) and other deserts (such as the Kalahari and the Namib Deserts), several ocean/atmosphere modes internal to the climate systems, to a vast distribution of limnological systems (Janowiak 1988, Marshall *et al.* 2001; Chang *et al.* 2006). Other modulating agents include complex aerosol-radiative forcing/feedback, vegetation dynamics/feedbacks, and land surface forcing, including horizontal distribution of soil moisture and albedo. Continuous anthropogenic perturbations to the built environment, over-exploitation of the continent's natural resources, unabated use of outdated technology, etc., which directly or indirectly reinforce the negative tendencies of greenhouse gas radiative forcing on the climates, cannot be overstated. These interactive factors substantially and differentially, influence the micro-, meso-, and synoptic-scale climate dynamics of any climatic setting over the continent. There is substantial evidence of climate-driven ecological, environmental, socio-economic impacts, as well as human conflicts, on a region, the negative consequences of which require strategic, remedial actions in the face of climate change. For instance, climate-induced human conflicts have been documented (Hsiang *et al.* 2013).

Naturally, the differences in geographical locations of the regions in a vast continent also contribute to their inherent but unique complexities and vulnerabilities to climate variability and change. Eltahir and Gong (1996) have presented the governing equations to demonstrate that West Africa is relatively more vulnerable to regional and global environmental change in comparison to other tropical regional climates. Several hypotheses and/or theories were propounded to explain the sensitivity, especially of the West African Sahel, to local, regional, and global forcings. Among these, was the eminent theory by Charney (1975), which was, however, challenged by critics on some grounds (Tucker *et al.* 1991; Eltahir and Gong 1996). Asnani (2005) has presented a treatise on climate variability and climatological features over the continent. These, together with a plethora of other scholarly research, testify that there appears to be a lack of unified theory which can fully explain the dynamical complexities across the African climate systems as a whole (e.g. Piexoto and Oort 1993; Asnani 2005). A modest appreciation of the climate systems is realized via regional climate studies, which have employed empirical and numerical (dynamical) models, including several downscaling techniques to deal with coarse resolutions of General Circulation Model outputs. Undeniably, the upsurge of dynamical models has improved our understanding of the geophysical mechanisms associated with each regional climate. Nonetheless, such models are imperfect, suggesting that our understanding of the continent's climates is far from perfect, especially for the nonlinear components of the climate systems.

Recently, applications of Computer Science disciplines, such as artificial intelligence, machine learning or data mining, to climate data have become a complementary path to unraveling the regional climate variability, predictability and prediction and the associated stochasticities (Pendse *et al.*; Chen *et al.* 2013; Gonzalez *et al.* 2015). Mainstream climate scientists have acknowledged these potentials and there is telling evidence of Computer Science–Climate Science five-year (2010–2015) Expedition collaborative research outcomes. The $10 m (US) project was sponsored by the USA National Science Foundation on the theme: 'Expedition in Computing. Understanding Climate Change – A Data-Driven Approach' (2015). The project, leaving exemplary footprints in the climate science community, deserves to be mentioned.

Over the geopolitical boundaries of the continent, the following regional climate systems may be distinguished on the basis of their unique climatological features: (i) Northern African Climate System (NACS), (ii) West African Climate System (WACS), (iii) Eastern African Climate System (EACS), (iv) Southern African Climate System (SACS), and Central African Climate System (CACS). However, it should be emphasized that climate knows no political boundaries because teleconnection and transboundary fluxes may have several ramifications which can preferentially influence specific regional climate systems or the continent as a whole. The differential influences from a set of complex, interactive processes are determinants of different rainfall patterns, one of the key economic drivers of the continent, as well as important atmospheric features monitored and evaluated in climate change projections. The next section summarizes the key rainfall features over the regional climate systems.

Regional climates

NACS

The NACS is essentially a desert environment, with complex climate dynamics. Some of the key features intrinsic in a desert are as follows: (i) a major heat source, (ii) lack of moisture and vegetated lands, (iii) lower cloud cover, (iv) dry dynamics – notably subsidence, which is part of the descending branch of the tropical Hadley circulation, (v) heat lows of large amplitudes, (vi) mineral aerosols – in an atmosphere with such dust-laden cloud condensation nuclei which aggressively suppress the growth of rain particles, and (vii) high albedo, among other factors (Rodwell *et al.*1996; Asnani 2005; Chauvin *et al.* 2010).

Different classification systems may be used to describe deserts which, some with key features, will be briefly highlighted here. According to Köppen's system, a desert is characterized by mean annual precipitation (MAP) less than 250 mm, with high surface air temperature. Thornthwaite's system is based on hydrological balance, in which MAP is normalized by mean annual potential evapotranspiration. According to this system, deserts may be described as hyper-arid, arid, semi-arid, and sub-humid where their respective aridity indices (AIs) correspond to <0.03, $0.03 < AI < 0.20$, $0.02 < AI < 0.05$ and $0.50 < AI < 0.75$ (Asnani 2005). Budyko's system is based on an energy balance equation, where a net annual radiation (NAR) incident on the earth's surface is computed in relationship to MAP. Lettau's system describes a desert based on dryness ratio (DR) where the ratio is defined as NAR normalized by the product of latent heat of vaporization and MAP. In this system, hyper-arid, arid, and semi-arid regions have DRs of >10, 7–10 and 2–6, respectively. Desertification, due to several factors, has become a major concern in the face of continental climate change.

The sub-Saharan African Climate Systems (SSACS)

The SSACS consist of the Western, Eastern, Southern, and Central African Climate Systems. Janowiak (1988), in analysing precipitation patterns using rotated empirical orthogonal function (EOF) solutions on seasonal and annual data, concluded that the continental precipitation loading patterns exhibited high spatial coherence, with several dipoles based on retained modes isolated from the eigenfunction spectrum. Rainfall dipoles are anomalies of opposite signs, differentiated by plus ('+') and ('–'), indicative of precipitation surplus and deficit, respectively, relative to a reference/base period. Nicholson (1986) had previously reported similar findings, but based on correlation analysis. Nicholson and Kim (1997) specifically identified 90 homogeneous rainfall patterns across the continent.

In this section, a brief description of the WACS will be used as a paradigm of the SSACS. This is justified on the basis of the West African Sahel's sensitivity to the vagaries of the global climate system, and became a spotlight in the global context, because of the protracted and devastating drought that prevailed for nearly 30 years in the latter part of the twentieth century. Furthermore, analyses of boreal summer (June–July–August–September: JJAS) in countless studies of

African rainfall have revealed that EOF 1 eigenvectors, which contribute most to the total explained variance, are located over the Sahel (Giannini et al. 2005; Polo et al. 2008). The centre of action of the loadings emphasizes the climatological significance of Sahelian mode in the context of climate change.

Several rainfall patterns have been observed over West Africa during the Northern Hemispheric summer. However, in general, four main categories of rainfall anomalies are recognized over the two main eco-climatological zones – the Sahel and the Gulf of Guinea Coast (GOGC) sub-regions (Fontaine et al. 1995; Nicholson and Grist 2001; Grossmann and Klotzbach 2009). These are: (i) anomalies with '+' ('−') signs centred over the Sahel (GOGC), and represent the regular West African rainfall dipole, (ii) inverted dipole with '−' ('+') signs centred over the Sahel (GOGC) sub-regions, (iii) ubiquitous '+' anomalies, constituting rainfall surplus, a non-dipole over the entire region, and (iv) ubiquitous '−' anomalies, indicative of rainfall deficit, a non-dipole over the entire region. These rainfall patterns have their characteristic time series ranging from interannual, subdecadal, decadal to interdecadal variability (Ward 1998; Giannini et al. 2005). These patterns are ascribed to several prevailing forcing agents, with contrasting local, regional, and global sea-surface temperature (SST) patterns and their associated low-to-upper level atmospheric circulations, being some of the prominent factors (Lamb 1978; Folland et al. 1986).

The main Atlantic oceanic modes responsible for the variations of rainfall character are the Atlantic Dipole Mode, Atlantic Niño, North Atlantic Horseshoe Variability and Atlantic Multidecadal Oscillation (Marshall et al. 2001; Chang et al. 2006). Teleconnection from the warm (cold) El Niño–Southern Oscillation (ENSO) events and the Indian Ocean Dipole play a significant role in the interannual/decadal variability of the West African climate. Key atmospheric patterns that are connected to the character of the rainfall are low-level Westerly Jet (850 hPa), African Easterly Jet (600-700 hPa), Tropical Easterly Jet (150-200 hPa) and extratropical intrusion of the North Atlantic Oscillation. The geophysical mechanisms associated with these ocean/atmosphere modes have been explained in detail in the literature (e.g. Hurrel 1995; Grist and Nicholson 2001). In a numerical modeling, orographic forcing emanating from A-AMC over the Saharan Desert was found to have contributed to at least 50 per cent of the Sahelian rainfall (Semazzi and Sun 1997). They also established that the presence of physiographic coastal terrain over the GOGC ensured that this sub-region was not overly dry in the summer season. These findings signify the contributory role of topography in climate dynamics.

For the sake of brevity, the other climate systems will be highlighted superficially to add flavour to the description of SSACS. The rainfall pattern over the EACS is bimodal, consisting of the long rains (March–April–May: MAM) and short rains (October–November–December: OND) seasons. These are distinguished on the basis of the rainfall intensities (Ogallo 1989; Ropelewski and Halpert 1987), with the MAM season superior to the OND season. The two seasons exhibit distinct patterns and high interannual variability (Ogallo 1989; Asnani 2005; Smith and Semazzi 2014). The role of local, regional and spatially remote factors, including contrasting SST patterns, have been linked to the character of the rainfall patterns. For instance, remote warm (cold) ENSO episodes are linked to wet (dry) spells over the region on interannual timescales. However, the role of the Indian Ocean Dipole (Saji *et al.* 1999) and the Atlantic (Marshall *et al.* 2001) are also considerable. The major rainfall season in Southern Hemisphere Africa is climatologically locked to the austral summer (December–January–February–March: DJFM). Janowiak (1988) has described the dominant rainfall anomaly patterns and their links to ENSO episodes and their associated planetary-scale atmospheric flows. Finally, the rainfall patterns over the CACS are widely heterogeneous, on the basis of peak rainfall. For instance, the region has been classified into four zones by some researchers (Balas *et al.* 2007; Farnsworth 2012). These are: (i) Zone 1 – July–August–September (JAS), (ii) Zone 2 – September–October–November (SON), (iii) Zone 3 – October–November–December (OND), and (iv) Zone 4- December–January–February (DJF). This zonation offers a better approach in handling the climate variability and change across the region.

Projected climate change and trends in Africa

The African continent is regarded to be among the vulnerable parts of the globe in terms of climate change due to human activity that interferes with the ecosystem. These activities result in the modification of the climate in terms of a projected temperature rise over the next hundred years, which would be capable of impacting both human welfare and the biophysical environment. While factors such as widespread poverty, recurrent droughts, inequitable land distribution and over dependence on rain-fed agricultural practices have been identified as major contributors to the impact of climate change on the continent, its location, shape and size also play a vital role in determining the climate (IPCC 2001). Within the twenty-first century, African temperatures have been projected to rise faster than the average world temperature (Hulme *et al.* 2001; Boko *et al.* 2007; Niang *et al.* 2014). In addition, near surface temperatures have been reported to have increased by 0.5°C or more over the last 100 years in most parts of the continent, with minimum temperatures warming more rapidly than maximum temperatures (Hulme 2001; Niang *et al.* 2014). According to IPCC (2001) and Collins (2011), the most recent period (1995–2010) shows more warming has occurred in Africa compared to the period 1979–1994 (Figure 1.1); this trend might have been influenced by other components of natural variability and human activity. Warming through the twentieth century has been observed at a rate of about 0.05°C per decade, with slightly greater warming in the June–July–August (JJA) and September–November seasons than in December–January–February (DJF) and March–May (IPCC 2001).

Climate change and human security in Africa

There is a series of observational evidence around the continent of Africa showing regional changes in climate, especially temperature increase and its

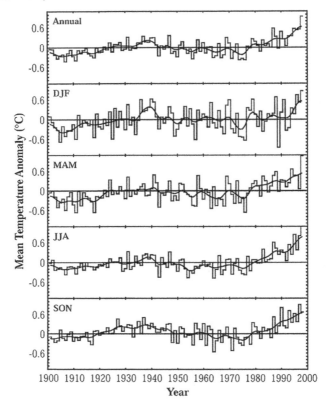

Figure 1.1 Mean surface air temperature anomalies for the African continent, 1901–1998, expressed with respect to 1961–1990 average, annual and four seasons (DJF, MAM, JJA, SON). Adapted from IPCC 2001.

diverse impact on physical and biological systems (Boko *et al.* 2007; Li 2011; Mohamed 2011) which, if left unmitigated, could undermine the stability of the continent. The IPCC (2001) report highlights several background factors that should be taken into consideration in the assessment of the vulnerability of Africa to climate change, which include: (i) diversity of climates, biota, culture and economic stand; (ii) tropical climate; (iii) development status; (iv) food supply; (v) disease burden; (vi) low capacity for interstate initiated interventions; (vii) armed conflicts and (viii) high external trade and aid dependence. These factors, if left unchecked, can lead to famine and disruption of the socio-economic well-being of the people, with a negative impact on people's capacity to cope with such change.

Jury (2013) affirmed in his study that understanding and predicting trends in climate is a difficult task. Despite the fact that seasonal forecasting has improved measures aimed at mitigating drought cycles, nevertheless, agricultural activities have witnessed a steep decline in yearly production in most countries of Africa. There are long established causal links between climate change and other factors. These include: consumption of fossil fuels; increased urban population; land degradation and increases in greenhouse gases and human security threats with potentially negative effects on individual well-being. Climate change undermines human security in different ways. This is partly because access to natural resources and services vary, and so also do the social determinants of adaptive capacity differ (Barnett and Adger 2007; Hendrix and Glaser 2007; Meier *et al.* 2007; Raleigh and Urdal 2007; Niang *et al.* 2014; Seter 2016). There is also evidence emerging of a connection between temperature increase and human violence (Niang *et al.* 2014). For instance, pastoral conflicts over natural resources is now endemic in many parts of Africa, and the effects of climate on pastoralism, rather than being considered in isolation, should be examined within a wider socio-economic framework (Meier *et al.* 2007). There is the need for stakeholders to take up the task of finding better measures to promote ecological stability, with the hope of affecting human security on the continent.

Loss of biodiversity

Another trend brought about by climate change relates to the changes in the distribution and dynamics of all forms of terrestrial ecosystems on the continent (Figure 1.2). The continent is now faced with desert encroachment, leading to the contraction of vegetated areas. This process is also encouraged by human activities through the expansion of agriculture, livestock grazing, and fuelwood harvesting (Niang *et al.* 2014). Biggs *et al.* (2004), Boko *et al.* (2007) and Bele *et al.* (2015) reported that in Zimbabwe, Malawi, eastern Zambia, central Mozambique and the Congo Basin, and the rainforests of the Democratic Republic of Congo, it had been revealed that deforestation had occurred in these locations at an estimated rate of about 0.4 per cent per year during the 1990s. In addition, Africa's forests are estimated to have contributed to about 80 to 90 per cent of the residential energy needs of rural low-income households on the continent (Boko *et al.* 2007). Additionally, the rate of forest degradation in the Congo Basin is estimated at 0.1 per cent (180,460 ha) per year due to commercial logging and clearing for agricultural demands (Bele *et al.* 2015). The trend in forest degradation and fragmentation on the continent is presenting a situation that needs to be addressed in order to halt the loss of fauna and flora.

Rainfall variability and extreme weather events over most of Africa have affected the agriculture sector and aggravated food insecurity among the urban poor, increasing the risk of malnutrition and its consequences. The rise in global food prices also contributed to the 30,000–50,000 malnutrition-related deaths among children in sub-Saharan Africa in 2009 (Hulme *et al.* 2001; Niang *et al.* 2014; Table 1.1). In addition, the demand for water in Africa is increasing, and it has been projected that by 2025, around 480 million people in Africa will be faced with water scarcity or stress, thereby increasing the potential for water conflicts (Medany *et al.* 2006).

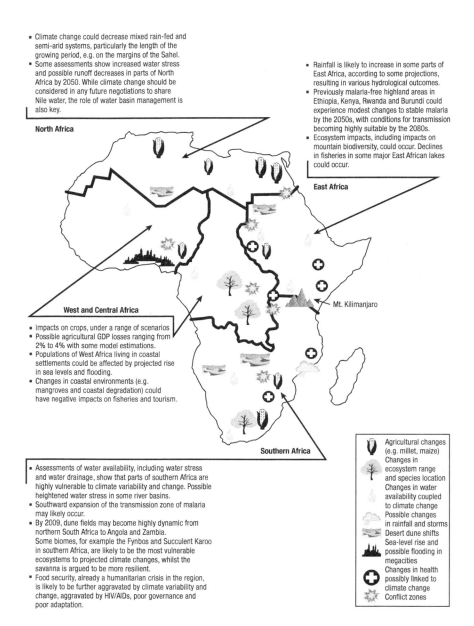

- Climate change could decrease mixed rain-fed and semi-arid systems, particularly the length of the growing period, e.g. on the margins of the Sahel.
- Some assessments show increased water stress and possible runoff decreases in parts of North Africa by 2050. While climate change should be considered in any future negotiations to share Nile water, the role of water basin management is also key.

North Africa

- Rainfall is likely to increase in some parts of East Africa, according to some projections, resulting in various hydrological outcomes.
- Previously malaria-free highland areas in Ethiopia, Kenya, Rwanda and Burundi could experience modest changes to stable malaria by the 2050s, with conditions for transmission becoming highly suitable by the 2080s.
- Ecosystem impacts, including impacts on mountain biodiversity, could occur. Declines in fisheries in some major East African lakes could occur.

East Africa

West and Central Africa

- Impacts on crops, under a range of scenarios
- Possible agricultural GDP losses ranging from 2% to 4% with some model estimations.
- Populations of West Africa living in coastal settlements could be affected by projected rise in sea levels and flooding.
- Changes in coastal environments (e.g. mangroves and coastal degradation) could have negative impacts on fisheries and tourism.

Mt. Kilimanjaro

Southern Africa

- Assessments of water availability, including water stress and water drainage, show that parts of southern Africa are highly vulnerable to climate variability and change. Possible heightened water stress in some river basins.
- Southward expansion of the transmission zone of malaria may likely occur.
- By 2009, dune fields may become highly dynamic from northern South Africa to Angola and Zambia. Some biomes, for example the Fynbos and Succulent Karoo in southern Africa, are likely to be the most vulnerable ecosystems to projected climate changes, whilst the savanna is argued to be more resilient.
- Food security, already a humanitarian crisis in the region, is likely to be further aggravated by climate variability and change, aggravated by HIV/AIDs, poor governance and poor adaptation.

Agricultural changes (e.g. millet, maize)
Changes in ecosystem range and species location
Changes in water availability coupled to climate change
Possible changes in rainfall and storms
Desert dune shifts
Sea-level rise and possible flooding in megacities
Changes in health possibly linked to climate change
Conflict zones

Figure 1.2 Examples of current and possible future impacts and vulnerabilities associated with climate variability and climate change for Africa. Note that these are indications of possible change and are based on models that currently have recognized limitations.

Source: Adapted from IPCC 2007.

Table 1.1 Undernourishment in Africa, by number and percentage of total population

Undernourished	1990–1992	1999–2001	2004–2006	2007–2009	2010–2012
Million	175	205	210	220	239
Percentage of total population	27.3	25.3	23.1	22.6	22.9

Source: Niang *et al.*, 2014.

The continent is vulnerable to a number of climate-sensitive diseases that include malaria, cholera, tuberculosis, meningitis and diarrhoea (Figure 1.3). The rise in temperature witnessed on the continent is also affecting the geographical distribution of disease vectors migrating to new areas and higher altitudes, thereby exposing large numbers of people that were previously not affected by such diseases (Medany *et al.* 2006; Boko *et al.* 2007; UNFCCC 2007). Heat stress and drought are also likely to have negative impacts on animal health, with the potential to impact food security (Medany *et al.* 2006).

The tourism industry in countries of Africa could be placed at risk due to climate change, which would be another setback, given the economic benefit of the industry in parts of the coastal zones and mountain regions (Boko *et al.* 2007; UNFCCC 2007). Data presented by Medany *et al.* (2006) showed that about 25 per cent of Africa's population inhabit land that is within 100 km of the coast, and the number of the population at risk from coastal flooding will increase from 1 million people in 1990 to 70 million in 2080. This scenario presents either a partial or complete threat to coastal infrastructures due to accelerated sea level rises in about 30 per cent of Africa's countries, including the Gulf of Guinea, Senegal, Gambia, Egypt and along the East-Southern African coast (UNFCCC 2007).

Ethnic and political unrest, and the devastating effect of El Niño rains in certain parts of the continent, are among the contributory factors to the poor performance of tourism in recent years. Climate change is having an impact on the continent's vegetation and ecological zones, which is affecting the distribution of wildlife. The southern African region has warmed by about 0.05°C per decade this century, while rainfall has decreased, resulting in several serious droughts on the continent. This trend is projected to continue into the future, with climate models suggesting that temperatures will continue to increase, which could also have an impact on rainfall (Viner and Agnew 1999).

It is difficult to predict how climate will change over the next decades in Africa, partly due to the poor understanding of the complex interactions between the drivers of change and partly due to a lack of local weather data. What is now a common trend is the increase in human migration on the continent due to environmental change, and the trend is projected to increase. The migration situation in Somalia and Burundi is a reminder of the interaction between climate change, disaster, conflict and displacement that encourages human movement within and between countries. For example, the Zambezi River floods that affected

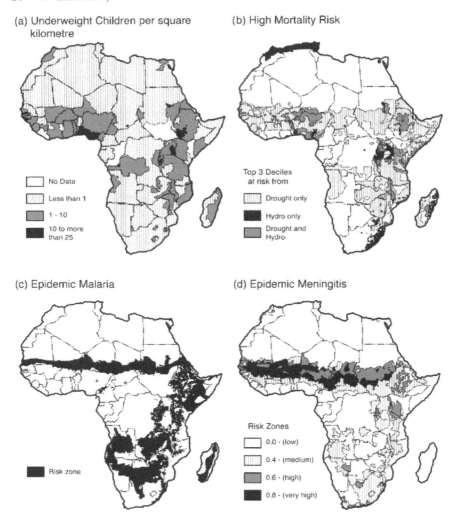

Figure 1. 3 Examples of current 'hotspots' or risk areas for Africa: (a) 'hunger'; (b) 'natural
hazard-related disaster risks'; (c) regions prone to malaria derived from historical
rainfall and temperature data (1950–1996); and (d) modelled distribution of
districts where epidemics of meningococcal meningitis are likely to occur, based
on epidemic experience, relative humidity (1961–1990) and land cover.
Source: Adapted from Boko et al., 2007.

Mozambique in 2007 displaced more than 90,000 of its inhabitants (Warner *et al.*
2010; Niang *et al.* 2014). The onset of famine indicates that when the threshold of
human endurance has been exceeded, populations are pressured to migrate to
other locations.

Conclusions

As this chapter has demonstrated, the impacts of climate change on African countries are substantial and cause damage to the livelihoods of millions of people across the continent. Apart from the global measures to reduce CO_2 emissions, there is a perceived need for intense adaptation efforts, with a view to reducing the economic losses and threats to health of Africa's populations. Community-based approaches to climate change represent an emerging area where action may be focused, ensuring that participatory methodologies are used so as to yield maximum benefits in respect of the success of adaptation measures.

References

Asnani, G. C. (2005) *Tropical Meteorology* (Revised edition) vols. 1, 2, and 3, Pune, India: Praveen Printing Press.

Balas, N., Nicholson, S. E., Klotter, D. (2007) 'The Relationship of Rainfall Variability in West Central Africa to Sea-Surface Temperature Fluctuations', *International Journal of Climatology*, 27: 1335–1349.

Barnett, J. and Adger, W. N. (2007) 'Climate Change, Human Security and Violent Conflict', *Political Geography*, 26(6): 639–655.

Bele, M. Y., Sonwa, D. J., and Tiani, A. M. (2015) 'Adapting the Congo Basin Forests Management to Climate Change: Linkages among Biodiversity, Forest Loss, and Human Well-Being', *Forest Policy and Economics*, 50, 1–10.

Biggs, R., Bohensky, E., Desanker, P. V, Fabricius, C., Lynam, T., Misselhorn, A. A., Musvoto, C. and Mutale, M., Reyers, B., Scholes, R.J., Shikongo, S. and van Jaarsveld, A.S. (2004) *Nature Supporting People: The Southern African Millennium Ecosystem Assessment Integrated Report*. Millennium Ecosystem Assessment, Pretoria: Council for Scientific and Industrial Research.

Boko, M., Niang, I., Nyong, A., Vogel, C., Githeko, A., Medany, M., Osman-Elasha, B., Tabo, R. and Yanda, P. (2007) 'Africa', in M. L. Parry, O. F. Canziani, J. P. Palutikof, P. J. van der Linden and C. E. Hanson (eds.) *Climate Change 2007: Impacts, Adaptation and Vulnerability. Contribution of Working Group II to the Fourth Assessment Report of the Intergovernmental Panel on Climate Change*, Cambridge UK: Cambridge University Press, pp. 433–467.

Chang, P., Yamagata, T., Schopf P., Behera, S. K., Carton, J., Kessler, W. S., Meyers, G., Qu, T., Schott, F., Shetye, S.-P. and Xie, S.-P. (2006) 'Climate Fluctuations of Tropical Coupled Systems – The Role of Ocean Dynamics', *Journal of Climate*, 19: 5122–5174.

Charney, J. G. (1975) 'Dynamics of Deserts and Drought in the Sahel', *Quarterly Journal of Royal Meteorological Society*, 101 (428): 193–202, doi: 10.1002/qj.49710142802.

Chauvin, F., Roehrig, R. and Lafore, J.-P. (2010) 'Intraseasonal Variability of the Saharan Heat Low and Its Link with Midlatitudes', *Journal of Climate*, 23: 2544–2561.

Chen, Z., Hendrix, W., Guan, H., Tetteh, I. K., Choudhary, A., Semazzi, F. and Samatova, N. F. (2013) 'Discovery of Extreme Events-related Communities in Contrasting Groups of Physical System Networks', *Data Mining and Knowledge Discovery*, 27: 225–258, doi: 10.1007/s10618-012-0289-3.

Collins, J. M. (2011) 'Temperature Variability Over Africa', *Journal of Climate*, 24(14): 3649–3666.

Eltahir, E.A.B. and Gong, C. (1996) 'Dynamics of Wet and Dry Years in West Africa', *Journal of Climate*, 9:1030–1042.

Farnsworth, A. J. (2012) *Rainfall Variability and the Impact of Land Cover Change over Central Africa*, Ph.D thesis, University of Reading, 198pp.

Folland, C. K., Palmer, T. N. and Parker, D. E. (1986) 'Sahel Rainfall and Worldwide Sea Temperatures, 1901–85', *Nature*, 320: 602–607.

Giannini, A., Saravannan, R., Chang, P. (2005) 'Dynamics of the Boreal Summer African Monsoon in the NSIPPI Atmospheric Model', *Climate Dynamics*, 25: 517–535.

Gonzalez II, D. L., Angus, M. P., Tetteh, I. K., Bello, G. A., Padmanabhan, K., Pendse, S. V., Srinivas, S., Jianing, Yu J., Semazzi, F., Kumar, V. and Samatova N. F. (2015) 'On the Data-Driven Inference of Modulatory Networks in Climate Science: An Application to West African Rainfall', *Nonlinear Processes in Geophysics*, 22: 33–46, doi:10.5194/npg-22-33-2015.

Grossmann, I. and Klotzbach, P. J. (2009) 'A Review of North Atlantic Modes of Natural Variability and their Driving Mechanisms', *Journal of Geophysical Research*, 114, 14 pp, doi: 10.1029/2009JD012728.

Hendrix, C. S. and Glaser, S. M. (2007) 'Trends and Triggers: Climate, Climate Change and Civil Conflict in Sub-Saharan Africa', *Political Geography*, 26(6): 695–715.

Hsiang, S. M., Burke, M. and Miguel, E. (2013) 'Quantifying the Influence of Climate on Human Conflict', *Science*, doi: 10.1126/science.1235367.

Hulme, M., Doherty, R., Ngara, T., New, M., Lister, D. (2001) 'African Climate Change: 1900–2100', *Climate Research* 17(2):145–168.

Hurrell, J. W. (1995) 'Decadal Trends in the North Atlantic Oscillation Regional Temperatures and Precipitation', *Science*, 269: 676–679.

IPCC (2001) '*Third Assessment Report: Climate Change*'. *Working Group II: Impact, Adaptations and Vulnerability*. Cambridge: Cambridge University Press.

IPCC (2007) 'Climate Change 2007: Impacts, Adaptation and Vulnerability, Contribution of Working Group II', in M. L. Parry, O. F. Canziani, J. P. Palutikof, P. J. van der Linden and C. E. Hanson (eds.) *The Fourth Assessment Report of the Intergovernmental Panel on Climate Change*, Cambridge: Cambridge University Press.

IPCC (2014) *Fifth Assessment Report: Climate Change. Working Group II: Impact, Adaptations and Vulnerability*, IPCC: Geneva.

Janowiak, J. E. (1988) 'An Investigation of Interannual Rainfall Variability in Africa', *Journal of Climate*, 1: 240–255.

Jennings, S. and McGrath, J. (2009) 'What Happened to the Seasons?', Oxfam Research Report. London: Oxfam.

Jury, M. R. (2013) 'Climate Trends in Southern Africa', *South African Journal of Science*, 109(1–2), pp.1–11.

Lamb, P. J. (1978) 'Large-Scale Tropical Atlantic Surface Circulation Patterns Associated with Subsaharan Weather Anomalies', *Tellus*, A30 240–251.

Leal Filho, W. (ed.) (2011) *The Economic, Social and Political Aspects of Climate Change,* Berlin: Springer.

Marshall, J., Kushnir, Y., Battisti, D., Chang P., Czaja A., Dickson R., Hurrell J., McCartney, M., Saravananand, R. and Visbeck, M. (2001) 'North Atlantic Climate Variability: Phenomena, Impacts and Mechanisms', *International Journal of Climatology*, 21 1863–1898.

Medany, M., Niang-Diop, I., Nyong, T. and Tabo, R. (2006) 'Background Paper on Impacts, Vulnerability and Adaptation to Climate Change in Africa', in the *African Workshop on Adaptation Implementation of Decision* (Vol. 1).

Meier, P., Bond, D. and Bond, J. (2007) 'Environmental Influences on Pastoral Conflict in the Horn of Africa', *Political Geography*, 26(6): 716–735.

Mohamed, A. B. (2011) 'Climate Change Risks in Sahelian Africa'. *Regional Environmental Change*, 11(1): 109–117.

National Science Foundation (2015) 'Expedition in Computing. Understanding Climate Change – A Data Driven Approach'. Available at: http://climatechange.cs.umn.edu.

Niang, I., Ruppel, O. C., Abdrabo, M. A., Essel, A., Lennard, C., Padgham, J. and Urquhart, P. (2014) 'Africa', in V. C. Barros, C. B. Field, D. J. Dokken, M. D. Mastrandrea, K. J. Mach, T. E. Bilir, M. Chatterjee, K. L. Ebi, Y. O. Estrada, R. C. Genova, B. Girma, E. S. Kissel, A. N. Levy, S. MacCracken, P. R. Mastrandrea, and L. L. White (eds.) *Climate Change 2014: Impacts, Adaptation, and Vulnerability. Part B: Regional Aspects. Contribution of Working Group II to the Fifth Assessment Report of the Intergovernmental Panel on Climate Change*, Cambridge, United Kingdom and New York, Cambridge University Press pp. 1199–1265.

Nicholson, S. E. (1986) 'The Spatial Coherence of African Rainfall Anomalies: Interhemispheric Teleconnections', *Journal of Climate and Applied Meteorology*, 25: 1365–1381.

Nicholson, S. E. and Grist, J. P. (2001) 'A Conceptual Model for Understanding Rainfall Variability in the West African Sahel on Interannual and Interdecadal Timescales', *International Journal of Climatology*, 21: 1733–1757.

Nicholson, S. E. and Kim, J. (1997) 'The Relationship of the El Niño–Southern Oscillation to African Rainfall', *International Journal of Climatology*, 17: 117–135.

Ogallo, L. J. (1989) 'The Spatial and Temporal Patterns of the East African Seasonal Rainfall Derived from Principal Component Analysis', *International Journal Climatology*, 9: 145–167.

Peixoto, J. P. and Oort, A. H. (1993) *Physics of Climate*, New York: American Institute of Physics, 520 pp.

Pendse, S. V., Tetteh, I. K., Semazzi. F., Kumar, V. and Samatova, N. F. (2012) 'Toward Data-Driven, Semi-Automatic Inference of Phenomenological Physical Models: Application to Eastern Sahel Rainfall' in Proceedings of the 12th Society for Industrial & Applied Mathematics (SIAM) Conference on Data Mining, SDM 2012: 35–46.

Polo, I., Rodriguez-Fonseca, B., Losada, T., García-Serrano, J. (2008) 'Tropical Atlantic Variability Modes (1979–2002). Part I: Time-Evolving SST Modes Related to West African Rainfall', *Journal of Climate*, 21 6457–6475.

Raleigh, C. and Urdal, H. (2007) 'Climate Change, Environmental Degradation and Armed Conflict', *Political Geography*, 26(6): 674–694.

Rodwell, M. J. and Hoskins B. J. (1996) 'Monsoons and the Dynamics of Deserts', *Quarterly Journal of Royal Meteorological Society*, 122: 1385–1404.

Ropelewski, C. F. and Halpert, M. S. (1987) 'Global and Regional Scale Precipitation Patterns Associated with the El Niño Southern Oscillation', *Monthly Weather Review*, 115: 1606–1626.

Saji, N. H., Goswami, B. N., Vinayachandran, P. N. and Yamagata, T. (1999) 'A Dipole Mode in the Tropical Indian Ocean', *Nature*, 401: 360–363.

Semazzi, F.H.M. and Sun, L. (1997) 'The Role of Orography in Determining the Sahelian Climate', *International Journal of Climatology*, 17: 581–596.

Seter, H. (2016) 'Connecting Climate Variability and Conflict: Implications for Empirical Testing', *Political Geography*, 53: 1–9.

Smith, K. A., Semazzi, F.H.M. (2014) 'The Role of the Dominant Modes of Precipitation Variability over Eastern Africa in Modulating the Hydrology of Lake Victoria', *Advances in Meteorology*, Article ID 516762, 11 pp. http://dx.doi.org/10.1155/2014/516762.

UNEP (2005) *UNEP 2004/5 GEO Yearbook*, Nairobi: UNEP.

UNFCCC (2007) 'Climate Change: Impacts, Vulnerabilities and Adaptation in Developing Countries', United Nations Framework Convention on Climate Change: Bonn, Germany: UNFCCC Secretariat. Available at: https://unfccc.int/resource/docs/publications/impacts.pdf.

Viner, D. and Agnew, M. (1999) *Climate Change and its Impacts on Tourism*, Norwich: Climatic Research Unit, University of East Anglia.

Ward, M. N. (1998) 'Diagnosis and Short-Lead Time Prediction of Summer Rainfall in Tropical North Africa at Interannual and Multidecadal Timescales', *Journal of Climate*, 11: 3167–3191.

Warner, K., Hamza, M., Oliver-Smith, A., Renaud, F. and Julca, A. (2010) 'Climate Change, Environmental Degradation and Migration', *Natural Hazards*, 55(3), 689–715.

World Health Organization (2015) *World Malaria Report*, Geneva: WHO.

Zhou, G, Minakawa, N., Githeko, A.K. and Yan, G. (2004) 'Association between Climate Variability and Malaria Epidemics in the East African Highlands', *Proceedings of the National Academy of Sciences*, USA, 101 (8): 2375–2380.

2 Climate change and the Caribbean

Trends and implications

Michael A. Taylor, Jhordanne J. Jones and Tannecia S. Stephenson

Overview

The Caribbean region (Figure 2.1) lays claim to being amongst the most vulnerable to climate change. The Samoa Pathway (UN 2014) notes that the adverse impacts

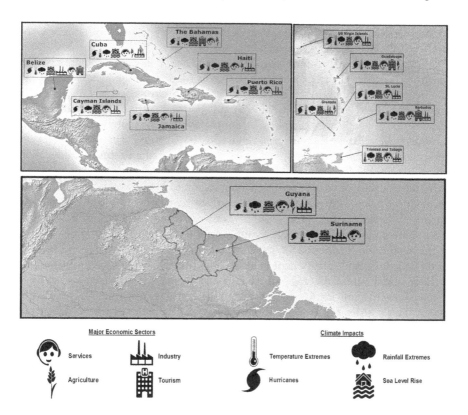

Figure 2.1 **Top left:** Map of the Caribbean. Major economic activities and climate vulnerabilities for selected territories are shown. **Top right:** Eastern Caribbean. **Bottom:** Guyana and Suriname.

of climate change compound existing challenges for Small Island Developing States like those which constitute the Caribbean, and place additional burdens on national budgets and efforts to achieve sustainable development goals. In this primarily science-based chapter, a brief overview of climate change is offered, followed by an examination of the historical and future trends in measures of climate relevant for the Caribbean region. The significance of the trends is discussed in the context of the aforementioned vulnerability. The chapter concludes by making a case for further research on the science of Caribbean climate variability given the strong linkages to Caribbean life, lifestyles and economies. Specifically, it is argued that the observed and future trends suggest the need for, and value of, expanded usage of climate information in order to counter some of the uncertainty resulting from the changing climate.

Understanding climate change

The distinction is made between weather and climate. Whereas weather describes the day-to-day variations in climatic variables (e.g. rainfall and temperature), climate is the mean state in those variables over periods of time for a given location. Depending on interest, the averaging period may vary from months or seasons through decades, centuries or longer.

The distinction is also made between climate variability and climate change. Year-to-year, groups of years and even decadal variations in the mean state of the climate variables are classified as climate variability. On the other hand, climate change describes large-scale and long-term shifts occurring over multiples of decades and longer. For example, the annual average temperature of the earth (land and ocean) over the last one-hundred years (Figure 2.2) shows differences between adjacent years or groups of years, with some being hotter or colder than others. This kind of climate variability can be linked to global climatic phenomena with known cycles of occurrence, for example, the El Niño, which is an abnormal warming by a few degrees of the sea's surface in the central and east-central equatorial Pacific. After onset, an El Niño generally peaks during northern hemisphere winter and causes significant disruptions in climate for various regions of the world for the period of its duration. Its three-to-six-year periodicity is therefore a discernible component in location specific climate records, for example, in the seasonal rainfall records of the Caribbean. Figure 2.2, however, also shows a distinct upward slant in the mean annual temperatures over the entire period of record. The positive linear trend is representative of a climate change signal – in this case, a long-term shift towards higher mean temperatures in the present. Global warming, or the upward trend in the mean surface temperatures of the earth (approximately 0.85° C between 1880 and the present), is one of a number of observations which provides evidence of a changing climate system. Other observed changes which are consistent with a warming globe are given in Table 2.1.

Factors that can cause the earth's climate to change on long time scales include: (i) changes in the amount of the sun's energy reaching the earth due to changes in the sun itself, or in the earth's orbit. This has been responsible for cold glacial periods in the past; (ii) changes in the reflective characteristics of the atmosphere

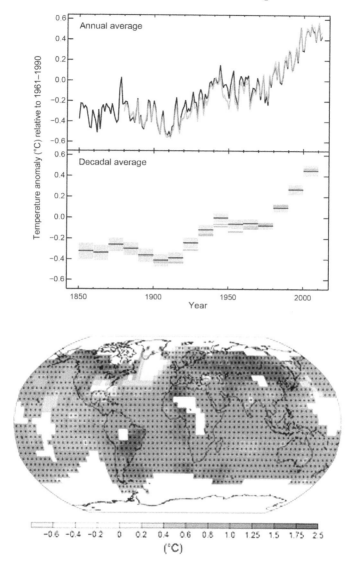

Figure 2.2 (a) Observed annual and decadal global mean surface temperature anomalies from 1850 to 2012 and (b) map of the observed surface temperature change from 1901 to 2012.
Source: IPCC (2013).

and/or the earth's surface, for example by explosive volcanic activity or melting sea ice; (iii) human-induced or anthropogenic changes in the concentration of greenhouse gases in the atmosphere and the enhancement of the 'greenhouse

Table 2.1 Six ways the global climate system has changed over the last century

Higher temperatures	The globally averaged combined land and ocean surface temperatures have warmed by approximately 0.85° C over the period 1880 to 2012.
Changing rainfall	Average Northern Hemisphere precipitation over the mid-latitude land areas has increased since 1901. There is lower confidence in trends for other area-averaged latitudes because of – amongst other things – limited data of sufficient length.
Sea level rises	The rate of sea level rise since the mid-19th century has been larger than the mean rate observed during the previous two millennia. Over the period 1901 to 2010, global mean sea level rose by 0.19 m.
More extreme events	Changes in many extreme weather and climate events have been observed since about 1950. For example, it is very likely that the number of cold days and nights has decreased and the number of warm days and nights has increased on the global scale. It is likely that the frequency of heat waves has increased in large parts of Europe, Asia and Australia. There are likely more land regions where the number of heavy precipitation events has increased than where it has decreased. The frequency or intensity of heavy precipitation events has likely increased in North America and Europe.
Ocean acidification	Since the beginning of the industrial revolution, the pH of surface ocean waters has fallen by 0.1 pH. This is equivalent to an increase in acidity of approximately 30%.
Retreating glaciers, shrinking ice sheets, changing snow cover	Glaciers have continued to shrink almost worldwide, and the Greenland and Antarctic ice sheets have been losing mass over the last two decades. Arctic sea ice and Northern Hemisphere spring snow cover have continued to decrease in extent.

Source: Adapted from the Fifth Assessment Report (AR5) of the Intergovernmental Panel on Climate Change.

effect' (see Figure 2.3). The Intergovernmental Panel on Climate Change (IPCC) notes that it is extremely likely that more than half of the observed increase in global average surface temperature from 1951 to 2010 was caused by the human-induced increase in greenhouse gas concentrations and other anthropogenic forcings. Human activities – primarily the burning of fossil fuels and changes in land cover (e.g. deforestation and urbanization) – have significantly increased the concentration of greenhouse gases since pre-industrial times. Carbon dioxide (CO_2), methane (CH_4) and nitrous oxide (NO_2) have increased by approximately 40 per cent, 150 per cent and 20 per cent, respectively, since pre-industrialized times (IPCC 2013) (Figure 2.4). The increase in CO_2 is particularly significant because of its long residence time ($\sim$1000 years) in the atmosphere. As the atmosphere warms in response, the amount of water vapour (also a greenhouse gas) it can hold also increases. The IPCC concludes that 'it is extremely likely that human influence has been the dominant cause of the observed warming since the mid-20th century' (IPCC 2013).

The developed countries of the world have so far been those responsible for most of the anthropogenic greenhouse gases, with 10 countries being responsible for more

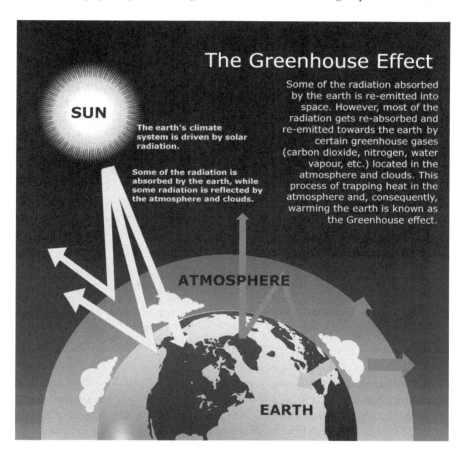

Figure 2.3 Warming the planet
As illustrated in the diagram above, the sun radiates energy. Approximately one third of the solar energy that reaches the top of Earth's atmosphere is reflected directly back to space, while the remaining two-thirds is absorbed by the earth's surface and to a lesser extent by the atmosphere. The earth in turn radiates its absorbed energy back to space, much of which is absorbed by greenhouse gases in the atmosphere and reradiated back to Earth. By so doing the surface of the earth is further warmed. The whole process is called the greenhouse effect. Without the natural greenhouse effect, the average temperature at the Earth's surface would be too cold to facilitate life as we know it. Unfortunately, the effect of human activities, primarily the burning of fossil fuels and clearing of forests, is to greatly intensify the natural greenhouse effect, and cause global warming.

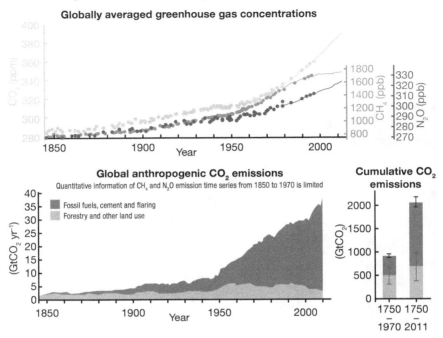

Figure 2.4 **Top:** Atmospheric concentrations of the greenhouse gases carbon dioxide (CO_2, top line), methane (CH_4, middle), and nitrous oxide (N_2O, bottom) determined from ice core data (dots) and from direct atmospheric measurements (lines). **Bottom:** Global anthropogenic CO_2 emissions from forestry and other land use as well as from burning of fossil fuel, cement production, and flaring.
Source: IPCC (2014).

than 60 per cent of greenhouse gas emissions in 2011 (World Resources Institute, Climate Analysis Indicator Tool 2.0). In contrast, the Caribbean's share of total global GHG emissions is very small and estimated at less than 1 per cent. The distributions shift, however, with respect to vulnerability to impact from, and adaptive capacity to, climatic variations. With respect to those measures, regions like the Caribbean carry the larger burden as they are disproportionately impacted by climate change.

An unfamiliar climate

An examination of historical records suggests that the climate of the Caribbean region has changed in significant ways over the recent past.

First, there has been a distinct warming of the Caribbean over the past 100 years (Jones *et al.* 2015). Mean temperatures, as well as day time and night time temperature records, exhibit statistically significant warming (Figure 2.5) characterized by: (i) an increase in the average day time temperature by approximately 0.19°C/decade since 1960; (ii) an increase in the average night time

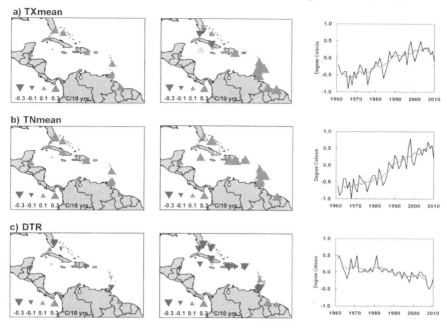

Figure 2.5 Trends in (a) day time temperatures (TXmean), (b) night time temperatures (TNmean) and (c) diurnal temperature range (DTR). Left panels show the trends for 1961–2010; middle panels show the trends for 1986–2010; and right panels present the time series for area averaged anomalies for 1961–2010 relative to a 1981–2000 climatology. Upward (downward) pointing triangles indicate positive (negative) trends. Solid triangles correspond to trends significant at the 5% level. The size of the triangle is proportional to the magnitude of the trend. Grey colour indicates warming, dark colour indicates cooling trends in (a) and (b); dark colour indicates that the daily minimum is increasing more than the daily maximum in (c). The grey line in the right panels is a 7-point running mean.
Source: Stephenson *et al.* (2014).

temperature by approximately 0.28°C/decade since 1960; (iii) a decrease in the diurnal temperature range (DTR), i.e. the difference between day time and night time temperatures; (iv) an increase in the number of extremely warm days by 3.31 per cent/decade since 1960; and (v) a decrease in the occurrence of very cool nights by 2.55 per cent/decade since 1960 (Jones *et al.* 2015; Stephenson *et al.* 2014; Alexander *et al.* 2006).

Second, regional rainfall records also show statistically significant trends in the intensity, frequency and duration of daily events and in the occurrence of extreme events (floods or drought). Stephenson *et al.* (2014) note that whereas Caribbean rainfall records do not show any statistically significant increases in annual total amounts, both heavy rainfall events and the intensity of daily rainfall have risen significantly over the past 25 years. They also indicate small and gradual increases in consecutive dry days, particularly over the northwestern (Bahamas, Cuba, Jamaica, Cayman) and southeastern (Trinidad and Tobago, Curacao, Guyana, Suriname) Caribbean. In the mean, the Caribbean has neither become wetter nor drier over the last 50–60 years, as the regional rainfall record is dominated by interannual (year-to-year) and decadal variability driven by strong associations with large-scale drivers of global climate such as El Niño events (Jones *et al.* 2015, Stephenson *et al.* 2014). The increase in the frequency, severity, and duration of El Niño events since the 1970s (Stahle *et al.* 1998; Mann, Bradley and Hughes 2000) has therefore translated into an increased occurrence of regional rainfall extremes (floods and droughts) over the same period. In very recent times, the region has experienced two significant El Niño related droughts in 2009–10 and again in 2015.

A third noticeable climate-related change has been an increase in the number of observed tropical storms and hurricanes in the tropical Atlantic. Between 1995 and 2009, the number of named tropical storms and hurricanes has averaged 14.5 and 7.6 per year, respectively, as compared to 11.6 and 6.1 per year between 1980 and 1994 (Pulwarty, Nurse and Trotz 2010). For Jamaica, this has meant that 11 storms and hurricanes have tracked within 200 km of the island since 2000, compared to only 4 storms and hurricanes between 1980 and 1999. The attribution of the increase primarily to climate change is still under scientific scrutiny, particularly since there are other known influences, e.g. the swing into the positive or warm phase of the Atlantic Multidecadal Oscillation in the early 1990s (Goldenberg *et al.* 2001).

Finally, tidal gauge observations indicate that sea levels in the Caribbean have risen at a rate of between 1.7 and 1.9 mm/year between 1950 and 2009 (Table 2.2) (Church *et al.* 2004; Palanisamy *et al.* 2012; Torres and Tsimplis 2013). The mean Caribbean rate of sea-level rise is near the global mean of 1.9 mm/year for the period 1901 and 2010 (IPCC 2013). Non-uniformities across the region, as captured in Table 2.2, are in part due to differential tectonic displacement within the basin (Hendry 1993; Gamble 2009). It is to be noted, however, that in the last 20 years, the global rate of sea-level rise (and likely that for the Caribbean) has increased significantly, and is estimated to be closer to 3 mm/year as determined from satellite altimetry (IPCC 2013).

Taken together, the historical climate records of the Caribbean suggest the emergence of a 'new' climate regime marked by warmer temperatures, a more variable rainfall pattern (characterized by intense rainfall events after longer dry spells and more frequent floods and droughts), the passage of more hurricanes and tropical storms and higher sea levels. One implication of the new climate regime is the introduction of the 'unfamiliar', that is, an era where the climate seems to be behaving outside of what would be 'expected' or perceived as 'normal' for the region. Gamble *et al.* (2010) noted this as the perception amongst farmers in St. Elizabeth, Jamaica who felt that there was a discernible increase in drought conditions in recent years due to changes in the rainfall patterns of the early (April–June) and principal (August– November) growing seasons. Specifically, Gamble *et al.* (2010) noted that the farmers commented in interviews that drought conditions were becoming more prevalent and that this was something they were neither used to nor prepared for. The warmer regime and changes in the nature of how rain events occur are also seemingly translating into perceptions that: (i) the days and nights are hotter than before; (ii) night time offers little relief from hot day time temperatures; (iii) summer is starting earlier and persisting longer; (iv) the wet season is becoming drier and the dry season is becoming wetter; and (iv) the number of dry days between rain events has increased, but when rain does occur, it pours (Taylor 2015).

The sense of 'unfamiliarity' is also being triggered by the magnitude and/or intensity of the climate extremes seen under the 'new' climate regime in recent times. At the time of its occurrence, the Meteorological Service of Jamaica noted that in the 25 years up to its occurrence, the drought of 2009–2010 was the worst

Table 2.2 Tide gauge observed sea-level trends for Caribbean stations

Station and Country		Span years	% of data	Trend	Months	Gauge corrected
Puerto Limon	Costa Rica	20.3	95.1	1.76±0.8	216	2.16±0.9
Cristobal	Panama	101.7	86.9	1.96±0.1	566	2.86±0.2
Cartagena	Colombia	44	90	5.36±0.3	463	5.46±0.3
Amuay	Venezuela	33	93.4	0.26±0.5	370	0.26±0.5
Cumana	Venezuela	29	98.6	0.96±0.5	331	0.76±0.6
Lime Tree	US Virgin Islands	32.2	81.9	1.86±0.5	316	1.56±0.5
Magueyes	Puerto Rico	55	96.2	1.36±0.2	635	1.06±0.2
P. Prince	Haiti	12.7	100	10.76±1.5	144	12.26±1.5
Guantanamo	Cuba	34.6	89.9	1.76±0.4	258	2.56±0.6
Port Royal	Jamaica	17.8	99.5	1.66±1.6	212	1.36±1.6
Cabo Cruz	Cuba	10	90	2.26±2.8	108	2.16±2.8
South Sound	Cayman	20.8	87.6	1.76±1.5	219	1.26±1.5
North Sound	Cayman	27.7	89.2	2.76±0.9	296	2.26±0.9
C. San Antonio	Cuba	38.3	76.7	0.86±0.5	353	0.36±0.5
Santo Tomas	Mexico	20	85.4	2.06±1.3	205	1.76±1.3
Puerto Cortes	Honduras	20.9	98	8.66±0.6	224	8.86±0.7
Puerto Castilla	Honduras	13.3	100	3.16±1.3	160	3.26±1.3

Source: Adapted from Torres and Tsimplis (2013).

experienced and resulted in inadequate rainfall to satisfy the water demand of many parishes, including the highly populated Kingston and St. Andrew (Trotman and Farrell, 2010). The subsequent re-occurrence of a prolonged and severe region-wide drought in 2015–16 reinforced the sentiments of a new normal to which the region is yet to become acclimatized. Similarly, the Christmas Eve rains of 2013, which impacted St Vincent and the Grenadines, St Lucia and Dominica were as notable for their timing during the traditional dry season as well as for the severe flooding which resulted. Prime Minister Ralph Gonsalves of St Vincent and the Grenadines described the event as a 'disaster of a proportion the likes of which we have not seen in living memory'.

An unprecedented climate

Regional climate science also suggests that the climate of the Caribbean will continue to change in significant ways through to the end of the current century. Using global and regional climate models and storylines of future global development, the picture of the Caribbean under future climate change is set out below.

Much warmer temperatures

The Caribbean is expected to continue warming through to the end of the century, irrespective of the climate model used or scenario examined. Climate models indicate that by the end of the current century, the mean annual temperature of the Caribbean region will be warmer by 1.0° C to 3.5° C compared to present-day temperatures (Figure 2.6), with the probability of the occurrence of extreme warm seasons being 100 per cent. Nowhere in the region is exempt, with warming over both ocean and land surfaces, and larger magnitude warming over the bigger islands (Cuba, Hispaniola, and Jamaica) (Karmalkar et al. 2013, Campbell et al. 2010). Other things to note about the future warming are: (i) it is for every month of the year; (ii) the frequency of days and nights that are considered 'hot' in the current climate will occur on up to 95 per cent of all days by the 2090s (McSweeney et al. 2010); (iii) the frequency of days and nights that are considered 'cold' in the current climate will become exceedingly rare by the end of the century (McSweeney et al. 2010); and (iv) Caribbean land areas will warm more than ocean areas (Karmalkar et al. 2013, Campbell et al. 2010).

Much drier

By the end of the current century, global climate models project that the Caribbean will receive up to 20 per cent less annual rainfall (bottom panel, Figure 2.5). Regional climate models project even higher maximum mean drying in the main Caribbean basin – between 25 and 30 per cent – by the end of the century (Karmalkar et al. 2013; Campbell et al. 2010). The annual mean decrease in rainfall will be across the entire region, though the far north Caribbean (western Cuba and the Bahamas) may have smaller decreases in annual totals than the rest

Temperature change Caribbean (land and sea) Jan-Dec wrt 1986-2005 AR5 CMIP5 subset

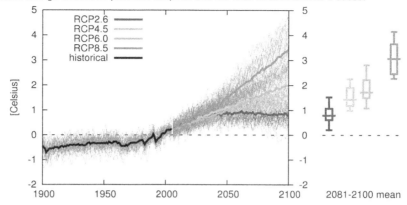

Relative Precipitation change Caribbean (land and sea) Jan-Dec wrt 1986-2005 AR5 CMIP5 subset

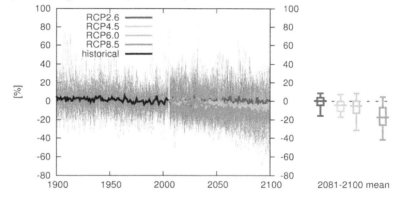

Figure 2.6 **Top:** Projected annual temperature change for the Caribbean relative to 1986–2005 for the four RCPs. **Bottom:** Projected percentage change in annual rainfall amounts for the Caribbean relative to 1986–2005 for the four RCPs.
Source: Diagrams generated using KNMI Climate Explorer.

of the basin. The projected drying will be most pronounced in the Caribbean wet season between May and October. Year-to-year and decadal variability will likely still be a dominant feature of the Caribbean rainfall record through to the middle of the current century. Thereafter, the projected mean drying pattern will become entrenched and variability will occur around a lower mean. By the end of the century, global climate models project only a 3 per cent chance of an extremely wet year compared to present-day conditions, but a 39 per cent chance of an extremely dry year.

Other indications from modelling studies (McSweeney *et al.* 2010, Campbell *et al.* 2010) are: (i) that the proportion of total rainfall that falls in heavy events for most of the Caribbean decreases towards the end of the century and there are more dry days; (ii) that the drying is robust in September, October and November, with these three months accounting for most of the annual drying; (iii) that the eastern Caribbean will experience larger decreases in rainfall amounts compared to the rest of the region by the end of the century; and (iv) that the northwest Caribbean will see slightly smaller decreases in annual rainfall than the eastern Caribbean, with some countries (e.g. the Bahamas) not seeing the establishment of the projected dry pattern until much later in the century.

More intense hurricanes

It is likely that whereas the region may not see an increase in the number of hurricanes and tropical storms in the future, the intensity of the storm events when they do occur will increase under global warming. The IPCC Special Report on Extremes (IPCC 2012) suggests that tropical cyclone related rainfall rates will increase under climate change as water vapour in the tropics increases due to warmer surface temperatures. Rainfall rates near the hurricane centre during the late twenty-first century may increase by +20 to +30 per cent in the hurricane's inner core, and +10% at radii of 200 km or larger. Modelling studies (e.g. Emanuel 2007; Knutson et al. 2010; Bender et al. 2010) are also consistent in suggesting that by the end of the twenty-first century, the maximum wind speeds associated with hurricanes will increase by +2 to +11 per cent. However, the studies do not offer consensus with respect to changes in hurricane genesis, location, tracks, duration, or areas of impact, or whether the global frequency of hurricanes will decrease or remain essentially unchanged. Some research suggests that Atlantic hurricane and tropical storms may reduce in number (e.g. Bender et al. 2010) even as the frequency of category 4 and 5 Atlantic hurricanes increases (Knutson et al. 2013).

Higher sea levels

The rate of mean sea-level rise in the Caribbean is not projected to be significantly different from the projected global rise. The IPCC (2013) projects that mid-century change (between 2046 and 2065) in global sea levels will be between 0.24 and 0.30 m, while the end of century change relative to 1986–2005 levels will be 0.40–0.63 m. Other studies suggest that the upper bound is too conservative and could be up to 1.4 m (Rahmstorf 2007; Rignot and Kanargaratnam 2006; Horton et al. 2008; IPCC 2013). Perrette et al. (2013) suggest a similar higher upper bound of up to 1.5 m for the Caribbean Sea by the end of the century.

Taken together, the future climate of the Caribbean as revealed by the modelling studies indicates an entrenchment of the emerging climate trends of the present noted previously. That is, there is: (i) continued warming of the region; (ii) significant variability in annual rainfall amounts, but superimposed on a gradual drying trend; (iii) further change in the intensity, frequency and duration of daily rainfall and more drought events; (iv) the likelihood of more intense hurricanes and tropical storms when they do occur; and (v) additional increases in sea levels. However, the magnitude of projected changes by the end of the current century is greater than the magnitude of change seen over the last century, i.e. future changes exceed the historical variations in climate already seen. Under the most severe projections, temperatures warm by a further three degrees (compared to a one-degree change seen over the last century); the region is up to 30 per cent drier; hurricane rain rates and wind speeds increase by 30 and 11 per cent, respectively; and sea levels are 0.5 to 1.5 metres higher. The picture is of a region characterized by 'unprecedented' climate change.

Corresponding research to investigate the impact of climate change of this magnitude on the Caribbean is lacking, fragmented and uncertain. In that regard, the chapters of this book add much-needed insights. The impacts are likely to be mostly negative, unevenly distributed and non-linear, and more pronounced on coastal infrastructure and cities, agricultural activities, water resources, biodiversity, tourism and the regional population's health (IPCC 2014). Studies that try to estimate the major aggregate economic costs of future climate change for the Caribbean yield various estimates, for example, from 5.6 to 34 per cent (Haites *et al.* 2002) or from 10 to 22 per cent (Bueno *et al.* 2008) of the Caribbean's GDP for change over 2025–2100. These estimates are considered to be conservative as the scope of the studies are largely confined to specific sectors and specific factors, such as the loss of land and infrastructure, declines in tourism and/or the impact of extreme weather events (ECLAC 2005).

An unreliable climate

It is the combination of an unfamiliar 'new' climate regime and projections for unprecedented further climate change that makes climate an unreliable factor in the Caribbean region's quest for developed status. Climate establishes itself as an important developmental consideration because of the region's high vulnerability to climate variations. This vulnerability arises from a number of factors.

On the one hand, there is an embedded sensitivity to climate resulting from the patterning (deliberate or otherwise) of Caribbean life around the distinct annual cycles of climate, particularly rainfall and temperature. There is a strong awareness of the timing of wet and dry and hot and cool seasons, and an anticipation of, and dependence on, annual patterns of climate such as the bimodal rainfall pattern and midsummer drying. The climate patterns are easily identifiable in indicators of Caribbean life and lifestyle, including disease incidence, energy production and consumption, water availability and usage, disaster preparedness procedures, planting and reaping cycles, forest fire frequency, seasonal employment statistics, and the timing of recreational and sporting activities. Planning in, and for, these and other spheres of Caribbean existence, then, often revolves around the expectation that the climate cycles will reappear in their usual form year after year.

The region's geographic characteristics further contribute to its vulnerability. The Caribbean includes a few mainland territories (Guyana, Suriname and Belize), but is mostly made up of many small islands and cays which are either low lying (e.g. Bahamas, most of the Grenadines, Barbuda), or volcanic with mountainous interiors and very short coastlines (e.g. St. Kitts and Nevis,

St. Lucia, St. Vincent, Dominica, Grenada, Montserrat), or combine hilly interiors and limited coastal plains (e.g. Antigua, Barbados, Haiti, Jamaica and Trinidad and Tobago) (Figure 2.1 and Table 2.3). Small size and complex topography force dependence on narrow coastal areas and/or steep hillsides for the location of major cities, key infrastructure (e.g. ports, airports, hospitals, major highways), large-scale agricultural plots, economic and industrial zones, and major population settlements (Pulwarty, Nurse and Trotz 2010; Simpson *et al.* 2010; Lewsey, Cid and Kruse 2004). There is, then, an inescapable exposure of the majority of the region's population and most of its infrastructure to climatic hazards such as hurricanes and tropical storms and their impacts including coastal erosion, coastal flooding and landslides. Mimura *et al.* (2007) estimate that more than 50 per cent of the Caribbean region's population resides within 1.5 km of the coast.

The vulnerability of the region arises because its economies rely heavily on (i) climate-sensitive sectors such as agriculture and tourism and (ii) rainfall for water. Tourism and agriculture employ approximately 30 per cent and 13 per cent, respectively, of the regional labour force (Pulwarty, Nurse and Trotz 2010; WTTC 2016), and contribute significantly to the GDP of most Caribbean countries. In their present forms, both sectors are very dependent on favourable climatic conditions, with direct and indirect linkages to climate documented by a number of studies (e.g. Ebi *et al.* 2006; Donner *et al.*; Knutson and Oppenheimer 2007; Simpson *et al.* 2010), including other chapters of this book. These studies emphasize the vulnerability of Caribbean economies to climate extremes and the consequent impact on livelihoods, quality of life, and individual and national economic well-being. The dependence on rainfall as the most important determinant of available water resources in the Caribbean also entrenches the vulnerability (Cashman *et al.* 2010). Most CARICOM Member States rely primarily on groundwater, surface water or rainwater harvesting, or various combinations of all three, for potable, industrial, sewerage and agricultural water supply (Table 2.3). Summer rainfall is particularly important for recharging water sources in advance of the dry season from December through April, and for ensuring that sufficient supplies exist until the onset of the rainy season the following May/June.

In a context, of extreme vulnerability, then, the challenge presented first by the emergence of an unfamiliar climate regime becomes even more evident. Table 2.4 lists some recent climatic events that have had a significant impact on Caribbean life, livelihoods and economies. The dislocations come as much from the unexpected magnitudes of the climatic events (e.g. the severity of the storm or the prolonged nature of the drought) as from the unexpected timing of the climatic event, or the unexpected changes in the frequency of occurrence of climate hazards or events. There has always been some consideration of climate norms in operational and contingency planning in the region, particularly with respect to the hurricane season. There is, however, growing recognition of the inadequacy of this methodology for factoring in climate simply because climate change is rendering the utilized historical norms and bounds unreliable.

Table 2.3 Economic and geographic characteristics and climate vulnerabilities for select Caribbean territories

Country	Major economic sectors (% contribution to GDP)	Geographic characteristics	Major source of water	Climate hazard	References
Anguilla	Services (49.5%) Tourism (18.2%) Goods and Manufacturing (15.4%)	Flat	Desalination	Sea Level Rise, Flooding, Increase in Temperature and Rainfall Extremes, Hurricanes, Drought	CARIBSAVE (2012); CDB (2010)
Antigua and Barbuda	Services (53.5%) Goods and Manufacturing (11.95%) Tourism (9.8%)	Mountainous, volcanic interior and limited coastal flatland	Groundwater, surface water	Sea Level Rise, Hurricanes, Drought, Coral bleaching	Government of Antigua and Barbuda (2011); USACE (2004a); Simpson et al. (2009)
Bahamas	Tourism (50%) Services (15%) Agriculture and Fisheries (3-5%)	Flat	Groundwater, Desalination	Sea Level Rise, Hurricanes, Increase in Temperature and Rainfall Extremes	USACE (2004b), Simpson et al. (2009); Chase (2008); Government of the Bahamas (2001)
Barbados	Services (38.4%) Goods and Manufacturing (30.6%) Tourism (15%)	Mountainous, volcanic interior and limited coastal flatland	Groundwater (79%) desalination (12%)	Sea Level Rise, Flooding, Increase in temperature and rainfall extremes, Hurricanes	Government of Barbados (2001); CARIBSAVE (2012); Chase (2008)

Table 2.3 Continued

Country	Major economic sectors (% contribution to GDP)	Geographic characteristics	Major source of water	Climate hazard	References
Belize	Services (40.2%), Goods and Manufacturing (25.1%) Tourism (17%)	Mountainous, volcanic interior and limited coastal flatland	Groundwater (95% rural areas), Surface water (90%)	Increase in temperature and rainfall extremes, Increase in Temperatures, Drought, Flooding, Hurricanes, Sea Level Rise, Degradation of Coral Reefs	Government of Belize (2012); Simpson et al. (2009)
British Virgin Islands	Services (38%), Tourism (14%)	Mountainous, volcanic interior and limited coastal flatland	Desalination (60%) Ground water (40%)	Sea Level Rise, Increase in Temperature and Rainfall Extremes, Hurricanes, Flooding	Chase (2008)
Cayman Islands	Services (94.9%), Goods and Manufacturing (3.9%), Mining (0.7%)	Flat	Desalination Ground water	Hurricanes, Sea Level Rise, Increase in Temperature and Rainfall Extremes, Flooding, Drought	DOE (2010); ESO (2014)
Cuba	Services (70%), Industry (23%), Agriculture and Fisheries (~4%)	Hilly, mountainous interior and coastal plains	Surface water (~74.2%) with 68% from regulated water resources (120 dams and 900 micro-dams) and 6.2% from unregulated resources; Ground water (25.2%)	Sea Level Rise, hurricanes, drought, Increase in temperature extremes	Ministerio de Ciencia Tecnología y Medio Ambiente (2001);

Country	Economic sectors	Topography	Water resources	Climate hazards	References
Dominican Republic		Hilly, mountainous interior and coastal plains		Sea Level Rise, Increase in Temperature and Rainfall Extremes, Drought	Government of the Dominican Republic (2009)
Grenada	Services (50%), Agriculture (11%), Industry (7%)	Mountainous, volcanic interior and limited coastal flatland	Surface water	Sea Level Rise, Hurricanes, Increase in Temperature and Rainfall Extremes	Simpson et al. (2009); Department of Economic Affairs (2001); Government of Grenada (2000)
Guadeloupe	Services Tourism Agriculture	Mountainous, volcanic interior and limited coastal flatland	Surface water	Sea Level Rise, Hurricanes, Increase in Temperature and Rainfall Extremes	INSEE (2015); Pouget and Dezetter (1993)
Haiti	Services (56%), Agriculture (24.1%), Industry (19.9%)	Hilly, mountainous interior and coastal plains	Surface Water Groundwater	Sea Level Rise, Increase in Temperature and Rainfall Extremes, Drought	Government of Haiti (2009); Simpson et al. (2009); CIA World Factbook
Jamaica	Goods and Services (72.9%); Manufacture and Construction (15.8%); Agriculture, Forestry and Fisheries (7.4%)	Hilly, mountainous interior and coastal plains	Groundwater resources (84%) Primarily from limestone aquifers Surface water (16%) 92% to (agriculture, tourism, domestic, industrial)	Drought, Increases in temperature and rainfall extremes, Hurricanes, Sea Level Rise	USACE (2001); Simpson et al. (2009); Chase (2008); CSGM (2012); Government of Jamaica (2002)

Table 2.3 Continued

Country	Major economic sectors (% contribution to GDP)	Geographic characteristics	Major source of water	Climate hazard	References
St. Kitts and Nevis	Services (71%), Industry (23.2%), Agriculture (5.8%)	Mountainous, volcanic interior and limited coastal flatland	Groundwater, Surface Water	Sea Level Rise, Increase in Temperature and Rainfall Extremes, Hurricanes	CARIBSAVE (2012), McSweeney et al. (2008); Government of St. Kitts and Nevis (2001)
St. Lucia	Services (76.9%), Industry (24.6%), Agriculture (4.9%)	Mountainous, volcanic interior and limited coastal flatland	Surface water	Sea Level Rise, Increase in Temperature and Rainfall Extremes, Hurricanes	Government of St. Lucia (2012)
Puerto Rico	Goods (58.4%), Services (13.3%), Agriculture (0.8%)	Hilly, mountainous interior and coastal plains	Surface water (83%) Groundwater (17%)	Increase in temperature and rainfall extremes, Drought, Sea Level Rise, Hurricanes	PRCCC (2013), USGS (2010), Government of Puerto Rico (2014)
Trinidad & Tobago	Services (44%); Petroleum (42.1%); Manufacturing (21.3%)	Hilly, mountainous interior and coastal plains	Surface water (52%) Groundwater (32%) Desalination (12%)	Increase in temperature and rainfall extremes, Drought, Sea Level Rise	Government of Trinidad and Tobago (2011, 2013); Central Bank of Trinidad and Tobago (2015)

Turks and Caicos	Tourism (44.3%) Services (38.6%) Goods and Manufacturing (8.7%)	Flat	Desalination Surface water	Increase in temperature and rainfall extremes, Drought, Sea Level Rise	CARIBSAVE (2012), Statistical Office (2014)
US Virgin Islands	Services (84%), Goods (16%)	Hilly, mountainous interior and coastal plains	Desalination Surface water	Increase in temperature and rainfall extremes, Drought, Sea Level Rise, Hurricanes	BEA (2014)

Table 2.4 Three examples of recent climate impacts within the Caribbean

A series of storms	A single storm or hurricane can have devastating impacts on the economy of an island. For example, the total cost of damage and losses associated with Hurricane Tomas (2010) in St. Lucia amounted to 42.4 % of GDP and 47% of public external debt (ECLAC, 2011a). Hurricane Ivan (2004) inflicted approximately 200% of GDP damage on Grenada and the Cayman Islands (CCRIF, 2010).
	A string of storms challenges the ability of an island to recover. Since 2000, Jamaica has been impacted by ten storms or hurricanes: Hurricane Michelle (2001) (0.8% of GDP), Hurricane Charley (2004) (0.002%), Hurricane Ivan (2004) (8.0%). Hurricanes Dennis and Emily (2005) (1.2%), Hurricane Wilma (2005) (0.7%). Hurricane Dean (2007) (3.4%), Tropical Storm Gustav (2008) (2.0%), Tropical Storm Nicole (2010) (1.9%), Hurricane Sandy (2012) (0.9%).
An out of season event	Flash floods in December 2013 during the traditional dry season significantly impacted infrastructures in St. Vincent and the Grenadines and St. Lucia. There was substantial damage to roads and bridges, with impact concentrated in areas with the highest levels of poverty. Damages amounted to 15% of GDP in St. Vincent and the Grenadines and 8% of GDP in St. Lucia. (World Bank Press Release, March 2014).
Two prolonged droughts in six years.	The 2009–10 drought saw stations in Trinidad, Grenada, St. Vincent, Barbados, St Lucia, Dominica, Jamaica recording their lowest ever February (2010) rainfall totals; stations in Anguilla, Grenada, Trinidad, Dominica and St. Vincent recording their lowest ever three-month (January to March, 2010) totals; stations in Tobago, Grenada, Barbados, St. Vincent, St. Lucia and Guyana recording their lowest six-month (October 2009 to March 2010) totals. The drought impacts included a reduction in the banana industry in Dominica (43% lower in 2010 than for 2009); 25 % loss in onion crop and 30 % loss in tomato crop in Antigua; a reduction in hydro power contribution in St. Vincent from 28.69% in Feb 2009 to 12.01% in Feb 2010; high costs in Guyana to deliver water (pumping and creation of canals) to one of its 10 regions; significant costs in every territory to provide water to communities and settlements; record numbers of bush fires throughout the Caribbean. (Trotman *et al.* 2010).
	2015–16 saw the onset of prolonged drought conditions again. Records show that 2015 was the driest year on record for the Eastern Caribbean. The drought impacts were similar to the last major drought of 2009–10.

Furthermore, with future trends suggesting the entrenchment of climate changes already underway, but at unprecedented levels, there is a need to deliberately account for climate in the development plans for the region. Unprecedented further change will exacerbate existing vulnerabilities and expose new ones as climate thresholds are attained and surpassed. Mora *et al.* (2013) determine the timing of 'climate departures' or the 'year when the projected mean climate of a given location moves to a state continuously outside the bounds of historical variability'. From their study, unprecedented climates which bring about disruptions in ecology and society occur earliest in the tropics and amongst low-income countries. The departure year for temperatures (the first year when even the coldest mean annual temperatures achieved thereafter is warmer than the warmest temperatures experienced to date), is in the early 2020s (2023 for Kingston, 2025 for Port-au-Prince, 2026 for Santo Domingo) through the mid-2030s (2031 for Havana, 2034 for Bridgetown and Belmopan) for most Caribbean cities. They suggest also that the departure date for ocean acidity has already passed in 2008, making the region's coral stock extremely vulnerable (Mora *et al.* 2013). It is, however, not only the biodiversity of the region which will come under greater threat. Taylor (2015) suggests a list of the 'emerging vulnerable' in the Caribbean under climate change which includes the urban poor, subsistence farmers, the physically challenged, children, the elderly, outdoor workers, athletes, small businesses, coastal infrastructure, and cultural and historical assets. To varying degrees, these groupings share, the characteristics of inherent sensitivity to climate variations, increasing exposure to harsher environmental conditions and limited capacity to cope with the impacts brought on by unprecedented climate change.

There is a case being made, then, for deliberate and urgent action. Climate change is already having a profound impact on the Caribbean region's geophysical, biological and socio-economic systems. It will only further deplete national budgets, compromise livelihoods and negate gains made in the pursuit of priority development objectives, including strides made with respect to education, food security and combating poverty, as well as access to basic services such as clean water, sanitary living conditions and energy. Climate change is transforming the natural environment into a hazard as opposed to its being an asset whose favourable and familiar characteristics can be exploited for economic development. In other words, the region's future sustainability is under threat if action in response to climate change is not prioritised (Taylor 2015).

If the required actions in response to climate change are to be transformative, they must be (amongst other things) anticipatory and responsive, urgent and timely, adaptive and mitigative, and targeted and tailored to sectoral and national or regional circumstance. Recent attempts to develop climate services premised on a greater understanding of Caribbean climate science have the potential to offset some of the uncertainty due to an 'unreliable' climate. That is, the predictability of Caribbean climate has advanced significantly in recent years through the collaborative efforts of a number of regional institutions (see for example Taylor *et al.* 2013 for a description of a regional climate modelling initiative). Significant efforts are underway to translate this predictive skill into useful climate services in sensitive sectors, including early warning systems. The onset of the 2015 regional drought was better forecast, although its severity was underestimated. Initiatives such as the Caribbean Drought and Precipitation Network (Trotman *et al.* 2008) and the Caribbean Precipitation Outlook (http://rcc.cimh.edu.bb/climate-monitoring/spi-monitor/) provide a measure of foresight which can potentially offset some of the dislocations associated with the changing climate regime, once take up can be encouraged and use of the climate products routinized. The case is being made for even greater scientific endeavours aimed at an improved understanding of, not only the changing climate, but also its direct and indirect linkages to Caribbean life, particularly on sub-regional and sub-national scales.

In conclusion, what is clear is that climate change must be afforded more than passing attention in the Caribbean. Climate considerations must be mainstreamed into the regional planning processes through deliberate and sustained efforts. In the face of unfamiliar, unprecedented and unreliable conditions brought on by climate change, it is only this approach which is likely to facilitate the region becoming resilient to its impacts.

References

Alexander, L. V., Zang, X., Peterson, T. C., Caesar, J., Gleason, B., Klein Tank, A., Haylock, M., Collins, D., Trewin, B., Rahimzadeh, F., Tagipour, A., Ambenje, P., Rupa Kumar, K., Revadekar, J., Griffiths, G., Vincent, L., Stephenson, D., Burn, J., Aguilar, E., Brunet, M., Taylor, M. A., New, M., Zhai, P., Rusticucci, M. and Vazquez-Aguirre, J. L. (2006) 'Global Observed Changes in Daily Climate Extremes of Temperature and Precipitation', *Journal of Geophysical Research*, 111: D05109, doi:10.1029/2005JD006290.

Bender, M. A., Knutson, T. R., Tuleya, R. E., Sirutis, J. J., Vecchi, G. A., Garner, S. T. and Held I. M. (2010) 'Modeled Impact of Anthropogenic Warning on the Frequency of Intense Atlantic Hurricanes', *Science*, 327:454–458.

Bueno, R., Herzfeld, C., Stanton, E. A. and Ackerman, F. (2008) 'The Caribbean and Climate Change: The Cost of Inaction', Medford, MA: Tufts University.

Campbell, J. D., Taylor, M. A., Stephenson, T. S., Watson, R. and Whyte F. S. (2010) 'Future Climate of the Caribbean from a Regional Climate Model', *International Journal of Climatology*, 31(12) 1866–1878. Available at: http://doi.wiley.com/10.1002/joc.2200.

Cashman, A., Nurse, L. and Charlery, J. (2010) 'Climate Change in the Caribbean: The Water Management Implications', *The Journal of Environment & Development*, 19(1): 42–67.

Church, J. A., White, N. J. and Coleman R., Lambeck, K. and Mitrovica, J. (2004) 'Estimates of the Regional Distribution of Sea-Level Rise over the 1950–2000 Period', *Journal of Climate*, 17: 2609–2625.

Donner, S. D., Knutson, T. R. and Oppenheimer, M. (2007) 'Model-Based Assessment of the Role of Human-Induced Climate Change in the 2005 Caribbean Coral Bleaching Event', *Proceedings of the National Academy of Sciences of the United States of America*, 104: 5483–5488.

Ebi, K. L., Lewis, N. D. and Corvalan, C. (2006) 'Climate Variability and Change and their Potential Health Effects in Small Island States: Information for Adaptation Planning in the Health Sector', *Environmental Health Perspectives*, 114:1957–1963.

Economic Commission for Latin America and the Caribbean (ECLAC) (2005) 'Comparison of the Socio-Economic Impacts of Natural Disasters on Caribbean Societies in 2004'. Available at: www.cepal.org/en/publications/27585-comparison-socio-economic-impacts-natural-disasters-caribbean-societies-2004.

Emanuel, K. (2007) 'Environmental Factors Affecting Tropical Cyclone Powder Dissipation', *Journal of Climate*, **20**, 5497–5509, doi: http://dx.doi.org/10.1175/2007JCLI1571.1.

Gamble, D. W. (2009) 'Caribbean Vulnerability: Development of an Appropriate Climatic Framework' in D. McGregor, D. Dodman, and D. Barker (eds.) *Global Change and*

Caribbean Vulnerability: Environment, Economy and Society at Risk? Kingston, Jamaica: University of the West Indies Press.

Gamble, D. W., Campbell, D., Allen, T. L., Barker, D., Curtis, S., McGregor, D. and Popke, J. (2010) 'Climate Change, Drought, and Jamaican Agriculture: Local Knowledge and the Climate Record', *Annals of the Association of American Geographers*, 100(4): 880.

Goldenberg, S., Landsea, C., Mestas-Nuñez, A. and Gray, W. (2001) 'The Recent Increase in Atlantic Hurricane Activity: Causes and Implications', *Science*, 293(5529): 474–479.

Haites, E., Pantin, D., Attzs, M., Bruce, J. and MacKinnon, J. (2002) 'Assessment of the Economic Impact of Climate Change on CARICOM Countries', World Bank Technical Paper, Toronto, Canada: Margaree Consultants Inc.

Hendry, M. (1993) 'Sea-Level Movements and Shoreline Change' in G. Maul (ed.) *Climatic Change in the Intra-Americas Sea*, London: Edward Arnold, 115–161.

Horton, R., Herweijer, C., Rosenzweig, C., Liu, J. P., Gornitz, V. and Ruane A. C. (2008) 'Sea Level Rise Projections for Current Generation CGCMs Based on the Semi-Empirical Method', *Geophysical Research Letters*, 35, L02715, doi:10.1029/2007GL032486.

Intergovernmental Panel on Climate Change (IPCC) (2012) 'Managing the Risks of Extreme Events and Disasters to Advance Climate Change Adaptation. A Special Report of Working Groups I and II of the Intergovernmental Panel on Climate Change', C. B. Field, V. Barros, T. F. Stocker, D. Qin, D. J. Dokken, K. L. Ebi, M. D. Mastrandrea, K. J. Mach, G-K. Plattner, S. K. Allen, M. Tignor, and P. M. Midgley (eds.), Cambridge, UK, and New York: Cambridge University Press, 582.

Intergovernmental Panel on Climate Change (IPCC) (2013) 'Climate Change 2013: The Physical Science Basis. Contribution of Working Group I to the Fifth Assessment Report of the Intergovernmental Panel on Climate Change' T. F. Stocker, D. Qin, G-K. Plattner, M. Tignor, S. K. Allen, J. Boschung, A. Nauels, Y. Xia, V. Bex and P. M. Midgley (eds.), Cambridge, UK and New York: Cambridge University Press, 1535 pp.

Intergovernmental Panel on Climate Change (IPCC) (2014) 'Climate Change 2014: Synthesis Report. Summary for Policymakers', Core Writing Team: R. K. Pachauri and L. Meyer (eds.), Geneva, Switzerland: IPCC. Available at: www.ipcc.ch/pdf/assessment-report/ar5/syr/SYR_AR5_SPMcorr2.pdf.

Jones, P. D., Harpham, C., Harris, I., Goodess, C. M., Burton, A., Centella-Artola, A., Taylor, M. A., Bezanilla-Morlot, A., Campbell, J. D., Stephenson, T. S., Joslyn, O., Nicholls, K. and Baur, T. (2015) 'Long-Term Trends in Precipitation and Temperature across the Caribbean', *International Journal of Climatology*, doi:10.1002/joc.4557.

Karmalkar, A. V., New, M., Taylor, M. A., Campbell, J., Stephenson, T., New, M., Centella, A., Benzanilla, A. and Charlery, J. (2013) 'A Review of Observed and Projected Changes in Climate for the Islands in the Caribbean', *Atmosfera* 26(2):283–309.

Knutson, T. R., McBride, J. L., Chan, J., Emanuel, K., Holland, G., Landsea, C., Held, I., Kossin, J. P., Srivastava, A. K. and Sugi, M. (2010) 'Tropical Cyclones and Climate Change', *Nature Geoscience*, **3**, 157–163, doi:10.1038/ngeo779.

Knutson, T. R., Sirutis, J. J., Vecchi, G. A., Garner, S., Zhao, M., Kim, H-S., Bender, M., Tuleya, R. E., Held, I. M. and Villarini, G. (2013) 'Dynamical Downscaling Projections of Twenty-First-Century Atlantic Hurricane Activity: CMIP3 and CMIP5 Model-Based Scenarios', *J. Climate*, **26**, 6591–6617, doi: http://dx.doi.org/10.1175/JCLI-D-12-00539.1

Lewsey, C., Cid, G. and Kruse, E. (2004) 'Assessing Climate Change Impacts on Coastal Infrastructure in the Eastern Caribbean', *Marine Policy* 28:393–409.

McSweeney, C., New, M., Lizcano, G. and Lu., X. (2010) 'UNDP Climate Change Country Profiles: Improving the Accessibility of Observed and Projected Climate Information for Studies of Climate Change in Developing Countries', School of Geography and the

Environment, University of Oxford. Available at: http://journals.ametsoc.org/doi/pdf/10.1175/2009BAMS2826.1.

Mann, M. E., Bradley, R. S. and Hughes, M. K. (2000) Long-Term Variability in the ENSO and Associated Teleconnections. Pp. 357–412 in H. F. Díaz and V. Markgraf (eds.), *ENSO: Multi-Scale Variability and Global and Regional Impacts*, New York: Cambridge University Press.

Mimura, N., Nurse, L., McLean, R. F., Agard, J., Briguglio, L., Lefale, P., Payet, R. and Sem, G. (2007) 'Small Islands. Climate Change 2007: Impacts, Adaptation and Vulnerability' in M. L. Parry, O. F. Canziani, J. P. Palutikof, P. J. van der Linden, and C. E. Hanson (eds.) *Contribution of Working Group II to the Fourth Assessment Report of the Intergovernmental Panel on Climate Change*, Cambridge, UK: Cambridge University Press 687–716.

Mora C., Frazier, A. G., Longman, R. J., Dacks, R. S., Walton, M. M., Tong, E. J., Joseph J., Sanchez, J. J., Kaiser, L. R., Stender, Y. O., Anderson, J. M., Ambrosino, C. M., Fernandez-Silva, I., Giuseffi, L. M. and Giambelluca, T. W. (2013) 'The Projected Timing of Climate Departure from Recent Variability', *Nature*, 502: 183–187.

Palanisamy, H., Becker, M., Meyssignac, B., Henry, O., and Cazenave, A. (2012) 'Regional Sea Level Change and Variability in the Caribbean Sea since 1950', *Journal of Geodetic Science*, 2(2): 125–133.

Perrette, M., Landerer, F., Riva, R., Frieler, K. and Meinshausen, M. (2013) 'A Scaling Approach to Project Regional Sea Level Rise and its Uncertainties', *Earth System Dynamics*, 4: 11–29.

Pulwarty, R. S., Nurse, L. A. and Trotz, U. O. (2010) 'Caribbean Islands in a Changing Climate', *Environment: Science and Policy for Sustainable Development* 52(6):16–27.

Rahmstorf, S. (2007) 'A Semi-Empirical Approach to Projecting Future Sea-Level Rise', *Science*, 315: 368–370.

Rignot, E. and Kanagaratnam, P. (2006) 'Changes in the Velocity Structure of the Greenland Ice Sheet', *Science*, 311(5763), 986–990.

Simpson, M. C., Scott, D., New, M., Sim, R., Smith, D., Harrison, M., Eakin, C. M., Warrick, R., Strong, A. E., Kouwenhoven, P., Harrison, S., Wilson, M. D., Nelson, G. C., Donner, S., Kay, R., Geldhill, D. K., Liu, G., Morgan, J. A., Kleypas, J. A., Mumby, P. J., Palazzo, A., Christensen, T.R.L., Baskett, M. L., Skirving, W. J., Elrick, C., Taylor, M., Magalhaes, M., Bell, J., Burnett, J. B., Rutty, M. K., Overmas, M. and Robertson, R. (2009) *An Overview of Modelling Climate Change Impacts in the Caribbean Region with Contribution from the Pacific Islands*. Barbados, West Indies: United Nations Development Programme (UNDP).

Simpson, M. C., Scott, D., Harrison, M., Silver, N., O'Keeffe, E., Harrison, S., Taylor, M., Sim, R., Lizcano, G., Wilson, M., Rutty, M., Stager, H., Oldham, J., New, M., Clarke, J., Day, O., Fields, N., Georges, J., Waithe, R. and McSharry, P. (2010) *Quantification and Magnitude of Losses and Damages Resulting from the Impacts of Climate Change: Modelling the Transformational Impacts and Costs of Sea Level Rise in the Caribbean* (full document), Barbados, West Indies: United Nations Development Programme (UNDP).

Stahle, D. W., Arrigo, R. D., Krusic, P. J., D'Arrigo, R. D., Krusic, P. J., Cleaveland, M. K., Cook, E. R., Allan, R. J., Cole, J. E., Dunbar, R. B., Therrell, M. D., Gay, D. A., Moore, M. D., Stokes, M. A., Burns, B. T., Villanueva-Diaz, J. and Thompson, L. G. (1998) 'Experimental Dendroclimatic Reconstruction of the Southern Oscillation', *Bulletin of American Meteorological Society* 79: 2137–2152.

Stephenson, T. S., Vincent, L. A., Allen, T., Van Meerbeeck, C. J., McLean, N., Peterson, T. C., Taylor, M. A. and co-authors (2014) 'Changes in Extreme Temperature and Precipitation in the Caribbean Region 1961–2010', *International Journal of Climatology*, 34(9) 2957–2971.

Taylor, M. A. (2015) '*Why Climate Demands Change*', The Grace Kennedy Foundation Lecture 2015, Kingston, Jamaica: Grace Kennedy Foundation.

Taylor, M. A., Centella, A., Charlery, J., Benzanilla, A., Campbell, J., Borrajero, I., Stephenson T., and Nurmohamed, R. (2013): 'The PRECIS-Caribbean Story: Lessons and Legacies', *Bulletin of the American Meteorological Society*, 94, 1065–1073, doi: 10.1175/BAMS-D-11-00235.

Torres, R. R., and Tsimplis, M. N. (2013) 'Sea-Level Trends and Interannual Variability in the Caribbean Sea', *Journal of Geophysical Research: Oceans*, 118: 2934–2947, doi:10.1002/jgrc.20229.

Trotman, A. R. and Farrell, D. A. (2010) 'Drought Impacts and Early Warning in the Caribbean: The Drought of 2009–2010', in Caribbean Institute for Meteorology and Hydrology: Technical Cooperation Workshop for Development of the Caribbean Regional Cooperation Programme in Multi-Hazard Warning System. Available at: https://www. wmo.int/pages/prog/drr/events/ Barbados/Pres/4-CIMH-Drought.pdf.

Trotman, A. R., Mehdi, B., Gollamudi, A. and Senecal, C. (2008) 'Drought and Precipitation Monitoring for Enhanced Integrated Water Resources Management in the Caribbean', in *Caribbean Environmental Forum*.

United Nations (UN) (2014) 'Resolutions Adopted by the General Assembly on 14 November 2014: Small Island Developing States (SIDS) Accelerated Modalities Action (SAMOA). Pathway' Available at: www.un.org/ga/search/view_doc.asp?symbol=A/RES/69/15&Lang=E.

World Travel and Tourism Council (WTTC) (2016) 'Travel & Tourism Economic Impact 2016: Caribbean'. Available at: www.wttc.org/-/media/files/reports. economic%20impact %20research/regions%202016/caribbean2016.pdf.

Part II

Rural livelihoods and adaptive responses to climate change

3 Assessing the vulnerability of Caribbean farmers to climate change impacts

A comparative study of cocoa farmers in Jamaica and Trinidad

Kevon Rhiney, Anton Eitzinger, Aidan D. Farrell and Michael A. Taylor

Introduction

Agriculture is undoubtedly one of the most vulnerable sectors in the world to climate change (IPCC 2007, Jarvis *et al.* 2010), and several studies have already predicted that global agricultural production could suffer progressive yield losses by the end of the century (Lobell *et al.* 2008, 2011; Challinor and Wheeler 2008; Challinor *et al.* 2009; Thornton *et al.* 2011). While an increasing number of studies illustrate the likely impact of long-term changes in the global climate on regional farming systems, there is a noticeable shortage of impact studies examining the vulnerability of agricultural systems in small island states (Nurse and Moore 2005; Tompkins *et al.* 2005; Mimura *et al.* 2007; Nurse *et al.* 2014). This is despite the fact that small island states are considered to be amongst the most vulnerable countries in the world to the adverse impacts of global climate change and are also regarded as major food security hotspots. This is quite evident in the case of the insular Caribbean, which is expected to be amongst the earliest and most impacted by climate change over the course of this century (Pulwarty *et al.* 2010; Simpson *et al.* 2009; Trotz and Lindo 2013).

Given current climate projections, there is a growing consensus that if the world continues on its current emission trajectory, we are likely to exceed a $+2°$ C rise in global mean surface temperature by the end of this century (IPCC 2014). In fact, some would argue that even drastic reductions of global greenhouse gas emissions now will be insufficient to avoid some of the impending impacts of future climate change (Magnan 2014). As such, adaptation to climate change is arguably the only foreseeable means of survival for many small island states – the majority of which are located in the Caribbean and the Pacific.

In the Caribbean, this need for adaptation is particularly evident in the agriculture sector as medium to longer-term changes in climate could potentially displace the livelihoods of thousands of smallholder farmers across the region. Any significant flux or change in the region's climate (especially in terms of temperature and rainfall) could have significant adverse effects on the sector, including a general reduction in agricultural productivity and an increase in the risk of crop failure. Studies have shown, for instance, that increasing global temperatures in other regions over the last three decades have already resulted in significant yield losses in many crops (Long and Ort 2010; Lobell *et al.* 2011). While this seems to be a likely scenario for the Caribbean, regional farmers are currently operating with only limited information on the likely impacts of future climate change and of the potential of available cultivars to withstand these changes.

This chapter primarily reports on a baseline study, which was conducted with cocoa farmers in Jamaica and Trinidad, to examine the likely impacts of predicted changes in climate on this high-value perennial crop, and to take stock of the associated socio-economic consequences, especially for rural smallholders. The study was part of a larger regional project that was aimed at enhancing the region's capacity to screen and select crop cultivars that are more resistant to drought and heat stress. Through a combination of plant varietal research and crop niche modelling, the project team was able to estimate how predicted changes in future climate could affect the yield performance of different varieties of tomato and cocoa commonly grown throughout the Caribbean. In general, results from the study indicate that there will be an overall reduction in the area of land suitable for crop cultivation as the region's climate gets progressively warmer and as rainfall becomes more variable. The largest reductions in suitability are expected in low-lying areas, particularly along Jamaica's southern coast and in Trinidad's southwestern region. In the case of cocoa, the impacts were found to be far less significant under a warmer climate. Reductions in dry season rainfall and overall changes in inter-seasonal precipitation patterns were found to be the most likely direct causes of declining crop yield for all the cocoa varieties tested. The local-scale implications of these results are wide-ranging, especially for small, resource-poor farmers, and will likely produce uneven vulnerability outcomes.

Methodology

The fieldwork informing this paper involved community-baseline surveys of farmers operating in established cocoa-growing regions in Jamaica and Trinidad (see Chapter 2, Figure 2.1). Northern Clarendon was chosen for the cocoa baseline survey in Jamaica, given the importance of this region in terms of cocoa production. Cocoa is grown in almost every parish in Jamaica, but the major cocoa-producing parishes are Clarendon, St. Mary, St. Catherine, St. Andrew and St. Thomas. Currently, an estimated 7,000 farmers are engaged in the farming of some 8,800 acres of cocoa across Jamaica, with Clarendon recording the highest average acreage. The majority of the surveys were carried out in Trout Hall, located at an elevation of approximately 250 metres above mean sea level. Trout Hall is one of Clarendon's most established cocoa-producing areas, along with communities like Smithville, Brandon Hill, Wood Hall and Park Hall.

In the Trinidad case study, surveys were conducted in eleven communities that were identified as major cocoa-growing areas. These included communities such as Moruga, Siparia, Point Fortin and Penal-Debe in the southwest and Cumuto, Sangre Chiquito and Coryal in the northwest. Cocoa is grown throughout most of

Trinidad, with a fairly high concentration of cocoa estates in the northern, central and southwestern sections of the island. The most recent estimates suggest that there are approximately 1,700 farmers growing cocoa and coffee in Trinidad and Tobago, cultivating an estimated 600 tonnes of cocoa beans per year (Bekele 2004). It is important to note that while cocoa produced in these two islands contributes very little to overall world cocoa production, the Caribbean region in general produces some of the world's finest and best varieties of cocoa, and generally commands a premium price on the international market.

Fieldwork for the baseline assessment was conducted simultaneously in both countries between November and December 2014. A total of 54 cocoa farmers were surveyed in Jamaica, compared to 40 farmers in Trinidad. A semi-formal instrument was used to conduct the surveys. Questions covered general farming practices, production challenges and socio-demographic characteristics of the farming population. The survey also assessed farmers' perceptions of climate and climate change, with particular emphasis on drought and heat-related stress.

In terms of the climate impact analysis, several regional climate models run under various IPCC emission scenarios were used in conjunction with downscaled climate information available for Jamaica and Trinidad, covering the period up to 2100. By combining the model results with the plant physiological data obtained from the plant-screening exercise done for the larger study, a suitability index was generated for each cultivar and then mapped using GIS.

The EcoCrop model and results from the screening trials were then used to determine and map the suitability of the different cocoa cultivars examined in the study. EcoCrop uses environmental ranges as inputs to determine the main niche of a crop, and then produces an overall crop suitability as a percentage, and separated suitability values for temperature and precipitation as output (Eitzinger *et al.* 2015a, 2015b).

Results and analysis

Modelling future climate change impacts on cocoa production

Climate change is not only likely to cause a decline in yields of some very important crops throughout the region, but the distribution of crop suitability within current production areas will change as well. According to analysis of climatic data for the RCP 8.5 emissions scenario (a scenario of comparatively high greenhouse gas emissions) for both Jamaica and Trinidad, several changes in climatic characteristics are to be anticipated. In general, model predictions forecast a gradual increase in temperature and a moderate decrease in rainfall. In comparison to a current annual daily mean temperature of 26.5°C, by 2050, the annual mean temperature is projected to increase by between 2 and 2.1°C. Additionally, the average temperature of the warmest month will potentially increase by 2.1 to 2.2°C by 2050, while in the coldest month, the minimum temperature is forecast to increase by between 1.8 and 1.9°C. In terms of precipitation, the models predict that by the 2050s, annual rainfall may decline by between 700 mm and 800 mm; this is in comparison to a current average rainfall of 2,219 mm per year for Jamaica and

2,000 mm per year for Trinidad. Even more important are the anticipated inter-seasonal variations in rainfall, which may see a reduction in wet season rainfall and dry periods becoming even drier and more extensive across the region.

Amidst these model predictions, water shortages and thermal stress associated with increases in evapotranspiration and higher daily mean temperatures are generally expected to present a major challenge for agricultural production throughout the Caribbean. The impacts on different crops will not be uniform, however, as this partly depends on the capacity of local varieties to withstand these longer-term changes in climate (which has implications for their spatial distribution and range), and the ability of individual farmers to adjust their crop-management practices. According to our crop model, the production areas for cocoa will not have significant suitability changes under a warmer climate, due largely to the wide temperature range of the cocoa plant itself. However, projected reductions in annual precipitation, as well as inter-seasonal variations in rainfall distribution, will

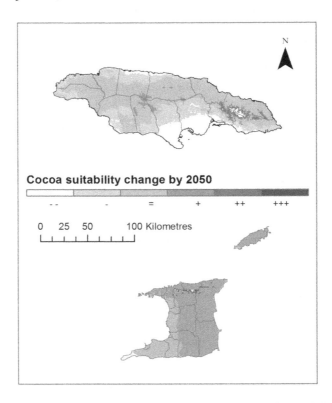

Figure 3.1 Modelled suitability change of cocoa in Jamaica (top) and Trinidad (bottom) by 2050. Darker shaded areas are predicted to have increasing (+ signs) suitability change in the future, while lighter shades are predicted to have decreasing (– signs) suitability change, for the specific crop. Number of signs shows magnitude of increase/decrease, equals sign means no predicted future change of suitability.

Source: International Centre for Tropical Agriculture (CIAT) 2016.

more than likely result in declining cocoa yields in coming decades. According to the model results, cocoa production will suffer suitability losses of between 10 and 15 per cent by 2050 especially in lower, drier zones in Jamaica and Trinidad.

These results have significant implications for the viability of the cocoa industry in the Caribbean and present a severe threat to the livelihood of thousands of farmers and their families. Nevertheless, these projections only present part of the story as vulnerability is also socially produced. The ability of farmers to adequately respond to these climatic stresses will partly depend on their existing capacities and capabilities to adapt. Implicit in this is the recognition that climate change will be more likely to produce uneven vulnerability outcomes. These outcomes will also be highly contingent on wider societal and developmental issues, as well as the social and economic conditions of the individual farmers themselves. These conditions often vary from the degree of exposure and sensitivity to climate-related hazards, to varying capacities in adaptation, which are usually influenced by differences in gender, age, knowledge and risk perception, and inequalities in access, control and ownership over resources (Cardona 2011; Rhiney 2015).

Farmers' exposure and sensitivity to climate-related stress

One of the main purposes of the farmer survey was to capture baseline data, informed by farmers' own local knowledge and experiences, to ground-truth the scientific model results and outputs. This involved ascertaining the socio-demographic characteristics of the farmers that were typically involved in cocoa cultivation, as well as identifying the underlying factors driving their vulnerability to climate-related hazards, the main production challenges and the existing coping strategies being employed by disadvantaged farmers. Essentially, the baseline was designed to take stock of the current situation, particularly regarding farmers' level of awareness of relevant climate-change-related issues, as well as to give some idea of the state of readiness of local farmers to adapt to the new climatic conditions.

It is clear from the survey that cocoa is typically produced on small and medium sized farms, with the majority of individual estates amounting to less than five acres of land. The cocoa estates in Trinidad were noticeably larger in comparison to the estates in Jamaica. The average farm size in Jamaica was 3.7 acres, with nearly a quarter of the farmers (24.1%) operating on plots amounting to one acre or less in size. The average size for the cocoa estates in Trinidad was 7.2 acres and the minimum recorded estate was 2.5 acres.

The majority of farmers had been involved in farming for over 25 years in both case studies. This is a reflection of the average age of the farmers surveyed, the majority of whom were over 40 years of age. While the questionnaire provided a generally good measure of farmers' experience and knowledge base, as much as 92 per cent of the farmers surveyed had no formal training in agriculture, and participation in farmers' organizations was not the norm – amounting to less than 25 per cent of the sampled population in Jamaica and 31 per cent in Trinidad.

Another key area of enquiry for the baseline surveys was to explore farmers' perceptions of long-term climate change. Numerous studies have shown that farmers' perceptions of climate are inseparable from their years of accumulated local knowledge, through which they negotiate their daily activities (Roncoli et al. 2002; Vedwan 2006). As pointed out by Gamble et al. (2010: 2) 'although farmers might not understand the science behind climate change, their continual observation of and interaction with the surrounding environment heightens their awareness of even minor deviations from what is perceived to be normal weather and climate conditions'. This seems to be the case based on the findings of this study. A majority of the farmers indicated that they have, in fact, noticed changes in weather patterns in recent decades. Most of the farmers in Jamaica (around 78%) reported observing changes in rainfall patterns over the last 20 years. An even greater number of the Jamaican respondents (84.7%) indicated experiencing changes in the timing of the traditional rainy season. The results were strikingly similar for Trinidad. Approximately 80 per cent of the farmers in Trinidad indicated that they have observed annual changes in rainfall over the past 20 years, while 76 per cent reported observing changes in the timing and duration of the traditional rainy season.

In terms of observed trends in annual rainfall distribution, 64 per cent of the cocoa farmers in Jamaica indicated observing a declining trend in recent decades. On the contrary, the majority of farmers in Trinidad (approximately 60%) reported that rainfall had increased over the last few decades. When quizzed further, farmers seemed to have been experiencing greater variations in inter-seasonal rainfall as opposed to a general increase or decrease. This seems to be the case for farmers in the two countries studied. Farmers generally complained about the growing unpredictability of the rainy season, which poses a major limitation to routine farm-management practices. This is especially important since the large majority of cocoa farmers surveyed had no form of irrigation on their farms.

In terms of impacts, a few farmers pointed to the erratic nature of the rains they had been receiving in recent years. These had resulted in greater incidence of local-level flooding, especially for farm holdings located in low-lying areas. Other impacts, believed to be associated with the observed changes in rainfall, included noticeable changes in the growing and fruiting cycles of individual cocoa trees, shedding of flowers and the outbreak of diseases such as the black pod or cherelle wilt. During prolonged dry periods, cocoa pods took a much longer time to ripen, resulting in either fruit abortion or the production of smaller-sized pods. All of these impacts can have a severe negative effect on farmers' income and could potentially displace the livelihoods of the most resource-poor farmers.

As it pertains to farmers' responses, or adjustments to these perceived changes in rainfall, the results were mixed. In the case of Jamaica, only 15 per cent of the cocoa farmers have made adjustments on their farms in response to the observed changes. Similarly, only approximately 20 per cent of the farmers surveyed in Trinidad indicated that they had made some form of adjustment to their farming practices in response to the observed changes in rainfall. These included practices such as:

- mulching to regulate soil moisture loss during dry periods;
- removal of shade trees under humid conditions to prevent the spread of diseases such as the black pod;

- increasing the application of certain inputs such as fertilizers and fungicide (though very costly) or altering the time these inputs are normally applied;
- constructing new drains on farms to reduce the risk of flooding, or expanding/ cleaning existing drains; and
- employing a range of on-farm irrigation and water storage practices.

Approximately 68 per cent of the farmers surveyed in Jamaica and 58 per cent of the farmers in Trinidad indicated that they had also observed a noticeable change in mean air temperature over the last 20 years. The large majority of farmers in Jamaica (approximately 60%) held the view that the mean temperature has increased over the period. While this compares to only 35 per cent of the farmers in Trinidad, the field data suggest that higher air temperatures could become a problem over time if combined with other factors. So while cocoa trees generally display a high heat tolerance, they are less able to cope under warmer, drier conditions. Farmers who reported observing an increasing trend in air temperature pointed to impacts such as wilting of cocoa trees, increased incidence of fire outbreaks, root damage (usually linked to wild fires), stunting, reduction in the size of cocoa pods, longer ripening periods, and in extreme cases, fruit abortion and the premature shedding of flowers.

Only a handful of farmers indicated that they have made some adjustment to their farm-management practices in lieu of the perceived changes in temperature. A common coping practice amongst farmers was to increase the amount of water normally applied to tree crops. Since it was not a common practice to irrigate cocoa estates in the Caribbean, this meant farmers had to actually purchase water during extended dry periods. Of course, not all farmers were able to sustain this practice, given how expensive it is to purchase water. Studies have also shown that during periods of severe drought, this vulnerability can be further compounded by inefficiencies in state-led relief efforts and the prohibitive cost of accessing water from informal water truck operators (McGregor *et al.* 2009).

While these results paint a generally homogenous picture, it is also quite evident that the aggregate impacts of a changing climate will not be felt uniformly, even amongst farmers specializing in the same crops. Indeed, the cumulative impacts of a changing climate regime will ultimately depend on the individual farmer's capacity to respond to unstable market forces and localized climatic (and non-climatic) shocks and stresses, including the ability to adjust planting schedules or diversify into new resistant crop varieties in response to erratic crop yields and weather patterns. If the regional climate should get drier and warmer, then it will become increasingly difficult for many farmers to cope, much less adapt. Unequal access to critical farm inputs, capital, information and other resources will certainly produce different vulnerability outcomes.

Being a perennial crop means that cocoa requires far more time and a substantially greater amount of investment compared to annual crops that take a much shorter time to mature. As such, cocoa farmers could very well be at a disadvantage in the long run, given how long it takes a cocoa plant to mature and hence its potentially greater exposure to climate-induced shocks and stresses. Also, farmers who invest in the cultivation of perennial crops, such as cocoa or coffee, may find it more difficult to respond to changing temperature and precipitation patterns and market price signals because of the significantly higher costs associated with the uprooting and replanting of these crops (Slater *et al.* 2007).

On the other hand, tree crops have a built-in resilience to climate fluctuations as they have established root systems, energy stores and more hardy woody tissue. Indeed, cocoa demonstrated a generally higher tolerance to heat stress compared to most other crops. This suggests that cocoa farmers would be less likely to suffer a significant fallout in income if mean temperate increases. The challenge however, is related to the other underlying problems affecting the industry. Often there are a host of things that could shape the long-term viability of a crop subsector, including for example, changing commodity prices, changing levels of government support, unstable input costs, and even changing consumption patterns globally. Even though cocoa is a high-value global commodity, in the large majority of cases, the environments in which smallholders in Jamaica and Trinidad have to operate have not done enough to stimulate innovation and diversification in the subsector. While Caribbean cocoa commands a premium price on the world market, the regional industry has been struggling in recent years to sustain production levels. This has been attributed to a combination of unfavourable weather conditions, coupled with poorly maintained fields and farmers' general dissatisfaction with farm-gate prices.

Concluding remarks

This chapter was primarily aimed at illustrating the varied ways that medium to long-term changes in both rainfall and ambient temperature could potentially impact cocoa production in Jamaica and Trinidad, as well as to elucidate the underlying factors driving the vulnerability of small-scale cocoa producers in the Caribbean to climatic shocks and stresses, and the implications these challenges pose for future adaptation action in the agricultural sector. Results from the study indicate that there will be an overall reduction in the area of land suitable for growing most crops, as the region's climate gets progressively warmer, with the largest reductions in suitability expected in low-lying areas. In the case of cocoa, however, the impacts were found to be far less significant under a warmer climate. Reductions in dry season rainfall and shifting rainfall patterns were found to be the most likely direct causes of declining crop yield for all the cocoa varieties tested. While these results point to a future characterized by enormous and unprecedented challenges, the local-scale impacts will more likely produce uneven vulnerability outcomes mediated against a range of ecological, socio-economic, institutional, political and cultural factors.

Therefore, there is an urgent need for devising agricultural adaptation measures that are not only better suited for both long and short-term climatic changes, but also more cost-effective and far-reaching in terms of their socio-economic impacts. There are inherent difficulties in effectively adapting to an unknown and uncertain future. Adaptation implies maintaining or strengthening resilience against current disruptions or disturbances, on the one hand, and being capable of effectively planning for the long term, on the other (Cardona *et al.* 2012; Magnan 2014). The latter point implies wagering on the future gains to be had from initiatives carried out today. In practice, it is very difficult to identify exactly what people are adapting to, or to tease apart whether they are responding to short or long-term environmental or socio-economic change. Engaging with these issues upfront could help in avoiding maladaptation and the social and environmental injustices that are often meted out against the most vulnerable groups in our societies. So while increasing on-farm access to irrigation can potentially aid in mitigating drought impacts or seasonal shifts in rainfall, if precipitation levels should continue to decline over the long run, water for irrigation purposes will become less available. Added to this, most cropping systems throughout the Caribbean are rain-fed and the adoption of irrigation systems (particularly amongst small-scale farmers) is extremely disjointed and slow. Arguably then, the promotion of irrigation schemes could actually exacerbate existing social inequalities amongst different groups of farmers – with small-scale farmers being the least likely to benefit. The same argument holds for other adaptation strategies that tend to be capital-intensive, such as greenhouse cultivation. And while breeding more climate-resilient crops contains tremendous potential for alleviating rural poverty and empowering local farmers, attention also has to be paid to underlying institutional, developmental and market forces that constrain farmers' ability to cope or adapt to both short and long-term environmental and socio-economic changes.

In closing, the authors seek to draw attention to the study's contribution to the regional food security discourse. It is argued here that under a variable and changing regional climate regime, food-production systems will come under increasing stress. This points more to the issue of availability, but has implications for the other pillars of food security as well. Any significant fallout in food production will certainly have implications for farmer and national incomes, as well as food prices and quality. An important and emerging theme, however, relates to the fact that promoting more resilient crop varieties will not necessarily solve the Caribbean's food insecurity problem unless attention is paid to the underlying systemic challenges affecting the regional agriculture sector.

Acknowledgement

This work was supported by a Caribsave-INTASAVE Caribbean grant (CIRCA: Impacts and Resilience in Caribbean Agriculture, No. CDKN/RC28).

References

Barker, D. (2012) 'Caribbean Agriculture in a Period of Global Change: Vulnerabilities and Opportunities', *Caribbean Studies*, 40 (2): 41–61.
Bekele, F. L. (2004) 'The History of Cocoa Production in Trinidad and Tobago', *Proceedings of the APASTT Seminar/Exhibition*, St. Augustine, Trinidad: Association of Professional Agricultural Scientists of Trinidad and Tobago.

Cardona, O. D. (2011) 'Disaster Risk and Vulnerability: Notions and Measurement of Human and Environmental Insecurity', in H. G. Brauch, U. Oswald Spring, C. Mesjasz, (eds.) *Coping with Global Environmental Change, Disasters and Security: Threats, Challenges, Vulnerabilities and Risks*, Berlin: Springer, 107–122.

CCCCC (2011) *2011–2015 Caribbean Regional Resilience Development Implementation Plan (IP)*, Belmopan, Belize: Caribbean Community Climate Change Centre (CCCCC).

Challinor, A. and Wheeler, T. (2008) 'Crop Yield Reduction in the Tropics under Climate Change: Processes and Uncertainties', *Agricultural and Forest Meteorology*, 148 (3): 343–356.

Challinor, A. J., Ewert, F., Arnold, S., Simelton, E., and Fraser, E. (2009) 'Crops and Climate Change: Progress, Trends, and Challenges in Simulating Impacts and Informing Adaptation', *Journal of Experimental Botany*, 60 (10): 2775–2789.

Eitzinger, A., Farrell, A., Rhiney, K., Carmona, S., van Loosen, I., and Taylor, M. (2015) 'Trinidad and Tobago: Assessing the Impact of Climate Change on Cocoa and Tomato', CIAT Policy Brief No. 27. Centro Internacional de Agricultura Tropical (CIAT), Cali, Colombia.

Eitzinger, A., Rhiney, K., Farrell, A., Carmona, S., van Loosen, I., and Taylor, M. (2015) 'Jamaica: Assessing the Impact of Climate Change on Cocoa and Tomato', CIAT Policy Brief No. 28. Centro Internacional de Agricultura Tropical (CIAT), Cali, Colombia.

Gamble, D. W., Campbell, D., Allen, T. L., Barker, D., Curtis, S., McGregor, D. and Popke, J. (2010) 'Climate Change, Drought and Jamaican Agriculture: Local Knowledge and Climate Change Record', *Annals of the Association of American Geographers*, 100 (4): 880–893.

IPCC (2007) *Climate Change. Impacts, Adaptation and Vulnerability. Contribution of Working Group II to the Fourth Assessment Report of the Intergovernmental Panel on Climate Change*, in M. L. Parry, O. F. Canziani, J. P. Palutikof, P. J. Van Der Linde, and C. E. Hanson (eds.), Cambridge: Cambridge University Press, 7–22.

IPCC (2014) Summary for Policymakers. In: *Climate Change 2014: Impacts, Adaptation, and Vulnerability. Part A: Global and Sectoral Aspects. Contribution of Working Group II to the Fifth Assessment Report of the Intergovernmental Panel on Climate Change.* C. B. Field, V. R. Barros, D. J. Dokken, K. J. Mach, M. D. Mastrandrea, T. E. Bilir, M. Chatterjee, K. L. Ebi, Y. O. Estrada, R. C. Genova, B. Girma, E. S. Kissel, A. N. Levy, S. MacCracken, P. R. Mastrandrea, and L. L. White (eds.), Cambridge: Cambridge University Press, pp. 1–3.

Jarvis, A., Lau, C., Cook, S., Wollenberg, E., Hansen, J., Bonilla, O. and Challinor, A. (2011) 'An Integrated Adaptation and Mitigation Framework for Developing Agricultural Research: Synergies and Trade Offs', *Experimental Agriculture*, 47(2): 185–203.

Knutti, R., and Sedláček, J. (2012) 'Robustness and Uncertainties in the Bew CMIP5 Climate Model Projections', *Nature Climate Change*, doi:10.1038/NCLIMATE1716.

Lobell, D. B., Burke, M. B., Tebaldi, C., Mastrandrea, M.D., Falcon, W. P., and Naylor, R. L. (2008) 'Prioritizing Climate Change Adaptation Needs for Food Security in 2030', *Science*, 319 (5863): 607–610.

Lobell, D. B., Schlenker, W, and Costa-Roberts, J. (2011) 'Climate Trends and Global Crop Production since 1980', *Science*, 333 (6042): 616–620.

Long, S. P. and Ort, D. R. (2010) 'More than Taking the Heat: Crops and Global Change', *Current Opinion in Plant Biology*, 13 (3): 240–247.

McGregor, D.F.M., Barker, D. and Campbell, D. (2009) 'Environmental Change and Caribbean Food Security: Recent Hazard Impacts and Domestic Food Production in Jamaica', in D.F.M. McGregor, D. Dodman and D. Barker (eds.) *Global Change and Caribbean Vulnerability: Environment, Economy and Society at Risk?* Kingston: UWI Press, 197–217.

Magnan, A. (2014) 'Avoiding Maladaptation to Climate Change: Towards Guiding Principles', *S.A.P.I.EN.S*, 7(1).

Mimura, N., Nurse, L., McLean, R. F. (2007) 'Small Islands', in M. L. Parry, O. F. Canziani, J.P. Palutikof, P. J. van der Linden and C. E. Hanson, (eds.) *Climate Change 2007: Impacts, Adaptation and Vulnerability. Contribution of Working Group II to The Fourth Assessment Report of the IPCC*, Cambridge, UK: Cambridge University Press, 687–716.

Mintz, S. W. (1985) 'From Plantations to Peasantries in the Caribbean', in S. W. Mintz and S. Price (eds.) *Caribbean Contours*, Baltimore: Johns Hopkins University Press, 127–54.

Nankishore, A., and Farrell, A. D. (2016) 'The Response of Contrasting Tomato Genotypes to Combined Heat and Drought Stress', *Journal of Plant Physiology*, 202: 75–82.

Nurse, L. and Moore, R. (2005) 'Adaptation to Global Climate Change: an Urgent Requirement for Small Island Developing States', *Review of European Community and International Environmental Law* 14 (2): 100–107.

Nurse, L., McLean, R., Agard, J., Briguglio, L. P., Duvat, V., Pelesikoti, N., Tompkins, E., and Webb, A. (2014) 'Climate Change 2014: Impacts, Adaptation and Vulnerability', in *Contribution of Working Group II to the Fifth Assessment Report of the Intergovernmental Panel on Climate Change*, Cambridge: Cambridge University Press.

Pulwarty, R. S., Nurse, L. A. and Trotz, U. O. (2010) 'Caribbean Islands in a Changing Climate', *Environmental Science and Policy for Sustainable Development*, 52(6): 16–27.

Rhiney, K. (2015) 'Geographies of Caribbean Vulnerability in a Changing Climate: Issues and Trends', *Geography Compass*, 9(3): 97–114.

Roncoli, C., Ingram, K. and Kirshen, P. (2002) 'Reading the Rains: Local Knowledge and Rainfall Forecasting in Burkina Faso', *Society and Natural Resources*, 15:109–427.

Simpson, M. C., Scott, D., New, M. (2009) *An Overview of Modelling Climate Change Impacts in the Caribbean Region with Contribution from the Pacific Islands*, Barbados, West Indies: United Nations Development Programme (UNDP).

Slater, R., Prowse, M., Kaur-Mann, N. and Peskett, L. (2007) *Climate Change, Agricultural Growth and Poverty Reduction*, United Kingdom: Overseas Development Institute. Available online: www.odi.org/sites/odi.org.uk/files/odi-assets/publications-opinion-files/1882.pdf.

Thornton, P. K., Jones, P. G., Ericksen, P. J., and Challinor, A. J. (2011) 'Agriculture and Food Systems in Sub-Saharan Africa in a 4 C+ world', *Philosophical Transactions of the Royal Society A: Mathematical, Physical and Engineering Sciences* 369 (1934): 117–136.

Timms, B. F. (2008) 'Development Theory and Domestic Agriculture in the Caribbean: Recurring Crises and Missed Opportunities', *Caribbean Geography*, 15(2): 101–117.

Tompkins, E., Nicholson-Cole, S. A., Hurlston, L. A. (2005) *Surviving Climate Change in Small Islands: a Guidebook*. Norwich: Tyndall Centre for Climate Change Research, University of East Anglia.

Trotz, U. and Lindo, S. (2013) 'Vulnerability and Resilience Building in CARICOM Countries', *Small Island Digest*, 2: 25–39.

Vedwan, N. (2006) 'Culture, Climate and the Environment: Local Knowledge and Perception of Climate Change among Apple Growers in Northwestern India', *Journal of Ecological Anthropology*, 10: 4–18.

4 Liquid gold or poverty in a cup?

The vulnerability of Blue Mountain and High Mountain coffee farmers in Jamaica to the effects of climate change

Anne-Teresa Birthwright

Introduction

Over recent decades, there has been a growing acceptance of the evidence of global climate change and its unequivocal impacts due to anthropogenic causes (IPCC 2013). The undesirable consequences of climate change threaten all countries, but more so the economies and livelihoods of vulnerable developing regions and Small Island Developing States (SIDS) such as in the Caribbean. Overall, the projected climatic changes will have serious negative consequences for the Caribbean, with differentiated impacts being felt in the individual territories (Rhiney 2015; Barker 2012). Additionally, these external stressors of climate change exacerbate existing local social, economic, institutional and political vulnerabilities of island states, which have been characterized by colonial plantation systems, limited physical size, reliance on fragile biophysical environments, amongst other shared features – further compromising their ability to cope and/or adapt to the vagaries of the changing climate.

For Jamaica, livelihoods have become increasingly sensitive to climatic changes as various sectors within the country are already experiencing a greater frequency and severity of climate-related events such as variable rainfall, droughts, hurricanes, extreme temperatures, severe water shortage and the increased incidence of pests and diseases (Taylor 2015; McGregor *et al.* 2009). Jamaica is chiefly dependent on primary production, with the major economic sectors utilizing natural resources; one such sector is agriculture. Agriculture has remained an important sector despite the increased liberalization of the economy in response to the challenges of a globalized and competitive marketplace and vulnerability to threats from meteorological hazards. Overall, agricultural production has remained vital to food security, employment, income and sustaining rural livelihoods (Tarleton and Ramsey 2008).

Coffee is widely grown across Jamaica, and the Coffee Industry Board (CIB), which regulates the production of coffee, designates two major grades of coffee – Blue Mountain and High Mountain (also called non-Blue Mountain). They are categorized on the basis of the altitude at which the coffee is grown: Blue Mountain coffee is produced at altitudes of 300 m to over 1,500 m above sea level within the

Blue Mountain range, and High Mountain coffee is assigned to hilly areas above 300 m outside of the Blue Mountain range. Since coffee is a key export commodity and one of the largest earners of foreign exchange, earning approximately US$ 17.9 million (over J$ 1.5 billion) in 2012 (Bank of Jamaica 2015), it is of major importance within the Jamaican agricultural sector. Even though not a major global producer, the product's competitive advantage is benchmarked by its high quality, the taste and appearance of the bean, contributing to it being ranked the number one brand on the international market.

Generally, the micro-environmental conditions (geology, topography and climate), which determine the quality grade of coffee, differ significantly between the Blue Mountain and the High Mountain areas, with coffee from the former acknowledged to be of superior quality. This has resulted in little attention and investment being directed to the High Mountain area; most of the investments – whether foreign or local – having been put into the improvement of the quality and quantity of the Blue Mountain brand. Regardless of the difference in the prestige of the different brands of coffee, both the Blue Mountain and High Mountain areas have been buffeted by climatic variability and economic change over the last 30 years. The comparative decline in production across both grades provides some evidence of the plight (Figure 4.1).

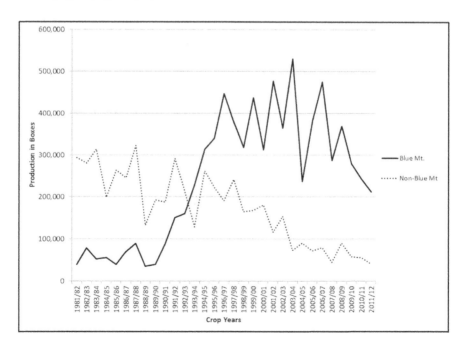

Figure 4.1 Blue Mountain and non-Blue Mountain coffee production (1981–2012).
Source: The Coffee Industry Board of Jamaica.

This chapter focuses on the outcomes of climate change and economic change across the two coffee-producing regions. The arguments presented are set within the wider context of the multidimensional nature of vulnerability and livelihood experiences. Both groups of farmers have been faced with the opportunities and challenges of an increasingly uncertain future climate and the impacts of economic globalization. Smallholder farmers are often not only doubly exposed to climatic and economic challenges, but also face multiple internal stresses which increase their vulnerability and influence their decisions (Abid *et al.* 2016; O'Brien *et al.* 2004); hence, the 'impacts of non-climatic stimuli on adaptation decision are amongst the main complications in the process of farm level adaptation' (Abid *et al.* 2016: 448). The empirical research draws on fieldwork data collected in 2014–2015 using a sequential explanatory mixed methods design, including focus group sessions and detailed questionnaires in the communities of Frankfield in the parish of Clarendon and Spring Hill in Portland. The chapter examines how farmers have responded to the combinations of climatic stresses and market shocks which they experienced, as well as an examination of the relationships between their perceptions of these issues and their adaptive responses.

Farm-level vulnerability

Vulnerability is a complex, crosscutting concept, central in the research fields of natural hazards, climate change, food security and political ecology, each developing individual models which address similar problems, but utilizing differing terminology based on their associated field of study (Fellmann 2012; Füssel 2007). In the human–environment nexus discourse, vulnerability is recognized as a function of a system's exposure, sensitivity and adaptive capacity (Fellmann 2012). Adger (2006: 268) defines vulnerability as 'the state of susceptibility to harm from exposure to stresses associated with environmental and social change and from the absence of capacity to adapt'. Recently, the IPCC (2014: 5) has defined vulnerability as 'the propensity or predisposition to be adversely affected', thus highlighting a central theme in the vulnerability literature where the focus is on the sensitivity and adaptive capacity of a system.

As a context-specific state, vulnerability is expressed differently between and within nations, communities, social groups, households and even farms (Adger *et al.* 2004). However, in the context of climate change, these systems must have the capacity to adapt or 'adjust to actual or expected climate stresses, or to cope with the consequences' (O'Brien *et al.* 2004: 304). The adaptive capacity of a system is often determined by its socio-economic characteristics (Brooks and Adger 2004; Smit and Pilifosova 2003), which can vary over time depending on changes in political, social and economic conditions. Enhancement in economic performance, technology, financial and information resources, institutions, local interactions and social services can lead to a gradual increase in adaptive capacity (Smit and Wandel 2006; Smit and Pilifosova 2003).

Regardless of external interventions, local communities and farmers often develop their own strategies to reduce the impacts of climate variability. The indigenous and traditional knowledge of various coping practices and adaptive responses have usually been autonomous and generational, as documented by Selvaraju (2013) and Beckford and Barker (2007) in relation to farmers' activities in Jamaica.

Site selection

The analysis presented here is informed by work in two study sites in communities dominated by small farmers principally dependent upon coffee production for income (Figure 4.2). At an elevation above 400–800 m, Frankfield is considered to be a High Mountain coffee-growing community. It is located in northwestern Clarendon in central Jamaica, which experiences the lowest annual rainfall for the island, registering less than 1,500 mm per annum. Farmers in this area are also involved in the cultivation of cocoa and other export-oriented crops, such as yam.

Located in the Blue Mountains in the parish of Portland, Spring Hill is characterized by its distinct ecological setting, created by the densely forested, mountainous topography and the highest annual rainfall on the island. Coffee production takes place on farms located on the steep, cloud-covered slopes within the Blue Mountain area and is the mainstay of the majority of farmers in these interior communities.

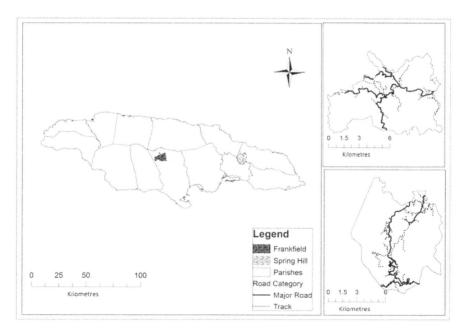

Figure 4.2 Location of study areas: Spring Hill, Portland (top right), and Frankfield, Clarendon (bottom right).

In both locales, the majority of the farms are small or medium sized, on individually owned plots. The average farm size in Frankfield is about five acres and three acres for Spring Hill; farms are fragmented, with an average of two to three plots per farm, including a house plot. Regardless of the distinct geographic locations of these coffee-producing areas, it was found that the impacts of climate change and economic globalization has not only impeded crop production, but has also affected the rural livelihoods of farmers engaged in production.

Implications of climate change for coffee production

Climate change has emerged as a global concern and one of the most challenging issues in recent decades, reflected in conditions such as increased temperatures, more variable rainfall regimes and increased severity of weather events, such as droughts and hurricanes (Taylor *et al.* 2012). According to Mimura *et al.* (2007) warming across the Caribbean region has taken place within a range of 0–0.5°C per decade between 1971 and 2004. Additionally, since the 1960s, there has been a noticeable increase in the percentage of days having warm maximum and minimum temperatures, with a decrease in the percentage of cold days (Taylor *et al.* 2012). It is expected that during warm El Niño events, there will also be an exacerbation of any warming and drying trends already present (Taylor 2015).

One of the greatest concerns with regard to the impact of climate change is its effect on agricultural production, where changes in temperature and rainfall patterns ultimately affect a nation's food security and individuals' livelihoods. Climate change has not only increased the unfamiliarity, unpredictability and unreliability of seasonal weather patterns around which farmers have tailored their farming activities, but also increased the frequency and intensity of severe weather events, such as droughts and hurricanes, and changed the locality and prevalence of pest and disease outbreaks due to shifts in temperature and rainfall (Altieri and Koohafkan 2008), hence increasing the cost of production.

In the context of agricultural production, it has been argued that 'coffee growers are by far the most numerous group that is directly affected and the most vulnerable' to the impact of climate change (ITC 2010: 2). This is due to the high value placed on temperature and rainfall conditions that not only define potential coffee yield, but develop crop phenology, which is inherent in productivity and quality (Haggar and Schepp 2012). This assertion was similar to that advanced by DaMatta and Ramalho (2006), who noted that drought conditions posed a major climatic stress on coffee production, where high temperatures, especially during the blossoming periods, may significantly wilt flowers, thus preventing the bearing of the plant. In some places, rising temperatures and altered seasonal rainfall patterns are expected to render certain previously producing areas unsuitable for the economic viability of coffee production (Ovalle-Rivera *et al.* 2015). This may trigger chain reactions, whereby irrigation and water management systems are placed under greater stress, which in turn further compromises the livelihoods and social well-being of the farming communities. The ramifications of any such changes in Jamaica is particularly pressing because the coffee produced is *Arabica typica*, which is more sensitive to temperature increase than *Robusta* (Bunn *et al.* 2014); thus, projected temperature increases would pose a major challenge to farmers.

Perceptions of climatic and economic conditions by smallholder coffee farmers

Climatic challenges

Most farms are rain-fed, with approximately 90 per cent depending entirely on rainfall. The rain-fed nature of agriculture in the communities increases the importance of any deficits or variance in predictability and volume of rainfall. Under these circumstances, continual observation of, and interaction with, environmental conditions is necessary and heightens farmers' awareness of even minor deviations from what is perceived to be normal weather conditions (Gamble *et al.* 2010). With many of the respondents of both areas residing in the communities from birth and having lived through experiences on which to draw, it was telling that the majority had observed an increase in temperature and a decrease in rainfall activity over the last 20 years, particularly during the April/ May period, which is critical to the initial flowering and berry development (Figure 4.3). Thus, in the midst of perceived rising temperatures and decreasing rainfall, farmers were experiencing increased water stress and they were unable to effectively water their crops.

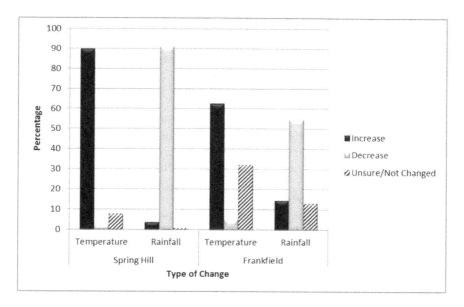

Figure 4.3 Farmers' perceptions of temperature and rainfall changes over 20 years (1991–2012).

The perception of increasing rainfall variability is accompanied by the view amongst farmers that droughts had become more common; 85 per cent of Spring Hill farmers perceived that droughts were worsening and 27 per cent had made similar observations in the Frankfield area. Nevertheless, 87 per cent of farmers in both areas complained of decreased coffee production due to issues such as burnt coffee berries, delays in the bearing season and an increase in pests and diseases, such as the coffee berry borer, coffee leaf rust and coffee leaf minor, which thrive under conditions of high temperatures. Recently, the coffee-cropping season faced two consecutive years of drought (2013/2014 and 2014/2015), which not only resulted in immature coffee berries and underdeveloped beans, but the lack of rains also increased the effects of the coffee leaf rust disease, heightening the challenges faced by farmers to stay economically afloat within the industry.

The recent rise in the infestation of coffee leaf rust severely decreased production and threatened the farmers' economic livelihoods. It is caused by the fungal disease (*Hemileia vastatrix*), which destroys the section of the leaf on which it grows, resulting in premature leaf fall. This compromises the tree's photosynthetic ability, resulting in roots, berries and shoots being starved of plant food. The end result is a reduction in the number of bearing nodes and, consequently, a reduction in crop production. This disease is one of the most potentially devastating threats to the global coffee industry. The International Coffee Council (ICC 2014) reported that for the 2012/2013 crop year, coffee production in some Central American countries was severely affected by one of the worst recorded outbreaks of leaf rust. Some of the countries that were severely impacted were Costa Rica, Guatemala, Honduras, Nicaragua and El Salvador. According to Serju (2012), the coffee industry in Jamaica also saw its worst case of coffee leaf rust in the 2012/2013 cropping season, which was described as 'larger than usual' by the CIB. The outbreak affected some of the major coffee-producing areas in both the Blue Mountain and High Mountain areas (in the parishes of Portland, St. Thomas, Manchester, St. Catherine and Clarendon). Farmers stated that the outbreak coincided with the passage of tropical storm Sandy in October 2012; the storm caused the coffee sector farm-gate losses of J$ 110 million (approximately US$ 920,000) from a combined crop loss of 32 per cent (PIOJ 2013). It is believed that the humid conditions brought on by the storm facilitated a widespread dispersal of the fungal spores to areas and altitudes that previously had been unaffected. Losses due to coffee leaf rust may have been as high as US$ 10 million between 2011 and 2014 (JIS 2014).

Another pest which severely limits coffee production, and has shown an increase throughout various coffee-producing regions, is the coffee berry borer (*Hypothenemus hampei*). This is a small beetle that survives only in coffee berries. In Jamaica, the level of infestation had, until recently, remained below the national average of 10 per cent (Martin-Wilkins 2012). However, in 2012, an upward trend was observed, moving the average to 13 per cent. Shocks such as these can have a significant impact on food security. With rising temperatures allowing the berry borer to extend its range, the emergence of a new climate regime may affect the viability of coffee production in certain regions, particularly those at lower elevations.

Economic challenges

Economically, coffee farmers face a myriad of both internal and external challenges, especially as the industry lacks any form of farm or crop insurance protection. A common experience was also the weak social ties with extension officers, where 74 per cent of farmers in Frankfield stated that they had received no assistance from extension officers, while 42 per cent of farmers in Spring Hill reported similar experiences. In the past, local government played an important role in lessening the sensitivity of coffee farmer livelihoods by providing access to farm inputs, information through continuous research and development, and extension services. However, the privatization of the coffee industry has limited the state's influence. Presently, there is a strong sense of distrust between farmers and agricultural agencies, as 89 per cent and 77 per cent of Frankfield and Spring Hill farmers, respectively, said that they had received no government support in the previous five years.

Farmers not only expressed their frustration at the lack of support from the state, they also referred to the low farm-gate prices for their coffee berries since the 2008 global economic downturn. Generally, when demand and prices are high, coffee has had the reputation of providing a stable and high income for farmers, however during times of 'bust', hunger and increased poverty have been experienced. Within the coffee industry, farmers are dependent on the farm-gate prices offered by local coffee dealers, as well as the continued support of major consuming countries such as Japan, which purchases 70 per cent of the island's Blue Mountain coffee. This persistent dependence on individuals and agencies in the higher levels of the coffee value chain, together with declining government support, has left farmers feeling helpless. Additionally, the critical reliance on one of the main markets for export of agricultural products such as coffee, underscores its economic vulnerability.

Amongst the farmers surveyed in Frankfield, 32 per cent indicated that they had abandoned, or intended to abandon, their farms due to the frustrations associated with keeping their coffee farms economically profitable; frustrations were fuelled by the high cost of farm inputs and employed labour, low farm-gate prices and delayed payments from coffee dealers for coffee berries. Discouraged by low demand and lack of investments, these farmers have turned to other export commodities, such as cocoa (48% of the farmers said that they had increased their cocoa production in the previous 10 years), sugar cane and yams, for their main source of income. The year-round production and reaping potential of these crops make them lucrative alternatives.

The irony is that despite a dramatic increase in farm-gate prices for both Blue Mountain and High Mountain coffee in recent years, many farmers had not been able to take advantage of this because of the record low production levels resulting from consecutive years of droughts, flare-ups of the coffee leaf rust and abandonment of coffee plots.

Adaptive responses by smallholder coffee farmers

Coffee farmers operate in a multifaceted environment characterized by political, economic, social, institutional and ecological conditions which often create a disabling environment. The impact of these multiple negative factors usually influenced farmers' perceptions and hence the decisions they made in terms of adaptation to climate change and related risks (Abid *et al.* 2016). Therefore, how farmers perceived changes in weather patterns was important in gaining an understanding of their vulnerability, coping and adaptation to climate change (Senaratne and Scarborough 2011). The responses of the coffee farmers in this study were: (a) to plant new coffee cultivars, such as *Arabica gesha* (a genetically modified disease-resistant coffee cultivar) instead of the previously grown *Arabica typica* variety); (b) change farm-management practices (such as altering fertilizer/pesticide input mixes and implementing farmer-made irrigation technologies); (c) incorporate new land-management measures (such as soil conservation and intercropping temporary and permanent shade plants and delaying the application of fertilizer and fungicide/pesticide, due to the variability and unpredictability of rainfall, and applying mulch to the roots of coffee plants – a technique commonly associated with lower, hotter, drier rain shadow areas); and (d) change their livelihood options, which included farm diversification.

Although seen in the industry as merely 'local best practices', a number of these techniques served multiple risk-minimization purposes. The intercropping not only provided shade for trees, ensuring moisture retention, but it also allowed farmers to diversify, thus generating a secure additional income from another crop while also improving the contribution to household food security. For many farmers in areas like Frankfield who had abandoned, or were considering abandoning, their coffee farms, the decision to intercrop offered an alternative adaptation strategy. These farmers focused on intercropping with other high-value exportable commodities, such as cocoa, sugar cane and yams, given their characteristic year-round production, low initial capital investment and low-cost maintenance.

Food security and the vulnerability of the smallholder coffee farmer

With the progression of climate change, small farmers will be pushed towards new realities with increasing rainfall variability, pests and diseases and frequent drought conditions, heightening the risk of fire hazards. Consequentially these stressors can have significant impacts on food security (Ross and Riano 2012). Food security is acknowledged as a state in which 'all people, at all times, have physical, social and economic access to sufficient, safe and nutritious food to meet their dietary needs and food preferences for an active and healthy life' (FAO 2003: 28). However, dialogue on the prevalence of seasonal food insecurity amongst coffee farmers within the speciality coffee industry has been limited. In particular, there has been a failure to openly acknowledge the reasons why farmers in areas which produce the world's best coffee are constantly exposed to the risks of food insecurity. In the face of climatic and economic change, coffee farmers demonstrate a high level of vulnerability due to both socio-economic and physical factors (ICT, 2010). Firstly, coffee's perennial nature limits farmers' capacity to quickly adapt to changes in market conditions and/or the environment, especially since investments in coffee production at any given time may not be realized immediately (Eitzinger 2013). Furthermore, small-scale farmers suffering the direct and indirect consequences of poverty and marginalization, have relatively few resources with which to cope (Caswell, Méndez and Bacon 2012).

The seasonal food insecurity experienced by farmers in both coffee-producing areas in this study is shaped by climatic and non-climatic forces. For example, increased temperatures and drought conditions not only result in 'light' coffee berries (an absence of bean maturation), but also lead to a loss of income due to smaller quantities being purchased by coffee dealers during the on-farm quality assurance process. Coffee prices and timing of payments has also been a major contributor to the incidence of food insecurity, as these periods of hunger generally occur post-harvest when funds (however limited) have been reinvested into the farm, and/or pre-harvest months, when funds are redirected to cater to children and their academic needs. Hence, farmers continuously face decisions of managing on-farm requirements, household maintenance and unexpected hardships, as each competes for the limited available financial resources.

Farmers intercropped subsistence crops (including fruit, vegetables and root crops) to complement coffee production; some also engaged in livestock husbandry and depended on assistance from familial social networks as a means of creating coping strategies to help them through the 'hunger months'. This did not compensate farmers' reduced purchasing power for standard off-farm food staples. The farmers in both localities in this study were also vulnerable to the shocks of natural hazards, such as hurricanes or tropical storms. Farmers stated that after the passage of these events, the recovery period generally took years, even with the use of personal savings (where available). For some, this loss in income led to poverty and increased future vulnerability, given the absence of, or limited access to, social and financial safety nets, such as insurance schemes.

As the impacts of climate change have become more prevalent, the coping and/ or adaptive responses in which farmers have engaged were dominated by their attempts earn an income and cultivate food for the household. For farmers in Frankfield who engaged in the cultivation of various high-value exportable crops, these coping mechanisms not only assisted in meeting farmers' subsistence needs to offset crop failure arising from rainfall variability, pest and diseases and low farm-gate prices for coffee, but also assisted in income generation. In contrast, the Spring Hill coffee farmers have limited options in the diversification of exportable crops as coffee is the principal means of income generation. Hence, in periods of scarcity, farmers faced difficulties in ensuring both a healthy coffee crop and sustaining food for their households, even despite their informal support systems, such as the short-term assistance from family or friends.

With coffee production being a key determinant of household income for the farmers in the areas under discussion, the susceptibility of coffee production to climate variability, combined with economic challenges, highlights the fact that the coffee farmers occupy a fragile 'space of vulnerability' (Watts and Bohle 1993) within an industry innately shaped by broader socio-economic, political and institutional forces. The farmers were therefore faced with both an external risk from climate and economic shocks and stresses, and internal challenges in an environment that could either enable or inhibit the enhancement of adaptive livelihood strategies and outcomes.

Conclusion

This chapter highlighted the vulnerability of coffee farmers to climatic and economic challenges in the context of a disabling environment which shapes the industry. These challenges within the coffee industry not only impact coffee production (the primary income-generating crop), but also the household resources to support the subsistence component of farms. Informal networks and farmers' social capital were critical in managing the effects of crop failure, income loss and general food insecurity, especially given the absence of formal safety nets. Despite the apparent advantage of the Blue Mountain coffee farmers of Spring Hill over the High Mountain coffee farmers of Frankfield, based on the continued investment and access to the newly emerging niche markets of the Blue Mountain brand, this is not an indication that they are less vulnerable than those in Frankfield. The farmers in both areas will have to contend with, and adapt to, the continued effects of a changing climate, with incidences of drought and storms. Furthermore, in considering shifting from coffee to other crops as an adaptive strategy, farmers in the area most dependent on coffee, namely the Blue Mountain area, would not have the possibilities of those in Frankfield to turn to the production of alternative exportable commodities. Unlike Spring Hill, the diversity characterizing Frankfield farmers demonstrates their capacity to easily allocate resources into more profitable crops as a means of adaptation.

In the midst of the challenges faced by coffee farmers, no lack of agency was demonstrated. This assertion was similar to that of Barker (2012: 56) where he stated that 'though farmers are vulnerable, they are not passive in the face of adversity; they try to adapt and cope with changing conditions; they experiment and improvise, though not always successfully'. Despite the vulnerability of the coffee farmers in this study, they demonstrated their adaptive capacity, which was essential for sustaining coffee production. To date, managing adaptation to the combined effects of economic and climatic constraints has been a contentious issue. The debate revolves around the question of whether the focus should be on specific adaptations to the direct impacts of these stressors; or rather, should there be investments made to enhance the more general adaptive capacities of communities, social groups and even households. Enhancing the determinants of adaptive capacity at both the national and local level, through improvement in education, increased economic performance, diversified food supply, improvement in infrastructure, social capital and equity, would undoubtedly reduce vulnerability (Mertz *et al.* 2009; Brooks *et al.* 2005). Once this is accomplished, tailoring adaptation measures to fit specific locations and situations may be possible, where the ideal situation is not only surviving shocks and stresses, but being adaptive in the long term through building the ability to navigate change and making the necessary transformations to overcome the ongoing challenges.

References

Abid, M., Schilling, J., Scheffran, J. and Zulfiqar, F. (2016) 'Climate Change Vulnerability, Adaptation and Risk Perceptions at Farm Level in Punjab, Pakistan', *Science of The Total Environment*, 547: 447–460.

Adger, N. (2006) 'Vulnerability', *Global Environmental Change*, 16: 268–281.

Adger, N., Brooks, N., Bentham, G., Agnew, M. and Eriksen, S. (2004) 'New Indicators of Vulnerability and Adaptive Capacity', Technical Report 7. Tyndall Centre for Climate Change Research.

Altieri, M. and Koohafkan, P. (2008) *Enduring Farms*, Penang: Third World Network (TWN).

Bank of Jamaica (2015) 'Jamaica in Figures (2012)' Available at: www.boj.org.jm/uploads/ pdf/jam_figures/jam_figures_2012.pdf.

Barker, D. (2012) 'Caribbean Agriculture in a Period of Global Change: Vulnerabilities and Opportunities', *Caribbean Studies*, 40(2): 41–61.

Beckford, C. and Barker, D. (2007) 'The Role and Value of Local Knowledge in Jamaican Agriculture: Adaptation and Change in Small-Scale Farming', *The Geographical Journal*, 173(2): 118–128.

Brooks, N. and Adger, N. (2004) 'Assessing and Enhancing Adaptive Capacity' Technical Paper 7. New York: UNDP.

Brooks, N., Adger, W. N. and Kelly, P. M. (2005) 'The Determinants of Vulnerability and Adaptive Capacity at the National Level and the Implications for Adaptation', *Global Environmental Change*, 15: 151–163.

Bunn, C., Läderach, P., Ovalle-Rivera, O. and Kirschke, D. (2014) 'A Bitter Cup: Climate Change Profile of Global Production of Arabica and Robusta Coffee', *Climatic Change*, 129 (1–2): 89–101.

Caswell, M., Méndez, V. E. and Bacon, C. M. (2012) 'Food Security and Smallholder Coffee Production: Current Issues and Future Directions', Agroecology and Rural Livelihoods Group (ARLG) Policy Brief 1. Burlington, VT: University of Vermont.

DaMatta, F. and Ramalho, J. (2006) 'Impacts of Drought and Temperature Stress on Coffee Physiology and Production: a Review', *Brazilian Journal of Plant Physiology*, 18(1): 55–81.

Eitzinger, A. (2013) 'Synergies, Climate Change Adaptation and Mitigation in Coffee', Decision and Policy Analysis Area (DAPA). Available at: http://dapa.ciat.cgiar.org/ synergies-between-climate-change-adaptation-and-mitigation-in-coffee-production.

FAO (2003) *Trade reforms and Food Security: Conceptualizing the Linkages,* Rome: Food and Agriculture Organization of the United Nations.

Fellmann, T. (2012) 'The Assessment of Climate Change-Related Vulnerability in the Agricultural Sector: Reviewing Conceptual Frameworks', *Building Resilience for Adaptation to Climate Change in the Agriculture Sector:* Proceedings of a Joint FAO/OECD Workshop.

Füssel, H. (2007) 'Vulnerability: A Generally Applicable Conceptual Framework for Climate Change Research', *Global Environmental Change*, 17(2): 155–167.

Gamble, D., Campbell, D., Allen, T., Barker, D., Curtis, S., McGregor, D. and Popke, J. (2010) 'Climate Change, Drought, and Jamaican Agriculture: Local Knowledge and the Climate Record', *Annals of the Association of American Geographers*, 100 (4): 880–893.

Gay, C., Estrada, F., Conde, C., Eakin, H., Villers, L. (2006) 'Potential Impacts of Climate Change on Agriculture: a Case Study of Coffee Production in Veracruz, Mexico', *Climatic Change* 79 (3–4): 259–288.

Haggar, J., and Schepp, K. (2012) 'Coffee and Climate Change Impacts and Options for Adaption in Brazil, Guatemala, Tanzania and Vietnam', Natural Resources Institute, Working Paper Series: Climate Change, Agriculture and Natural Resources No. 4.

ICC (2014) *World Coffee Trade (1963–2013): A Review of the Markets, Challenges and Opportunities Facing the Sector*, London: International Coffee Council (ICC).

IPCC (2013) 'Summary for Policymakers', in T. F. Stocker, D. Qin, G.-K. Plattner, M. Tignor, S. K. Allen, J. Boschung, A. Nauels, Y. Xia, V. Bex and P. M. Midgley (eds.) *Climate Change 2013: The Physical Science Basis*. Contribution of Working Group I to the Fifth Assessment Report of the Intergovernmental Panel on Climate Change, Cambridge and New York: Cambridge University Press.

IPCC (2014) 'Climate Change 2014: Impacts, Adaptation, and Vulnerability', in C. B. Field, V. R. Barros, D. J. Dokken, K. J. Mach, M. D. Mastrandrea, T. E. Bilir, M. Chatterjee, K. L. Ebi, Y. O. Estrada, R. C. Genova, B. Girma, E. S. Kissel, A. N. Levy, S. MacCracken, P. R. Mastrandrea, and L. L. White (eds.) *Part A: Global and Sectoral Aspects. Contribution of Working Group II to the Fifth Assessment Report of the Intergovernmental Panel on Climate Change*, Cambridge and New York: Cambridge University Press.

ITC (2010) 'Climate Change and the Coffee Industry', Technical Paper, Geneva: International Trade Centre.

Jamaica Information Service (JIS) (2014) 'Agriculture Ministry to Assist Coffee Farmers', Available at: http://jis.gov.jm/agriculture-ministry-assist-coffee-farmers.

McGregor, D., Barker, D., and Campbell, D. (2009) 'Environmental Change and Caribbean Food Security: Recent Hazard Impacts and Domestic Food Production in Jamaica', In: D. McGregor, D. Dodman and D. Barker (eds.) *Global Change and Caribbean Vulnerability: Environment, Economy and Society at Risk*, Kingston: UWI Press.

Martin-Wilkins, A. (2012) 'Berry Borer Blues: Beetle Threatens to Wipe out Half of Coffee Crop if Not Controlled', *Jamaica Observer*. Available at: www.jamaicaobserver.com/news/Berry-borer-blues_10764655.

Mertz, O., Haknaes, K., Jorgen, E. O., and Rasmussen, K. (2009) 'Adaptation to Climate Change in Developing Countries', *Environmental Management*, 43: 743–752.

Mimura, N., Nurse, L., McLean, R. F., Agard, J., Briguglio, L., Lefale, P., Payet, R. and Sem, G. (2007) 'Small Islands', in M. L. Parry, O. F. Canziani, J. P. Palutikof, P. J. van der Linden and C. E. Hanson (eds.) *Climate Change 2007: Impacts, Adaptation and Vulnerability*. Contribution of Working Group II to the Fourth Assessment Report of the Intergovernmental Panel on Climate Change, 687–716, Cambridge: Cambridge University Press.

O'Brien, K., Leichenko, R., Kelkar, U., Venema, H., Aandahl, G., Tompkins, H., Javed, A., Bhadwal, S., Barg, S., Nygaard, L. and West, J. (2004) 'Mapping Vulnerability to Multiple Stressors: Climate Change and Globalization in India', *Global Environmental Change*, 14 (4): 303–313.

Ovalle-Rivera, O., Läderach, P., Bunn, C., Obersteiner, M. and Schroth, G. (2015) 'Projected Shifts in Coffea Arabica Suitability among Major Global Producing Regions Due to Climate Change'. *PLOS ONE*, 10 (4).

PIOJ (2013) 'Jamaica Macro Socio-Economic and Environmental Assessment of the Damage and Loss Caused by Hurricane Sandy', Unpublished Report, Kingston: Planning Institute of Jamaica.

Rhiney, K. (2015) 'Geographies of Caribbean Vulnerability in a Changing Climate: Issues and Trends', *Geography Compass*, 9 (3): 97–114.

Ross, M. and Riano, N. (2012) 'Colombia's Vulnerable Agriculture – "Peak Coffee" Soon a Reality?' Online, *DAPA*. Available at: http://dapa.ciat.cgiar.org/colombias-vulnerable-agriculture-peak-coffee-soon-a-reality.

Selvaraju, R. (2013) *Climate Change and Agriculture in Jamaica*, Agricultural Sector Support Analysis, Rome: UN/FAO.

Senaratne, A. and Scarborough, H. (2011) 'Coping with Climatic Variability by Rain-Fed Farmers in Dry Zone, Sri Lanka: Towards Understanding Adaptation to Climate Change'. In: *Australian Agricultural and Resource Economics Society, Conference (55th)*, Melbourne, Australia.

Serju, C. (2012) 'Coffee Leaf Rust Threatens Industry', *Jamaica Gleaner*, December 15, 2012.

Smit, B. and Pilifosova, O. (2003) in, J. Smith, R. Klein and S. Huq (eds.) *Climate Change, Adaptive Capacity and Development*, London: Imperial College Press.

Smit, B. and Wandel, J. (2006) 'Adaptation, Adaptive Capacity and Vulnerability', *Global Environmental Change*, 16 (3): 282–292.

Tarleton, M., and Ramsey, D. (2008) 'Farm-Level Adaptation to Multiple Risks: Climate Change and Other Concerns', *Journal of Rural and Community Development*, 3(2): 47–63.

Taylor, M. (2015) *Why Climate Demands Change*, Grace Kennedy Foundation Lecture 2015, Kingston, Jamaica: Grace Kennedy Foundation.

Taylor, M., Stephenson, T., Chen, A. and Stephenson, K. (2012) 'Climate Change and the Caribbean: Review and Response', *Caribbean Studies*, 40(2): 169–200.

Watts, M. and Bohle, H. (1993) 'The Space of Vulnerability: The Causal Structure of Hunger and Famine', *Progress in Human Geography*, 17(1): 43–67.

5 Climate change adaptations by smallholder farmers in northern Nigeria to enhance food security

Adamu Idris Tanko

Introduction

The links between climate change, socio-economic development, health and environmental sustainability have become dominant and urgent global concerns. According to the Intergovernmental Panel on Climate Change (IPCC 2007), scientific consensus points to a quickening and threatening pace of human-induced climate change. But the questions that need to be answered on climate change may include: how the climate changes, or where and when its effects will be felt most acutely. While it may be clear to some people that the concept of climate change is a reality, it needs to be pointed out that it remains very vague to most people in rural Africa. This is alongside the fact that both cumulative impacts and the increased probability of extreme weather events that characterize climate change present heightened risks to vulnerable populations, economies and ecosystems globally. Under these conditions, understanding successful adaptation to climate change is essential to inform and to take action on how to respond socially and economically.

Global action, supported by evidence-informed strategies, is urgent in order to bolster the adaptive capacity of vulnerable populations, communities and/or social sectors in the face of the wide-ranging impacts of climate change in African countries. Nigeria, with a vast land space of 923,768 sq. km spanning different climatic regions, is regarded as being highly vulnerable to climate change. The country recording heightened dryness and aridity in the north, and flooding and coastal submergence in the south, therefore needs to be aware of the trends and the likely problems that will occur. In particular, mechanisms for mitigation and adaptation to change are urgently needed. It is towards this end that a study was undertaken with the hope that it would track, analyse and systematize the rudimentary adaptation strategies of small-scale agriculture to climate change in the village communities of northern Nigeria. Further, it is hoped that the results of the research would help in developing a comprehensive and integrated programme of support to enhance the sustainable adaptation of small-scale agriculture to climate change, thereby ensuring positive food security outcomes in the region and the country.

The study

Two villages in northern Nigeria were selected for study – Cifatake to the north and Aburom to the south of Kaduna State. Both villages are essentially agrarian.

Cifatake Village

Cifatake is located about 8–9 km northwest of Birni Yero (about 30 km along the Kaduna-Kano expressway). It began as a transit centre over 400 years ago, and was first settled by traders coming to Zaria from areas south of Kaduna. There was a pond called 'Cifatake' which was created by a stream. Over time, the people, mainly the Hausa tribe, continued to settle around the pond and engaged in agricultural activities, particularly crop cultivation and animal husbandry. The village is estimated to have a population size of 300,000, of which about 95 per cent are farmers. The villagers combine crop production with animal husbandry and trading. The village is today known primarily for the production of agricultural crops including maize, yams, tomatoes, rice, potatoes, peppers, cassava, groundnuts, onions, cucumbers, sorghum and millet (dauro).

The area is underlain by the basement complex rocks of Precambrian origin. The soils are essentially latosols, which are matured and good for the cultivation of many crops. On account of the high annual rainfall received of over 1,000 mm (Adesina *et. al.* 2009), soil erosion is extensive. The high rainfall, together with now-reduced vegetation cover, has exposed the lateritic hardpans which were at shallow depths. According to the villagers, the area was known to have a high density of many vegetation species.

Members of the village community travel long distances to market. For instance, they travel 7–8 km to Birnin Yero three days per week, 10–12 km to Mararabar Jos every Saturday, 20–25 km to Sabon Birni every Sunday, 65 km to Gadan Gayan every Friday, 20–22 km to Kamfanin Zango livestock market (every Monday) and to Kawo-Kaduna every Tuesday.

Aburom Village

The village is located about 30–35 km southwest of Kachia town in southern Kaduna. It has a total population of about 3,000 (according to the villagers), the majority of whom are crop cultivators, primarily cultivating ginger (*Citta, Hausa*), yams, sorghum and millet.

The villagers indicated that they patronized only one market, namely, the Kachia market. Firewood is the only source of energy in the village, thus, trees are lost mainly due to cultivation, household use and also the need for ash which, according to the villagers, is essential due to lack of chemical fertilizers. Thus, despite the fact that the area was originally covered with dense forest, the very high demand for fuelwood led to the loss of trees. Currently, soil erosion is a big threat to sustainable agriculture. The area has very high soil quality and is good for the cultivation of all crops, but with lowered vegetation cover, accelerated erosion is developing very rapidly.

The relationship between climatic conditions and agriculture in the study area

The climate is changing and is severely impacting agriculture, in particular, small-scale agriculture. This, in turn, has the potential to undermine food security at the level of the household as well as the country as a whole. Small-scale farmers – among them, women – are particularly vulnerable. Nevertheless, these farmers are responding to climate change by adapting in piecemeal fashion to its impact, oftentimes in ways which further increase their vulnerability.

Both villages are drought-prone, and this is associated either with the late arrival or an early cessation of the seasonal rains. These phenomena adversely affect all crops. Droughts in April and May, which are currently accepted as normal, prevent land preparation and ploughing activities from being conducted on time. They further delay sowing and broadcasting of seeds, as well as affecting the transplanting of other crops. When droughts extend up to early June, they destroy all crops and harvests become very poor. Inadequate rains through July–October cause severe hardship across the entire country. This is especially so as most of the large-scale agricultural irrigation schemes have virtually collapsed.

Major droughts in the north occurred in 1966, 1969, 1973, 1978, 1979, 1981, 1982, 1989, 1992, 1994, 1995 and 1998 (Buba 2009; 2014), causing a substantial reduction in food production. The droughts in consecutive years – 1978 and 1979 – had a direct and drastic effect on the nation's people, by substantially reducing harvests in the Kano region. Because farmers have been exposed to recurring droughts, they have had to adapt their farming systems from year to year in order to accommodate the different conditions that had been caused. For most farmers, agricultural adjustment is a costly option as investment is needed for re-sowing, crop replacement, intercropping and irrigation. Most resort to the disposal or mortgaging of assets, borrowing and, eventually, to migration.

Increasing climatic uncertainties are an additional threat in these drought-prone environments and also one of the major factors underpinning the need for risk-reduction measures. It forces farmers to depend on low-input and low-risk technologies. Failure to adopt new technologies, whereby maximum gains could be derived during favourable seasons, delays recovery after disasters. The investments made for poverty reduction are also lost within the high-risk areas due to regular hazard impacts. Increasing climate risks further undermine development efforts in northern Nigeria and aggravate poverty (Tanko 2013).

Several government programmes since the 1970s have sought to address climate risks (which were notable mainly because of drought). The development of the irrigation system in northern Nigeria in the 1970s and 1980s led to the increased production of horticultural crops as well as rice and wheat in the 1990s (Tanko 1994; 1999). However, because of the non-sustainability of the projects, the gains from them could not be continued (Olofin 1992). Some efforts are, no doubt, being made in order to reverse this trend. Government at different levels (federal, state and local) has initiated programmes towards promoting crop diversification. New ways and methods are also needed to better inform farmers to help them identify alternative, technically viable options for livelihood adaptation. Better access to climate information could encourage farmers to adopt new risk/opportunity-management practices under changing climatic conditions (Tanko 2013).

Thus, although the impacts of climate change on food production and food security are global concerns, they represent a particular threat for (northern) Nigeria. It is clear that agriculture is already under pressure. This could be, to a certain extent, due to an increase in demand for food, as well as the depletion of land and water resources. The prospects of continuing global climate change make this problem a priority for the country.

In order to avoid a worsening of the food insecurity situation, especially in rural areas, it has become necessary to:

a)   understand the adaptation and mitigation strategies of small-scale farmers;
b)   analyse and systematize these; and
c)   develop a sustainable strategy of adaptation and mitigation which enhances food security, guarantees livelihoods, contributes to poverty eradication, and increases access to gainful and functional employment for the majority.

Overall aim and objectives of the study

The overall aim of this chapter is to gain an understanding of the ways in which local farming communities in rural northern Nigeria perceive climate change and its impacts on their communities. This would point towards ways of enhancing food security by facilitating sustainable climate change adaptation and mitigation among small-scale farmers in the area. The objectives targeted by the study were to:

a)   investigate the effect of changing climatic conditions on agricultural production (i.e. from planting to crop yield);
b)   outline the level of vulnerability to climate change in the target communities;
c)   investigate the local adaptive techniques of the small-scale farmer in these communities;
d)   investigate the traditional responses to climate change (e.g. planting method, irrigation and crop protection) in order to boost food production and income;
e)   outline modern professional adaptive strategies that can be used by these local farmers to mainstream gender throughout the industry.

Methodology

The study was conducted following a participatory rural appraisal (PRA) approach. The two communities were purposively selected, and 72 members from Cifatake villages participated in the research, while 35 members participated from Aburom village. Participants were led to discuss environmental conditions and issues and agricultural activities that were found in, and affected, the communities. Thus, a checklist was used and drafted to stimulate discussion on:

a)   the physical and human environment, including vegetation types and species, soil and soil quality, geology, water resources, landforms, total number of people in the communities, farmers, animal resources, transportation and sizes of household;

b)   agriculture, including primarily crop cultivation, length of rain days and rainfall storms;

c)   infrastructure available, in particular the present conditions as they had continued or varied with a period about 30–50 years previously.

For all these issues, the study sought to find out about the changes in environmental factors as well as socio-economic conditions that had occurred, and what adaptive measures were devised over time.

Following data collection, analysis took cognizance of the levels of vulnerability, for which a scheme to indicate the level of vulnerability as devised by Adesina (2009) was used. Key indicators of vulnerability included income, access to key services (particularly in rural areas), life expectancy, frequency of malaria attack, sense of community and the number of household members that sleep in a room.

Finally, for both communities, assessments of current vulnerability were made from the questions that sought to address the following areas: a) Where does this community stand with respect to vulnerability to climate risks? b) What factors determine this society's current vulnerability? c) How successful are the efforts to adapt to current climate risks?

Results and discussion

Understanding climate change

Evidently, members of the two communities had a good understanding of climate change and its effects. Members at Cifatake promptly indicated that climate change has a lot to do with 'heat' and 'increasing heat'. Some of them described it as conditions of drought and desiccation. Collectively, they all pointed out that it had to do with constraining agricultural production and lower incomes. Although the Aburom community could not show this high level of understanding, they did understand climate change as having to do with 'seasonality' and with drought, which they promptly attributed to God's design (*ikon Allah*).

From the members of the two communities, it was very obvious that climate change had been observed as leading to the shortened length of the rainy season. In Cifatake, the eldest members recalled that rainfalls around the area used to begin in March and lasted up to November (meaning an equal number of rain days and dry days: 180 days each per annum). However, at present, rainfall was only established in May and lasted only until October (about 120 rain days annually). In the Aburom community, people were unanimous in expressing that they could not observe change in the number of rain days. Their initial response was that the annual length of the rain period had always been six months followed by six months of dry conditions. Despite this general understanding, a young man (of about 38–40 years) disagreed. He indicated that rainfall some years previously began in early May. This had changed in recent years. The community was now experiencing rainfalls only from late May. Many other members then agreed with him.

The effect of changing climatic conditions on agricultural production and traditional adaptive techniques in the two communities

The two communities established their understanding of the changing climatic conditions by explaining its effect on agricultural production. At Cifatake, members were categorical that present conditions were drier – hence it could not be possible to cultivate same crop types as in the previous 30–50 years. As a consequence, they had introduced many other crop varieties during this time. For instance, in the previous 30–50 years, the village knew only of a few crops – sorghum, white yam, cotton and groundnut. Because of the changing climate, farmers had begun to grow varieties of both food and cash crops including tomatoes, rice, peppers, sweet potatoes and cassava. In another explanation, in order to continue to cultivate the older (i.e. indigenous) food crops they had to change the seeds, adopting improved varieties. Moreover, some improved varieties did well in conditions where chemical fertilizers were used. Where this happened, farmers obtained better harvests from which they could sell the excess at markets in different parts of Kano state.

At Aburom, responses to the effect of changing climatic conditions on agricultural production were similar. As a community prominent for ginger cultivation (*Citta*), they changed the variety mainly because of the changing climate. The indigenous species they had was the *Citta yatsun biri*, which they abandoned over 25–30 years previously, adopting a newer variety called *Citta tafin giwa*. Likewise, they had shifted to a new variety of cowpea, from their native brown type to the white variety.

Agricultural inputs could only be accessed in the open market, often at exorbitant rates beyond the affordability of the famers. In addition to this, the conditions of bad roads and increased transportation costs raised the overall cost of such products even more when they had to be brought long distances. The implication of these factors included the rampant and constant bush and tree burning needed, not only for farming space, but also for the production of ash as a necessary farming input to improve the quality of the soil.

Effects of climate change and adaptations for food security in the study areas

The last two decades of the twentieth century have been noted for the frequency and intensity of extreme weather conditions. In Nigeria, temperatures have risen continuously (Buba 2009), with two periods of major anomalies over most of Nigeria's dryland. According to Buba (2014), the 1950s and 1960s were characterized by negative anomalies and the 1980s were marked by positive anomalies. He further indicated that the last decade (1990s) had shown more marked positive anomalies. This indicates that the temperature distribution over the area had fairly recently begun to show an upward trend consistent with ongoing global warming.

Rainfall in the study area usually started in the month of May and ended in October. This feature of the onset of the rain season was typical of the climate of West Africa, including the area in this study. This indicates that the time for the onset of the rainy season, according to the Nigerian Meteorological Agency (NIMET) and climatologists, has only changed slightly. Whereas the rain starts earlier and stops later in the southernmost parts, it starts later and ceases earlier in the northernmost parts of the region. This situation is influenced by the climatic factors that control the distribution of rainfall over Nigeria. Closely related to the duration of the rainy season is the amount of rainfall received. The amount continues to increase with the advancement of the rain season until a peak is reached in August. It decreases subsequently until it eventually ceases around October. Whereas mean annual rainfall varies significantly from one station to another (spatially), inter-annual (temporal) variation for individual stations is relatively small.

Impacts of climate change on food production and food security is a great threat for (northern) Nigeria. Agriculture is already under pressure due to an increase in demand for food, as well as to depletion of land and water resources. According to Tanko (2010), several adaptive practices or coping measures, and lack of any formal or semi-formal organization in the communities, render it impossible for formally organized measures to be adapted. Climatic factors are unfavourable and these combine to limit the local capacities and capabilities of the farmers. All farmers are vulnerable and are a long way from getting access to scientifically organized responses. For this reason, the farmers stand no chance of making a proper recovery from climatic hazards and they resort to seasonal rural-to-urban migration.

Rural-to-urban migration is a common feature of many developing economies as people travel to larger cities in search of better employment opportunities. In places where farmers must rely on seasonal crops for their livelihood, seasonal migration away from rural areas can help households increase their income and mitigate the risk inherent in an otherwise agriculture-dependent economy (Liman and Tanko 2015). Seasonal human migration in northern Nigeria is very common in relation to agricultural cycles. Migration is primarily of a type where members of village communities from different households migrate temporarily during the dry season, moving from their village of origin to some urban centres that may be near or far away from their villages. These seasonal migrants return to their villages at the onset of the rainy season.

Level of vulnerability to climate change in the two communities

Each community was assessed using variables relevant to the vulnerability of the agricultural sector to climate change. These variables included the relative area of land under cultivation, crop varieties, use of improved seeds, etc. These were measured against mobilization, institutional organization and regulations, and additional inflow of capital investments. Following this rating scheme, the following assessments were achieved for the two communities (Tables 5.1 and 5.2). Cifatake, with a vulnerability value of 0.57, showed more resilience to the impact of climate change than Aburom with a rating of 0.29.

Table 5.1 Vulnerability to climate change rating for Cifatake community

Issues in agricultural sector	Resource mobilization	Institutional organizations and regulations	Additional inflow of capital investment	Vulnerability all +s divided by 21
Land put to cultivation	+	0	0	12/21 = 0.5714
Crop varieties	+	+	+	
Use of improved seeds	+	?	?	
Harvest	+	?	0	
Improved technology for harvest	+	0	0	
Length of rain days	0	0	0	
Rainfall storms	0	0	0	
Water availability	0	0	0	
Vegetation cover	0	0	0	
Species varieties	+	0	0	
Available energy types	0	0	0	
Road infrastructure	0	0	0	
Time distances to market	0	0	0	
Available transportation	+	0	0	
Available markets	+	+	+	
Agro-Allied industries	0	0	0	

Scores (0 = no improvement has taken place, + = improvement has taken place, ? = improvement may have taken place)

Note: The vulnerability, as suggested by Adesina (2009) is a measure of all positive changes against all issues in the major land-based practice. In this study, the issues identified were those in the agricultural sector. All the positive changes were simply counted against 'a stability factor' (i.e. 21). The measure is then used as the indicator of the vulnerability.

Table 5.2 Vulnerability to climate change rating for Aburom community

Issues in agricultural sector	Resource mobilization	Institutional organizations and regulations	Additional inflow of capital investment	Vulnerability all +s divided by 21
Land put to cultivation	+	0	0	6/21 = 0.2857
Crop varieties	+	+	+	
Use of improved seeds	+	0	?	
Harvest	+	0	0	
Improved technology for harvest	?	0	0	
Length of rain days	0	0	0	
Rainfall storms	0	0	0	
Water availability	0	0	0	
Vegetation cover	0	0	0	
Species varieties	0	0	0	
Available energy types	0	0	0	
Road infrastructure	0	0	0	
Time distances to market	0	0	0	
Available transportation	0	0	0	
Available markets	0	0	0	
Agro-Allied industries	0	0	0	

Conclusion, general observations, lessons learnt and recommendations

From the study, it can be concluded that members of the farming communities in northern Nigeria have a good understanding of the concept of climate change and its impacts on their socio-economic circumstances and way of life, in particular, the impacts on agricultural activities. In both communities, members indicated that over the previous 15–30 years, they had introduced many other crop types, and spontaneously devised additional new farming techniques and inputs without necessarily formalizing their actions as 'adaptation'. The local responses can be categorized as: traditional or locally managed responses (e.g. additional crop types), state-supported responses (e.g. preparation and provision of improved seeds); and alternative innovative responses (e.g. more and alternative livestock and poultry/bird-rearing).

Generally, it was observed that the lack of formalized awareness and the lack of articulated knowledge for alternative adaptive responses led to the high vulnerabilities in local communities. It was found that several adaptive practices or coping measures were regularly considered by the farmers, but the lack of any formal or semi-formal organization in the communities rendered it impossible for the measures to be effectively adapted. Indeed, the study found that both the climatic conditions and the anthropogenic factors were contributing to the vulnerability to climate change in agrarian communities. Climatic conditions had become more unfavourable, and natural processes in the form of accelerated soil erosion occurred regularly. These further limited the local capacities and capabilities of the farmers. Moreover, the non-accessibility of the farming communities due to bad roads was a major challenge. All farmers and trading groups had become vulnerable. While the state-oriented adaptive responses may help in reducing vulnerabilities, communities that are remote from getting access to these measures may be left on their own, standing no chance of proper recovery from climate-related hazards.

A number of lessons can be learnt from the study, about strategies of adaptation to climate change in agricultural communities. Climate adaptation is a social learning process that creates the capacity to cope with climate-change-related impacts, and which makes multiple and integrated adaptation measures across sectors essential. Adaptation to climate change is a location-specific issue, and institutional capacity-building and organizational networking (with clear definitions of roles and responsibilities) are essential. Applying a livelihoods perspective is helpful in understanding and promoting local-level adaptation to climate change, so that there is the need to launch adaptation strategies with a focus on current variability and factor in climate change. Additionally, there is the need to better promote sustainable natural resource-management practices in the context of future risks. There is the need to monitor ongoing adaptation practices, provide alerts about the risks of maladaptation, and establish links with policy-making and, at the same time, to assess the value of indigenous knowledge in the context of managing future risks.

References

Adesina, F. A. (2009) 'A Synopsis of Adaptation Strategies of Action for Nigeria with Focus on the Frontline States', A Presentation to Climate Change Support Group, Abuja.

Adesina, F. A., Tanko, A. I., Ayuba, H., Adekunle, T. O., Orji, E., Adeyemi, K. and Tarfa, P. (2009) 'Recommendation for Nigeria's Position'. Technical Report submitted to Heinrich Boll Stiftung (HBS) on behalf of the Special Climate Change Unit (SCCU) of the Federal Ministry of Environment, Abuja.

Buba, L. F. (2009) *Evidence of Climate Change in Northern Nigeria: Temperature and Rainfall Variations*. Unpublished Ph. D. Thesis, Kano, Nigeria: Bayero University.

Buba, L. F. (2014) 'Climate Change' in A. I. Tanko and S. B. Momale (eds.) *Kano Environment, Society and Development*, London, Abuja: Adonis & Abbey Publishers Ltd. pp. 449–466.

IPCC (2007) 'Climate Change 2007: the Physical Science Basis' in S. Solomon, D. Qin, M. Manning, Z. Chen, M. Marquis, K. B. Averyt, M. Tignor and H. L. Miller (eds.) *Contribution of Working Group I to the Fourth Assessment Report of the Intergovernmental Panel on Climate Change*, Cambridge: Cambridge University Press.

Liman, M. and Tanko, A. I. (2015) 'Climate Change, Seasonal Migration and De-Agrarianization in West African Drylands', *Proceedings of 2015 International Conference of the Nigerian Meteorological Society*, 23–26 November 2015, Nigeria: Sokoto, pp. 292–297.

Olofin, E. A. (1992) 'The Gains and Pains of Putting a Water-Look on the Face of the Drylands of Nigeria', Inaugural Lecture Series, No. 1; 292–297, Bayero University, Kano.

Tanko, A. I. (1994) *An Evaluation of the Suitability of Water for Irrigation at the Kadawa Sector of the Kano River Project*, Unpublished M.Sc. Thesis. Kano: Department of Geography, Bayero University.

Tanko, A. I. (1999) 'Physical and Chemical Changes in Soils, and Agricultural Implications under Large-Scale Irrigation in the Kano Region, Northern Nigeria', *Eos Transactions, American Geophysical Union* (AGU) 80 (46), Fall Meet. Supplement, F98, 1999.

Tanko, A. I. (2010) 'Mega Dams for Irrigation in Nigeria: Nature, Dimension and Geographies of Impact', in S. Brunn (ed.) *Mega Engineering Projects in the World*, Dordrecht, Heidelberg, London, New York: Springer Publishers, pp. 1617–1631.

Tanko, A. I. (2013) 'Agriculture, Livelihoods and Fadama Restoration in Northern Nigeria', in A. Wood, A. Dixon and M. McCartney (eds.) *Wetland Management and Sustainable Livelihoods in Africa*, London and New York: Routledge, Taylor and Francis, Earthscan, pp. 205–228.

6 Smallholder adaptation to climate change

Dynamics, constraints and priorities of coastal Guyana

Linda Johnson-Bhola

Introduction

A 2009 International Food Policy Research Institute (IFPRI) Report on Global Food Policy suggested that by 2050, the global population will reach 9.0 billion and that climate change will pose a serious threat to lives and livelihoods. Pardey *et al.* (2010) noted that African and Latin American and Caribbean countries are likely to be severely affected by climate change as these countries have the highest population growth rates and limited financial and technical resources. These conditions are expected to progressively degenerate if measures are not taken to reverse the trends. According to the IPCC (2001), despite advances in technology, including improvements in crop variety and irrigation methods, climate remains a critical variable for agriculture.

Latin America and the Caribbean are experiencing increased episodes of disasters associated with climate change, resulting in millions of dollars of damage to agriculture and seriously threatening the region's food and nutrition security (Ramirez *et al.* 2013). Therefore, limited knowledge amongst farmers about climate change and its impacts could place them at great risk as more frequent and intense droughts and floods are predicted. Coastal Guyana is particularly vulnerable to climate change since approximately 60 per cent of Guyana's population of 700,000 lives on the Low Coastal Plain where most of the fertile farmlands are located. Over the past few decades, floods and droughts have laid bare the vulnerability of small-scale farmers who operate on the coast. Guyana had one of its worst floods in 2005 and this was followed by floods and droughts in 2007 and 2014, and then a drought in 2015 (US Army Corps of Engineers 2006; Guyana Sugar Corporation (GUYSUCO) 2009). While it is anticipated that the Rupununi Savannah is likely to experience drier conditions associated with climate change, the Low Coastal Plain, which is between one and three metres below the mean spring tide level, is expected to experience wetter conditions attributed to heavy and continuous rain. This is against the background of inefficient drainage and irrigation systems, and inflows of saline water from the Atlantic Ocean.

Guyana's agrarian structure was shaped by the post-slavery situation in which ex-slaves left the plantations and squatted on land, each household cultivating less than one hectare of land and using family labour. Weak policies and short-term approaches to small-scale agriculture have also led to inconsistencies in acreage restrictions imposed in later land development schemes. Despite the proliferation of small farms and the relative importance of such farms for domestic food supplies, smallholders are amongst the most disadvantaged and vulnerable groups in Guyana. Research has shown that smallholders bear the brunt of damage to farms at times of severe climate events, and yields are severely compromised, leading to immediate as well as long-term effects of such crises for households (ECLAC 2005; Development Policy and Management Consultants 2009).

Effects of climate change on agriculture

Climate change is likely to compound many of the existing challenges smallholders face in Guyana, ranging from increased flooding of farmed lands to higher incidence of pest infestation resulting in poverty, and the farmers' limited capacity to adopt new technology. The IPCC (2012) concluded that the effects of climate change are virtually certain to be 'overwhelmingly negative' for Guyana as a result of the geographical, social and economic conditions and limited ability to respond. The Initial National Communication and Action Plan in response to Guyana's commitments to the United Nations Framework Convention on Climate Change (UNFCCC) (2002), through the National Climate Committee (NCC), noted that a mean relative sea level rise of 10.2 mm per annum is expected for Guyana. This is estimated to be about five times the global average. The global circulation models (GCMs) indicate average rises of 2–4 mm per year in the first half of the twenty-first century and rises of 3–6 mm per year in the latter half.

Sea level is therefore projected to rise by about 40 cm to 60 cm by the end of the twenty-first century and could result in the breaching and overtopping of the sea defences. These scenarios point to the likelihood that productive lands could become inundated by sea water in various locations in Guyana, leading to a significant decline in agriculture (Downes *et al.* 2009). Temperature alterations are likely to directly affect crop growth rates, increase the incidence of pests, affect water supplies in soil and reservoirs, place crops under drought-stress and impede river flows which support the transportation of agricultural produce.

Guyana's Initial National Communication and Action Plan outlined a number of adaptation responses in the event of a mean relative sea level rise of 10.2 mm/year, together with increased intensities of rainfall leading to higher runoff and increased flooding. The responses included the following: (i) the use of salt-tolerant plant varieties; (ii) increased water management to prevent saline intrusion; (iii) improved sea and river defences protection; (iv) land use changes; (v) increased public awareness about climate change, the role of mangroves and efficient waste-management techniques; (vi) increased storage capacity of conservancies; (vii) acquisition and deployment of more water pumps; and (viii) better maintenance of drainage outfalls.

The nature of smallholder farming in Guyana

The heavy concentration of commercial undertakings in the country has not reduced the proliferation of smallholdings. The Food and Agriculture Organization

(FAO) (2012) estimated that more than half (approximately 60 per cent) of the country's farms were less than 5 hectares in size and that smallholdings occupied about 14 per cent of the total 21,496,901 hectares of lands in the country. Traditionally, smallholder farmers specialized in the cultivation of cash crops for domestic consumption. By 2012, some farmers had begun to shift from the production of cash crops for subsistence and domestic markets only, to include production to sustain the relatively small overseas market in the Caribbean, North America and Europe with vegetables and fruits. Today, small-scale arable farming still remains one of the dominant economic activities undertaken mainly in two of the five physiographical regions of the country; traditionally the Low Coastal Belt which is positioned on the northern section of the country, and more recently the Rupununi Savannah in the south.

A number of policies, regulations and action plans govern the administration of agriculture in Guyana. The National Development Strategy (2000–2010) outlined the issues faced by the agriculture sector at that time. The National Agricultural Strategy of 2013–2020 which emphasized the expansion of subsistence agriculture, entrepreneurial initiatives and agricultural diversification, identified food security as a way to end poverty and hunger by 2025, and it outlined the F-5 Strategic Approach for Agriculture. The F-5 Strategic Approach focuses on Food security, Fiber and nutritious Food accessibility to citizens, Fuel production development of alternative fuel sources, Fashion and health Products – (An Agro-Process Industry which creates a new industry) and furniture and crafts.

While the country's agricultural land policy initiatives could be considered short-term, with the approach limited in scope and significance, there are some *Acts* and *Statutes* that guarantee the right to have interest in land for farming. For example, Guyana's approach towards legitimizing titles to agricultural land is controlled by the *Agrarian Land (Prescriptive and Limitation) Act, Chap. 148* (Laws of British Guyana now Laws of Guyana, *Section 3; Chap. 60:02*). Provision is made also under the *State Land Act, Chap. 59:05* for acquisition of state land for agricultural purposes. Generally, land administration is managed by the Guyana Lands and Survey Commission (GL&SC) under the directive of the Ministry of Agriculture. Some smallholders benefit to a great extent from the services of institutions such as the National Agricultural Research and Extension Institute, the University of Guyana, and the government. The Guyana Marketing Corporation buys some of the produce and, in some cases, the government assists in the marketing of produce.

Distribution of farms in Guyana by size

The size of farm for smallholders is determined by tenure arrangement, labour availability and financial capability. If small farms were defined as those less than 4.047 hectares, then 60 per cent of the total farms could be considered small. Twenty-five per cent of farms occupied a maximum of 1 hectare of land while 60 per cent of the total farms occupied less than 14 per cent of the total hectares of land distributed mainly in rural areas on the coastal zone. Estimates showed that about 50 per cent of farmlands on the coast were privately owned (FAO 2012). Family plots that had been inherited for generations and kept as single blocks of land for the use of multiple family members, had been subdivided for individual families. Subdivision of communal lands, passed down through many generations, has sometimes resulted in two issues: it has created tension within families regarding the ownership of titles; and it has also resulted in the further fragmentation of land and the preponderance of small plot sizes. It is customary to find small land holdings of between 2.023 to 6.070 hectares. Labour on the plots is provided primarily by family members to offset production costs.

Productivity and production

According to the Guyana Office for Investment (GO-Invest 2012), approximately 90 per cent of the country's agricultural exports come from commercial undertakings. If export from commercial farming amounts to about 90 per cent of the total agricultural export for the country, it can be inferred that smallholder farming accounts for about 10 per cent of agricultural exports. The predominant crops grown on smallholdings are root crops, vegetables and fruits. In order to maintain high-quality yields and increase production levels, small-scale farmers are dependent on efficient drainage and irrigation systems provided by the Neighbourhood Democratic Councils (local authority). This is the same as for commercial farming activities, although the magnitude of the demand for drainage and irrigation services for the smallholder sector is far less. Nevertheless, these farmers require efficient water control measures to guard against contrasting weather conditions, namely dry spells and heavy and prolonged rains which, over the years, have resulted in huge losses to the farmers. Crops cultivated perish in both conditions since small farmers have not been able to benefit from varieties resistant to extreme weather conditions. From 2008, the government increased investment in drainage and irrigation by restoring drainage to many areas.

Implications of climate change for food security

Guyana's coast and near inland areas are highly susceptible to flooding caused by three interrelated and often-reported factors: geomorphological, marine and tidal events, and variable weather and climatic conditions. It is well established that climate change is significantly altering temperature and rainfall patterns across the country. In the specific circumstances of the areas under investigation, however, the large areas of low-lying pegasse (swampy) soil utilized by farmers, combined with the tidal effect of water intrusions from the Atlantic Ocean, serve to exacerbate the flooding of farmlands, especially where the drainage systems are inefficient. The result is that there are often periods of severe crop losses, impacting on the country's capacity to meet its local needs, as well as those of the export market. Although Guyana is a net exporter of food, the country continues to experience uncertainty in food availability. In this context, therefore, food security becomes a pertinent issue for farmers and their families as it relates to accessibility, utilization of food and natural and economic shocks on food supply systems due to climate change phenomena.

For the farmers in the study area, their almost total dependence on agriculture for their livelihood has left them particularly vulnerable to climate change. While evidence suggests that farmers have been exposed to training in various adaptive strategies to combat the effects of climate change, this invariably does not fully solve the problems they encounter as they often have to rely on institutional and family support in the event of climate-change-related disasters, such as droughts and floods. However, available data indicate that these kinds of assistance are limited; they do not go far enough to meet their needs, and are not sustainable. In addition, while it is generally understood that climate change disproportionately affects smallholders, it nevertheless has the overall effect of creating uncertainty and long-term vulnerability of all categories of small-scale farmers.

In the case of smallholders, for instance, who traditionally produce crops all year round for domestic consumption and to supply local markets, their inability to produce bountiful harvests throughout the year due to climate-change-related effects has resulted in many farmers losing their traditional markets – and, consequently, earnings – due to the erratic supply of produce. Although the farming households depend to a great extent on their produce as the main source of dietary nutrients from vegetables and root crops, they supplement their diets by using income from the sale of produce to purchase rice, cereals and other staples which do not form part of their production. Consequently, in times of floods and droughts, for example, when earnings are low due to poor crop production, the farmers are confronted with the escalation of food prices locally and nationally. This significantly hampers smallholders' ability to purchase vegetables, fruits and other staples to supplement their families' dietary intake.

Research methodology

Purpose of the study

The purpose of the study on which this chapter is based, was twofold. First, it was designed to identify the farmers who engaged in small-scale cash crop cultivation and who were affected by climate change. Second, it intended to assess the farmers' perceptions of the ways in which climate change was impacting farming activities, and how they were adapting, or proposed to address the impacts.

Selection of the study area

Two criteria were used in the selection of the study areas and villages. The criteria were the extent of small-scale farming undertaken, and the level of vulnerability of the farmers to the impact of climate change. The assumption was that the aforementioned criteria would determine both the extent to which climate change affected the farmers, and the strategies they implemented to address them.

According to the 2002 Population and Housing Census, the population of Tapacuma and Canal No. 2 Polder was 500 and 3,000, respectively. More than three-quarters of the population at Tapacuma and Canal Polder No. 2 engaged in agriculture.

A random sample was selected resulting in a total sample size of 174 (81 and 93, respectively) calculated at the 95 per cent confidence level. Of the total, 88 small farmers (41 and 47 respectively) participated in the survey. All respondents were between the ages of 22 and 65.

Data collection and processing

Data for this study were collected over a period of four days from a total of eighty-eight smallholders who were selected from the two communities. A questionnaire was designed, pre-tested and then administered to the farmers selected in Tapacuma and Canal No. 2 Polder. A team of six assistant researchers carried out the survey. The data were analyzed using the Statistical Package for Social Sciences (SPSS). Group interviews were also conducted to gather general information about the villages.

The dynamics and constraints associated with smallholder adaptation to climate change at Tapacuma and Canal No. 2 Polder

Demographic and socio-economic characteristics of smallholders

Studies conducted by Downes *et al.* (2009) and the Caribbean Community Climate Change Centre (2009) that focused on the effects of climate change on the agriculture sector in Guyana, have shown that there is a strong positive correlation between the socio-economic characteristics of farmers and both their levels of vulnerability to the impacts of climate change and the strategies employed to deal with the impacts.

The largest number of the respondents from Canal No. 2 Polder were Indo-Guyanese, the second largest were people of mixed race and, third, were Afro-Guyanese. Of the 41 smallholders in Tapacuma who participated in the survey, 30 (73%) were Indo-Guyanese, 9 of mixed race (22%) and 2 Afro-Guyanese (5%). For Canal No. 2 Polder, 31 (67%) of the 47 smallholders interviewed were Indigenous Peoples and 14 (30%) were of mixed race. Altogether, more males than females were surveyed and all of the respondents were heads of households. In terms of education, the majority of the respondents had attained primary education and this amounted to 68 respondents from both study areas combined. For Canal No. 2 Polder, 38 (80%) of the respondents had received formal education up to secondary school, while for Tapacuma, 37 (90%) had received secondary education. Altogether, this represented a total of 75 out of 88 (85%) of respondents who had obtained at least secondary-level education. Only one respondent had attained university-level education.

Amongst the key factors that determined the quantity of crops produced was the size of holdings. A common feature found in both study areas was the small size of holdings. Fifty-seven out of eighty-eight respondents cultivated less than one hectare, much of which was leased. Sharecropping was predominant amongst Canal No. 2 Polder farmers and much of the income from the sale of produce to mainly domestic markets was generally low and was used to support many families financially. In some instances, the sale of produce to middle men and relatively high investments in farming activities were common features impacting on the smallholders' earnings. Average annual investment ranged from G$ 80,000 (US $194) to more than G$ 200,000 (US $970). Less than half (30) of the total number of respondents from both study areas combined indicated that farming was the only source of income for the family. The survey results showed that 60 per cent of the smallholders within the age cohort 30 to 50 years obtained the highest incomes. Crops were harvested three times per year and the average annual income acquired from the sale of produce exceeded G$ 120,000 (US $583). Twenty-nine of the respondents did not state their income and noted that they did not keep records.

Smallholders' perceptions of climate change

The survey showed that all of the farmers experienced changes in weather conditions and they believed the changes were associated with a greater atmospheric system since the changes lasted for longer periods. Respondents between the ages of 20 and 30 years noted that the changes will continue and have far-reaching effects on their livelihood. Most of them identified increased incidence of pest infestation and dry spells as main effects. Others noted heavy and prolonged rains causing flooding of farms. The data in Table 6.1 show that from 2005 to 2014, flooding was the single most recurrent problem. Eighty-five respondents stated that the floods had affected their farms severely.

The past flooding episodes affected productivity and production since the results were flooded lands, loss of crops, loss of income and, ultimately, economic hardship for most of the affected families, most of which had an average of five members, including children of school age. Others experienced psychological issues since the only source of income had been destroyed. Those families that

Table 6.1 Flooding from 2005 to 2014 – severity of floods

Year	Severity of floods					
	Very severe	Moderately severe	Severe	Not severe	Not stated	Total
2005–2007	26	14	7	1	0	48
2008–2010	2	4	4	0	1	11
2011–2014	13	10	2	0	1	26
Not stated	2	0	1	0	0	3
Total	43	28	14	1	2	88

Source: Author's field survey.

were dependent on the produce as their source of food had consumed food of lower nutrient content. It took some families more than one year to be able to replant. With the absence of flood insurance and savings, the respondents relied on assistance in the form of grants, fertilizers and technical support from agricultural associations and government to prepare plots, procure planting materials and set up better drainage.

Main constraints smallholders faced in adopting technology in light of climate change

Key constraints which smallholders had encountered fell into two categories: economic and social. Exposure to prolonged rainfall led to water-logging, poor soils and pest infestation, while the dry spells caused inadequate water supply for crops. The high cost of drainage and irrigation technology, or underinvestment in technologies to boost production, caused many crops to fail over the years. The results of the survey showed that this situation had led to loss of income for almost thirty families who depended mainly on subsistence farming for their livelihood. Table 6.2 illustrates the steps smallholders at Canal No. 2 Polder proposed in order to acquire technology. Close to 25 per cent of the respondents indicated that they intended to have crop insurance. However, up to the time of the study, this facility had not been provided by insurance companies in Guyana. Similar steps were identified by smallholders from Tapacuma, except that they noted two other means, and these were increasing savings from successful harvests and finding alternative forms of employment that could assist them to acquire and use more effective technologies.

The constraint of not having access to effective technology was amplified by the lack of knowledge about climate change and agronomy as a means of reducing the incidence of crop failure, and thus adapting to the effects of climate change. According to the survey, only 11 out of 68 respondents had received technical or tertiary education. Since the majority of the respondents acquired secondary

Table 6.2 Steps to address the problem of technology usage (Canal Polder)

Steps taken	Technology usage			
	Yes	No	Not stated	Total
Crop insurance	8	2	1	11
Government assistance	8	2	0	10
Assistance from farmers' union	2	1	0	3
Loans from financial institutions	8	0	0	8
Other	2	1	0	3
Not stated	4	1	0	5
Multiple responses	7	0	0	7
Total	39	7	1	47

Source: Author's field survey.

Table 6.3 Steps to prevent climate change-related issues (in Tapacuma and Canal No. 2 Polder)

	Issues			
Steps taken	Yes	No	Not stated	Total
Improved drainage	18	7	2	27
Climate resistant crops	3	2	0	5
Increased savings	23	2	1	26
Alternative employment	15	0	0	15
Not stated	6	6	0	12
Multiple responses	2	1	0	3
Total	67	18	3	88

Source: Author's field survey.

education, and they were between the ages of 22 and 65, the likelihood was that none of them had received formal education relating to climate change and its impact on agronomy. Despite the fact that some smallholders possessed very little knowledge about the availability and use of technologies to build their resilience to climate change, they employed safeguards such as improved drainage and cultivation of a variety of crops as insurance against crop failure. Table 6.3, below, shows two adaptation strategies that smallholders were considering in order to safeguard the crops against climate-related impacts. These were: improved drainage; and cultivating more flood and drought-resistant crops. Although increased savings and alternative employment were not technologies that could address climate change impacts, they were included in the responses provided in the survey. One possible explanation for the inclusion could be the cost associated with the acquisition of the technologies.

Determinants of the choice of adaptation methods

For the smallholders who used the two adaptation measures, the choice of such measures depended on a number of factors. These were whether or not the technology was available, affordable and accessible and the age, farm size, source of information and the farmer's level of education and awareness. Most respondents stated that even if other technologies were available to them, the cost of those technologies would have been beyond the capacity of smallholders. Some of the farmers varied the crops cultivated in relation to the weather pattern over a given four-month period. Improved draining meant using pumps for irrigation and drainage, and removing excess water from crop land by digging ditches. These initiatives attracted minimal costs to the farmer. With respect to the utilization of drought or flood-resistant crops, peas, beans, cucumbers, watermelon and tomatoes were cited. However, it is questionable whether these were the best choices since research has shown that those crops are drought-resistant, so not necessarily best suited to wet conditions.

Conclusion

Reports from the Ministry of Agriculture in Guyana, the United States Army Corps of Engineers, the Caribbean Community Climate Change Centre and other agencies, show that climate change is already affecting Guyana. Even though the farmers' perceptions of climate change were not necessarily substantiated by the actual phenomenon, some of the adaptation measures employed were consistent with those proposed by the official organizations.

The study showed that smallholders relied on their personal experience of climate variations to determine the adaptation measures that they employed, although they had received no formal training or information on these issues. Smallholders also faced many constraints adapting to technology to address climate change. These included the high cost of drainage and irrigation technology, lack of insurance and limited financial resources. Consequently, most farmers had not used any adaptation measures at all, and had thought about seeking government assistance in order to address the challenges of technology.

Over the years, the government has assisted some small farmers in response to the effects of El Niño and La Niña, as articulated in the Climate Change Adaptation Policy, and in the country's Climate Change Action Plan in response to its commitments to the United Nations Framework Convention on Climate Change (*UNFCCC*). However, the assistance given has been *ad hoc* rather than providing a systematic approach to addressing the concerns of small farmers. Apart from direct government assistance to upgrade infrastructure, such as canals and embankments which protect against flooding, some stakeholder organizations have provided support to small farmers. Amongst the stakeholder groups that have offered technical, financial and other support to the small-scale farmers, was the Guyana Agricultural Producers' Association (GAPA). This association has continued to provide assistance in the areas of productivity, management, research, training and marketing as well as administering funds through its own efforts, government or donor programmes to assist farmers in the development of agriculture.

References

Caribbean Community Climate Change Centre (2009) *National Adaptation Strategy to Address Climate Change in the Agriculture Sector in Guyana, Synthesis and Assessment Report,* Belmopan: Caribbean Community Climate Change Centre.

Development Policy and Management Consultants (2009) 'National Adaptation Strategy to Address Climate Change in the Agriculture Sector in Guyana', Synthesis and Assessment Report. Prepared for the Caribbean Community Climate Change Centre, Belmopan, Belize.

Downes, A. and Pemberton, C. (2009) 'Climate Change and the Agricultural Sector in the Caribbean', in ECLAC (ed.) *The Economics of Climate Change in the Caribbean.* Santiago, Chile: ECLAC.

FAO (2012) 'Land Market Dynamics in Latin America and the Caribbean: A Case Study of Guyana', in FAO (ed.) *Organizacion de las Naciones Unidas para la Alimentacion y la Agricultura.*

GO-INVEST (2012) Agriculture/Agro-processing Sector. Available at: www.goinvest.gov.
gy/sectors/agricultureagroprocessing/.

Government of Guyana (2000–2010) 'National Development Strategy'. Available at: www.
guyana.org/NDS/NDS.htm.

Guyana Bureau of Statistics (2002) *Population and Housing Census*. Available at: www.
statisticsguyana.gov.gy/pubs.html#statsbull.

Guyana Sugar Corporation (GUYSUCO) (2009) 'Vulnerability and Capacity Assessment:
Impacts of Climate Change on Guyana's Agriculture Sector', Report for the Caribbean
Community Climate Change Centre, Belmopan, Belize.

IICA (2008) 'IICA's Contribution to the Development of Agriculture and Rural
Communities in the Americas', ICCA Annual Report, Puerto Rico: IICA.

IPCC (2001) *Climate Change 2001: Impacts, Adaptation & Vulnerability: Contribution of
Working Group II to the Third Assessment Report of the IPCC*, J. J. McCarthy, O. F.
Canziani, N. A. Leary, D. J. Dokken and K. S. White (eds.), Cambridge: Cambridge
University Press.

IPCC (2014) 'Fifth Assessment Report'. Available at: www.odi.org/sites/odi.org.uk/files/
odi-assets/publications.

Laws of Guyana (1998) *Title to Land (Prescriptive and Limitation) Act*, Section 3; Ch. 60:02.
Available at: www.guyaneselawyer.com/lawsofguyana/Laws/cap6002.pdf.

Pardey, P. G., Alston, J. M. and Wood, S. (2010) 'Agricultural Productivity', in P. G. Pardey,
S. Wood and R. Hertford (eds.) *Research Futures: Projecting Agricultural R&D Potentials for
Latin America and the Caribbean'*, Washington, D.C. and St. Paul, MN: International Food
Policy Research Institute (IFPRI), International Development Bank (IDB) and
International Science and Technology Practice and Policy (InSTePP), pp. 85–113.

Ramirez, D., Ordaz, J. L., Mora, J. and Acosta, A. (2013) *Belize: Effects of Climate Change
on Agriculture*, Mexico: ECLAC/CCAD/DFID.

United Nations Economic Commission for Latin America and the Caribbean (ECLAC)
(2005) *Guyana Socio-Economic Assessment of the Damages and Losses Caused by the
January–February 2005 Flooding*, Santiago: ECLAC.

United Nations Framework Convention on Climate Change (UNFCCC) (2001) *Guyana Climate
Change Action Plan in Response to its Commitments to the UNFCCC – Actions for Addressing
Climate Change, 2001*. Available at: www.unfccc.int/resource/docs/nap/guynap01.pdf.

United Nations Framework Convention on Climate Change (UNFCCC) (2002). *Report of
the Conference of the Parties on its Seventh Session*. Available at: http://unfccc.int/resource/
docs/cop 7/13a01.pdf.

United States Army Corps of Engineers (2006) *Guyana*. Available at: www.sam.usace.
army.mil/en/wra/Guyana/Guyana%20WRA.pdf.

7 Perceptions of changing climatic conditions in rural Kano, Nigeria

Effects on harvests and farmers' adaptive coping strategies

Halima Abdulkadir Idris

Introduction

Climate change is one of the all-encompassing global environmental changes likely to have deleterious effects on natural and human systems, including economies and infrastructure. The risks associated with it call for a broad spectrum of policy responses and strategies at the local, regional, national and global levels. The United Nations Framework Convention on Climate Change (UNFCCC) highlights two fundamental response strategies – mitigation and adaptation. While mitigation seeks to limit the effects of climate change through the reduction of greenhouse gases (GHG) and enhancing 'sink' opportunities, adaptation will alleviate the adverse impacts through a range of system-specific actions (Fussel and Klein 2002).

Much emphasis is on the African continent's vulnerability, primarily due to low adaptive capacity and its sensitivity to many projected changes (Stringer 2009). Records, dating as far back as the 1680s, have shown the region's marked decline in rainfall and its recurrent droughts of such magnitude and intensity that destruction caused by them has been on the increase over the last 100 years (Hulme *et al.* 2001; Tarhule and Lamb 2003, cited in Hein and deRidder 2006). Most prominent among these droughts was that of the early 1970s, during which hundreds of thousands of people and millions of animals died (Mortimore 1998).

Available evidence shows Nigeria has been experiencing diverse ecological problems directly linked to climate change (Borokini 2010). The southern ecological zone of Nigeria, is currently confronted with an irregular rainfall pattern, while the Guinea Savannah has been experiencing gradually increasing temperatures (Bello *et. al.* 2012).

This chapter focuses on the farmers' perceptions of climate change and the effects of the changing climatic conditions on their harvests, with a view to understanding their adaptive and coping strategies.

Climate change and agriculture

Nigeria is particularly prone to the devastating impacts of climate change due to its geo-physical position and socio-economic characteristics. The country extends from the wet coastal south through mangrove and delta to the dry, arid north. Its economy is predominantly agricultural, with about 70 per cent of its labour force in the agriculture sector. Although the wet southern environment provides the potential for cultivating tuber and tree crops, it is constrained by high population density and soil acidity. The dry north has vast land resources, but agriculture is constrained by soil desiccation and aridity (Tanko 2010). Responding to climate change through adaptation initiatives will require Nigeria to engage in a concerted effort over the short and long term, to seek out opportunities and design actions to reduce the vulnerability of the people to climate-change impacts. This will require building a climate-resilient society that is able to withstand, or recover quickly from, difficult conditions caused by the adverse effects of climate change (Oladipo 2010). The constraints posed by climate change on agriculture in this region range from pronounced seasonality of rainfall (which confines cultivation to short periods of three to five months), to severe and recurrent droughts (which disrupt the usual pattern of seasonal water availability). Most of the droughts also exhibit such characteristics as false onset of the rains, late onset of the rains, pronounced breaks during the rainy season, and early cessation of the rains. These lead to drastic alterations in the pattern of seasonal rainfall distribution (Adefolalu 1986; Anyadike 1993; Ekpoh 1999; Anyanwale 2007).

Food production is particularly sensitive to climate change because crop yields depend directly on climatic conditions (temperature and rainfall patterns). In tropical regions, even small amounts of warming will lead to a decline in the amount of crops harvested. In cold areas, crop harvests may increase at first with moderate increases in temperature, but then fall. Higher temperatures will lead to a large decline in cereal (for example, rice and wheat) production around the world (Stern 2006, cited in Pender 2008).

An important feature of drylands is low seasonal rainfall and high rainfall variability. High rainfall variability – as manifested in variable onsets and rainfall amounts – dry spells, recurrent droughts and floods are intrinsic characteristics of many sub-Saharan Africa (SSA) regions, especially the arid and semi-arid regions. This implies that rain-fed agriculture already has to accommodate these various conditions (Speranza 2010).

Coping and adaptation to climate change

Indigenous knowledge has been defined as institutionalized local knowledge that has been built upon and passed on from one generation to the other by word of mouth (Osunade 1994; Warren 1992). Such knowledge adds value to climate change studies in the following ways: First, indigenous knowledge systems create a moral economy. It identifies a person within a cultural context, thus providing decision-making processes or rules of thumb to be followed based on observed indicators or relationships within events (Adugna 1996; Woodley 1991). Second, in an effort to reconcile current food deficits with future environmental debt, most food-deficit regions face the challenge of identifying appropriate technological and policy approaches that are affordable, that best meet food security objectives and provide opportunities for smallholder farmers to adapt to climate change (Antle and Diagana 2003, cited in Ajayi *et al.* 2008). Third, in terms of practice, there are several ways to adapt to climate change at the farm level. These different ways are mainly complementary as they address different components of the smallholder farming system (Speranza 2010).

The study conducted in rural Kano

Research methods

Purposive sampling was employed in the selection of locations for study in the northern and southern parts of Kano State. This sampling method was selected because rainfall amount varies between the northern and southern parts of Kano, with the south receiving more rains. These samples were taken at four different segments of the state using the cardinal points as a guide, where Kano State was divided into northeast, northwest, southeast and southwest. From each of these segments, a community from one Local Government Area was selected, based on its accessibility and its being a rural, smallholder farming area. The communities selected within these areas were Gurumu in Gabasawa Local Government Area, Badume in Bichi Local Government Area, Darki in Wudil Local Government Area and Dangora in Kiru Local Government Area (Figure 7.1). Using convenience sampling, 15 farmers were selected from each of the communities for the appraisal. The age range of respondents was 45–89 years.

The participatory rural appraisal (PRA) technique was used in the field to gather qualitative data to complement the quantitative data. This technique enabled vulnerable groups in a community to have a voice and express their views on issues as they understood them. In this study, group discussions and direct interviews with open-ended questions were employed to elicit farmer participation.

The responses to some of the direct questions in interviews were measured on a Likert scale. Participants were led to discuss conditions and issues of environmental and agricultural activities as they affect them and their communities. The discussions focused around a time frame of 30 years, over which the participants recalled and discussed their situations, experiences, observations and perceptions. A checklist was prepared to include primarily crop cultivation, and farmers' assessments of rainfall onset, cessation, length of rain days, changes in the amount of rain received, rain storms, changes in temperature, and how these factors affected their harvests.

Farmers' perceptions of climate change

The farmers were asked if they had noticed any changes in the temperature and rainfall over the previous 30 years. Their responses are indicated below: All of the respondents in Dangora (Kiru) and Darki (Wudil) strongly disagreed that rainfall onset was earlier, in Gururmu (Gabasawa), about one-eighth of respondents were of this view and in Badume (Bichi), about one-fifth of the farmers strongly

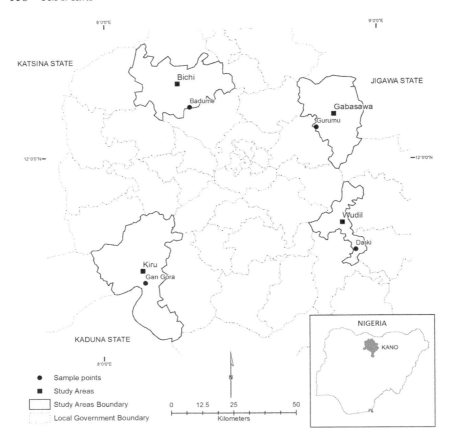

Figure 7.1 Kano State showing the study area.

disagreed as well. Most (more than four-fifths) of the respondents in Gurumu (Gabasawa) and Badume (Bichi) disagreed that rainfall onset had improved in the area. This indicated that the rainfall pattern had changed over time as observed and understood by the participants, rather than the actual situation of there being an earlier onset of rains, since late onset was the dominant situation experienced. Similarly, all participants from all the communities strongly agreed that there had been an earlier cessation of rains. This indicated that over the years, the farmers had been experiencing late starts and early cessation of rains, resulting in a shorter duration of the rainy season.

For Gurumu (Gabasawa), all participants disagreed that the number of rain days had increased and for Badume (Bichi), Dangora (Kiru) and Darki (Wudil), all participants strongly disagreed. This was an indication of observed changes in climate, confirming that the numbers of rain days had decreased greatly from what they had been about thirty years previously. Additionally, the amount of rainfall had also decreased, with the same pattern of responses by the communities. Thus, the participants from Badume (Bichi), Dangora (Kiru) and Darki (Wudil) strongly disagreed that there had been an increase in the amount of rainfall, while those from Gurumu (Gabasawa) disagreed. In other words, all the respondents believed that the rainfall amount had been decreasing over the years.

The decreasing duration of the wet season, number of rain days and amount of rainfall were seen by all the farmers to have negatively affected water availability in the study area, reflected in the fact that all of them strongly disagreed about improved water availability. On the other hand, all respondents in all the communities strongly agreed that there had been an increase in temperature over the years. Consequently, they strongly agreed that there had been a change in the climatic conditions in the area in terms of late start of rains, early cessation, shorter duration of the wet season and a more prolonged dry season with increasing shortages of water. All the responses recorded showed that there had been evidence of change in the seasonal pattern of rainfall as all the participants strongly agreed that rainfall cessation had happened much earlier than usual.

Climate change is one of the main challenges to be faced in the twenty-first century, and the existing poor historical data on climate from which projections can be made and food production adapted, exacerbate the vulnerability of countries such as Nigeria in terms of sustaining food security in the future. Scientific experts have pointed out that 60–70 per cent of the world's food is still produced from the 80 per cent of cropland that is rain-fed. The evidence is that in the past, extended periods of drought, unusually high rainfall or flooding in these areas have had devastating effects on the marginal levels of production, placing subsistence farming in jeopardy (Chikozho 2010).

Evidence of changes in climate

The number of rain days for a period of 30 years indicates the trend, and this raises questions about the implications for farming of any significant change or variation. The evidence is that the numbers of rain days were greater in the past than that recorded for 2011 and there has also been a decrease in the amount of rainfall (Table 7.1).

Table 7.1 Average number of rain days and average amount of rainfall (mm)

	Period/ Location	Gabasawa	Bichi	Kiru	Wudil
Average Number of Rain days (April–October)	1981 – 1991	28	36	40	41
	2001 – 2011	20	30	36	36
Average Amount of Rainfall (mm) (April–October)	1981 – 1991	164.8	153.25	176.5	184.8
	2001 – 2011	115.4	124	158	153

Source: Kano State Agricultural and Rural Development Authority (KNARDA), 2011.

Effects of changing climatic conditions on harvests

Changing climatic conditions were investigated in this study, based on changes experienced by the farmers pertaining to rainfall (rainfall onset, cessation, amount and number of rain days), temperature, water availability and seasonal patterns, which are the key elements of climate. The results, based on the observations and perceptions of the farmers, and the relationship that they have been able to establish with how conditions affect cropping practices regarding their harvests, are presented in this section.

About three-quarters of the participants disagreed that harvests had increased in relation to rainfall onset, while a quarter strongly disagreed. This tallied with the discussions held with the farmers who explained that late onset of rains had adversely affected productivity as they were unable to plant their crops early, thus shortening the length of the growing season and hastening the harvesting season. All these factors had affected the yield of their crops as the maturing period needed for high yields had been reduced.

Over 70 per cent of the participants strongly disagreed that harvests had increased on account of the decrease in the length of rain days and decrease in rainfall amount. This showed a direct association between the two climatic factors and harvests, emphasizing the dependence of harvests on amount of rainfall and the number of rain days. The farmers explained that temperatures had increased, which did not favour the germination, growth and maturity of their crops. From their observations, these increases in temperatures have had a negative effect on their products as they have continuously experienced decreases in yield over the past 30 years associated with the increase in temperatures.

Adaptive coping strategies of the farmers

The adaptive coping strategies of the farmers have to do mainly with farming operations and also some off-farm operations. Table 7.2 shows the coping strategies of the farmers in all the communities studied. The use of locally made organic fertilizer (compost) was more prevalent than chemical fertilizers, with 93.3 per cent of the farmers using organic fertilizer and only 6.7 per cent using a chemical fertilizer. This, they said, was attributed to the high cost of chemical fertilizers where they were available, but that in most cases they did not have access to them. The organic fertilizer was composed of kara (cornstalks), yayi (removed weed), domestic waste, animal dung and ash residue from use of fuel wood, which were put in a dug-out hole and left to rot and disintegrate. Later, the material was dried and used to fertilize their crops during the farming season.

The adoption of a shifting planting period, mixed cropping, intervals and spacing during planting were also some of the techniques used by the farmers. They also used improved seeds which required well-planned planting periods and methods in order to produce a better yield. About 46.7 per cent of the farmers used shifting planting periods, 35 per cent used intervals and spacing and relay planting, while 18.3 per cent used mixed cropping techniques. These, according to the farmers, helped in boosting their harvests, especially in times when rainfall was minimal.

All the farmers confirmed their use of improved seeds, which had resulted in better yields in recent times, despite the constraint of reduced rainfall. The improved seeds, which germinated and matured faster than the previously used varieties, was adapted to the new planting periods that were followed. Other issues discussed included storage and extension services. The farmers pointed out that about 65 per cent of them used modern storage facilities, such as the recently built stores, and 35 per cent used local storage, such as rumbu (silos) and tree tops. Additionally, 75 per cent of the farmers had access to extension workers, through whom they had been educated about planting periods, fertilizer application, harvest time, use of improved seeds, storage, and also how to link up with better markets for their products.

Table 7.2 Adaptive coping strategies

Adaptive coping strategies	Gurumu	Badume	Dangora	Darki	Total
	%	%	%	%	%
Use of organic fertilizer	100.0	73.33	100.0	100.0	93.33
Use of chemical fertilizer	0.0	26.67	0.0	0.0	6.67
Adoption of shifting planting periods	46.67	100.0	0.0	40.0	46.67
Use of intervals and spacing during planting and different planting periods	33.33	0.0	100.0	6.67	35.0
Mixed cropping	20.0	0.0	0.0	53.33	18.33
Use of improved seeds	100.0	100.0	100.0	100.0	100.0
Use of local storage facilities	100.0	0.0	0.0	40.0	35.0
Use of modern storage facilities	0.0	100.0	100.0	60.0	65.0
Access to extension workers	100.0	100.0	100.0	0.0	75.0
Planting trees	53.33	100.0	40.0	60.0	63.33
Use of relay planting techniques	100.0	100.0	100.0	100.0	100.0
Planting different varieties of crops	100.0	100.0	100.0	100.0	100.0
Addition of wild plants in diet	100.0	100.0	100.0	100.0	100.0

No. of respondents for each location (n) =15

Source: Author's field work, 2011.

Planting trees was also another coping strategy employed by farmers. These were reported to have helped in checking soil loss and also increasing soil fertility, resulting from the debris of fallen leaves. Additionally, the use of different planting techniques, such as planting times for different crops, was mentioned by the farmers, and they used various modes of soil tillage, as well as spacing to suit each crop. The planting of alternative varieties of crops was also practiced, as this allowed the farmers to harvest different crops at different times of the season, thereby providing some form of check and balance in case there were to be any losses from infestation by pests, diseases or invasive plants.

The decrease in harvest, as found in the study area, was an indication of the reduced availability of food, with food insecurity outcomes. These farmer households depended solely on agriculture for their livelihood, essentially depending on grain crops for their subsistence, including sorghum, millet and maize for which yields had all decreased. As a coping strategy, some of these farmer households had added wild plants to their diet – plants such as *Cassi tora*, *Leptadadia pyrotechnica* and *Moringa oleifera*.

Conclusion

There was conclusive evidence that farmers in the study had been aware of the changes in climatic conditions. Their observations were corroborated by the climatic data collated from Kano State Agricultural and Rural Development Authority (KNARDA) on the number of rainy days, mean amounts of rainfall for different time series, and the spatial and temporal trends of rainfall variability. Late onset of rains, early cessation of rains, increase in temperature, changes in seasonal patterns, among other changes, had been experienced by the farmers and understood as evidence of changes in climate which had affected their harvests negatively in recent years in comparison to harvests of 30 years previously. It was also observed that the farmers had adopted some coping strategies to ameliorate the adverse effects of the emerging harsher climatic conditions as it affected their harvests and also threatened the availability of food for their household survival. The adaptive responses included the use of locally made fertilizer, obtaining and using improved seeds, developing new planting period techniques, and adding wild plants to household diets.

One can conclude, therefore, that the emerging climate change scenario will impact negatively on agricultural production unless the farmers' capacities are built up through improved extension services and the availability of early maturing seeds. These are essential in order to add to and support the local efforts made, using indigenous coping strategies based on farmers' perceptions and experiences, in the effort to meet household food security requirements.

References

Adefolalu, D. O. (1986) 'Rainfall Trends in Nigeria', *Theoretical and Applied Climatology*, 37: 205–219.

Adugna, G. (1996) 'The Dynamics of Knowledge Systems Versus Sustainable Development', *Indigenous Knowledge Development Monitoring*, 4(2):31–32.

Ajayi, O. C., Akinnifesi, F. K., Sileshi, G., Chakeredza, S., Mn'gomba, S., Ajayi, O., Nyoka, I. Chineke, T. (2008) 'Local Solutions to Global Problems: the Potential of Agroforestry for Climate Change Adaptation and Mitigation in Southern Africa', paper presented at the Tropical Forests and Climate Change Adaptation (TroFCCA) Regional Meeting, Knowledge and Action on Forests for Climate Change Adaptation in Africa, 18–20 November, Accra, Ghana: ICRAF.

Anyadike, R.C.N. (1993) 'Seasonal and Annual Rainfall Variations over Nigeria', *International Journal on Climatology,* 13: 567–580.

Anyanwale, K. C. (2007) *Climate Dynamics of the Tropics,* Dordrecht: Kluwer Academic Publishers.

Bello, O. B., Ganiyu, O. T., Wahab, M.K.A., Afolabi, M. S., Oluleye, F., Ig S.A., Mahmud, J., Azeez, M. A. and Abdulmaliq, S. Y. (2012) 'Evidence of Climate Change Impacts on Agriculture and Food Security in Nigeria', *International Journal of Agriculture and Forestry,* 2(2): 49–55.

Borokini, I. T. (2010) 'Biodiversity Conservation and Climate Change in Nigeria' in F. Bojang and A. Ndeso-Atanga (eds.) *Nature & Faune,* Rome: Food and Agricultural Organization, 25(1): 75–85.

Chikozho, C. (2010) 'Applied Social Research and Action Priorities for Adaptation to Climate Change and Rainfall Variability in the Rainfed Agricultural Sector of Zimbabwe,' *Physics and Chemistry of the Earth,* 35 (13): 780–790.

Ekpoh, I. J. (1999) Estimating the Sensitivity of Crop Yields to Potential Climate Change in North-Western Nigeria. *Global Journal of Pure and Applied Sciences,* Vol. 5, No. 3:303–308.

Fussel, H. M., and Klein, R.J.T. (2002) 'Assessing the Vulnerability and Adaptation to Climate Change: An Evolution of Conceptual Thinking', paper presented at the UNDP Expert Group Meeting on Integrating Disaster Reduction and Adaptation to Climate Change, Havana, Cuba, 17–19 June 2002.

Hein, L. and deRidder, N. (2006) 'Desertification in the Sahel: a Reinterpretation' *Environmental Systems Analysis Group, Wageningen University, PO Box 47, 6700 AA, Wageningen,* Wageningen, The Netherlands: Plant Production Systems Group, Wageningen University.

Hulme, M., Doherty, R., Ngara, T., New, M., Lister, D. (2001) 'African Climate Change: 1900–2100', *Climate Research,* 17:145–168.

Idris, H. A. (2014) 'Adaptation Strategies to Climate Change by Smallholder Farmers in Rural Kano', Unpublished M.Sc. Thesis, Bayero University Kano, Nigeria.

Mortimore, M. (1998) *Roots in the African Dust: Sustaining the Sub-Saharan Drylands,* Cambridge: Cambridge University Press.

Oladipo, E. (2010) 'Towards Enhancing the Adaptive Capacity of Nigeria: A Review of the Country's State of Preparedness for Climate Change Adaptation', report submitted to Heinrich Boll Foundation Nigeria.

Osunade, M. A. (1994) 'Indigenous Climate Knowledge and Agricultural Practices in Southwestern Nigeria', *Journal of Tropical Geography,* 1: 21–28.

Pender, J. S. (2008) 'What Is Climate Change? And How it Will Effect Bangladesh'. *Briefing Paper (Final Draft),* Dhaka, Bangladesh: Church of Bangladesh Social Development Programme.

Speranza, C. I. (2010) *Resilient Adaptation to Climate Change in African Agriculture,* Bonn: Deutsches Institut für Entwicklungspolitik (German Development Institute Studies), 54.

Stringer, L C., Jen, C., Dyer, J. C., Reed, M. S., Dougill, A. J., Twyman, C. and Mkwambisi, D. (2009) 'Adaptations to Climate Change, Drought and Desertification: Local Insights to Enhance Policy in Southern Africa', *Environmental Science and Policy,* 12: 748–765.

Tanko, A. I. (2010) 'Facilitating Sustainable Climate Change Adaptation and Mitigation by Small Scale Farmers to Enhance Food Security in Kaduna State, Nigeria', Technical Report submitted to Tubali Development Initiatives on behalf of Heinrich Boll Stiftung (HBS), a German NGO working on climate change (April 2010).

Warren, D. M. (1992) 'Strengthening Indigenous Nigerian Organizations and Associations for Rural Development: The Case of Ara Community', *Occasional Paper No. 1*, Ibadan: African Resources Centre for Indigenous Knowledge.

Woodley, E. (1991) 'Indigenous Ecological Knowledge Systems and Development', *Agriculture and Human Values,* 8:173–178.

8 Perceptions and attitudes towards climate change

Strategies for food security amongst female farmers in rural Jamaica

Ayesha Constable

Introduction

Gender has become central to the discussions and work on development globally and there is a growing assessment of the linkages to the environment. The final decade of the last millennium witnessed increasing interest in the analysis of women–environment interactions and the gendered impact of environmental policies (Momsen 2002). In some contexts, there has been an overwhelming focus on the experiences of women because of the perceived and real inequities that place women in disadvantageous positions in some cultures and societies. The location of women in the decision-making hierarchy and the subjugation of women in some cultures are regarded by feminists as unfavourable for development and economic growth and a matter of injustice. At the twenty-first conference of the Parties to the United Nations Framework Convention on Climate Change (UNFCCC), members of the Women and Gender Constituency argued that the current global economic capitalist regime had been built on the backs of women. The last few decades have given rise to increased focus globally on climate studies with an emphasis on climate change and its connection with justice. In developing countries, climate change is having, and will have, devastating impacts on local economies because of the economic and geographic vulnerability of these countries. At the same time, a broader call to address gender in climate change policy has been taken up by several mainstream development organizations (for example, the United Nations' Food and Agriculture Organization, United Nations Development Programme Women's Environment and Development Organization and United Nations International Strategy for Disaster Reduction) (Bee *et al.* 2013).

Much emphasis has been placed on the fact that rural women, in developing countries in particular, interact more directly with their environment, and are disproportionately adversely affected by environmental degradation than are men (Dankelman 2002). Many of these countries have tried to diversify their economies, but remain dependent on agriculture to support rural livelihoods and bolster food security. At present, agriculture contributes 7 per cent to the Jamaican gross domestic product (GDP) and employs 17 per cent of the economically active labour force (FAO 2014), which is an increase from 5.3 per cent in 2005 and 6.5 per cent in 2000. Women represent 23 per cent of those employed in the agricultural sector. Although they play such important roles and make valuable contributions to the agricultural sector and to rural development, much of their contribution remains invisible because the food that they grow is in backyard gardens and on smallholdings. The unpaid labour that they do on family land and the produce that they sell in the market are not accurately recorded or reflected in national statistics (Ellis 2003).

Many organizations including the Women's Environment and Development Organization (WEDO) and the Women's Earth Climate and Action Network International (WECAN), maintain that women are disproportionately affected by climate change as a result of poverty, socially constructed gender inequalities, gendered work and family responsibilities, reliance on natural resources for livelihoods as part of 'women's work', and the limited financial, social and institutional resources available to women across the globe (Perkins 2014). Women do not lack agency in the environmental space; they hold critical local knowledge that can enhance climate adaptations and assist the development of new technologies to address climate variability in areas related to energy, water, food security, agriculture and fisheries, biodiversity services, health and disaster risk management (Alston 2014). Women are the cornerstone of the rural economy, especially in the developing world. They bear the greatest responsibility for food production, producing more than half of all food in the world (Smith 2015). Although both rural women and rural men have different and complementary roles in guaranteeing food security at the household and community levels, women often play a greater role in ensuring household nutrition, food safety and quality (FAO 2003). Climate change could potentially affect the ability of women to provide and secure food for their households.

The vulnerability of human populations and natural systems to the negative effects of climate change differs substantially across regions and populations within regions (Dankelman 2002). On the whole, the impacts of climate change on small islands, including Jamaica, will have serious negative effects, especially on socio-economic conditions and biophysical resources (IPCC 2014). Climate change impacts are already being observed in the Jamaican agricultural sector, resulting in lower yields due to the prevalence of more pests and diseases (Caribsave 2012). The Planning Institute of Jamaica reported that between 1973 and 2003, the agriculture sector suffered losses amounting to US$ 27.8 million because of severe weather events. Within the context of sustainable development, the government has recognized the importance of prudent management of Jamaica's natural resources in light of the potential negative impact of climate change (PIOJ 2015). While climate change is not the only factor causing major disruption, in combination with others it constitutes a major global challenge, and one that exacerbates gender inequalities (Alston 2014).

Jamaica's Rural Agricultural Development Authority (RADA) has, to date, registered 135,345 farmers, cultivating on 235,525 hectares of land under its farmer registration programme. Of these, 42,692 or 32 per cent were women, most within the age group 35–54 years. The average plot size cultivated by women is 1.4 hectares, in comparison with an average of 2.6 hectares cultivated by male farmers

(Gooden 2011). Crawford (2011) highlighted the multiple roles that women play in the agricultural process – as farmers, agricultural labourers, backyard gardeners, marketers, agro-processors.

This chapter highlights the dynamics in the way male and female farmers of Sherwood Content, Trelawny in Jamaica perceive and respond to climate change, with emphasis on the efforts made by women to ensure food security at the household level. Linking gender and climate change should go beyond demonstrating the vulnerability of women and their need for focused and tailor-made capacity development (Denton 2009).

Theoretical framework

The emerging climate justice movement has its roots in environmental justice. Recently, the environmental justice movement has focused on the implications of climate change for vulnerable people and communities and called for attention to be directed to climate justice (Israel and Sachs 2013). Agostino and Lizarde (2015) argued that the concept of climate justice emerged as a result of introducing a rights approach to the challenges posed by climate change. More recently, feminist interventions have called for the inclusion of gender in the climate justice debates (Israel and Sachs 2013).

Women are much more likely to be living in poverty, and are less likely to own land and resources that could protect them in a post-disaster situation. The IPCC (2007) makes special mention of the vulnerability of rural women who, in developing countries, are often dependent on natural resources for their livelihoods, and do most of the agricultural work, and bear responsibility for collecting water and fuel (Terry 2009). Furthermore, they have less control over production and income, less education and training, less access to institutional support and information, less freedom of association, and fewer positions on decision-making bodies than men (Alston 2014). Women's increased vulnerability following disasters may lead to the adoption of unsustainable coping strategies rather than long-term viable adaptation strategies (Alston 2013). Adaptation is different from coping, which, although it may ensure short-term survival, may not protect people from the future effects of climate change (Terry 2009).

The 2007 UNDP Human Development Report cautioned that gender inequalities intersect with climate risks and vulnerabilities, concluding that climate change is likely to amplify and exacerbate existing patterns of gender disadvantage (Aguilar 2013). Thus, women and the environment represent twin dimensions of exploitation that suffer from the current capitalist regime and patriarchal structures of domination. These linkages make environmental degradation especially consequential for women and are also believed to increase women's propensity to protect and preserve the environment, when they are afforded positions of power in society (McKinney and Fulkerson 2015). Worldwide, women are responsible for 70–80 per cent of household food production, chiefly as subsistence farmers, producing their own food. Traditional food-supply sources may become more unpredictable and scarce as climate changes affect women (Parikh 2007).

Women produce much of the world's food, yet the majority of the world's hungry are women and children (Gaard 2015). As stated in the People's Earth Declaration in Rio 1992 (Living Economies Forum 1992), women's roles, needs, values and wisdom are especially central to decision-making on the fate of the earth (Agostino and Lizarde 2015). A more recent permutation by Gaard (2015) advanced the view that climate change and first-world overconsumption are produced by masculinist ideology, and will not be solved by masculinist techno-scientific approaches. It is a feminist ethical approach to climate justice – challenging the distributive model that has ignored relations of gender, sexuality, species and environments – that has yet to be fully developed (*ibid.*).

Double vulnerability

In Jamaica, FAO (2010) examined local perceptions of the impacts of climate change in its Livelihood Assessment Tool-Kit training of the Rural Agricultural Development Authority (RADA). The major impacts noted by local communities were higher agricultural prices, food shortages and scarcity, reduction of local food production, famine and hunger, damage to, and loss of crops and livestock, and devastation of income streams through pests and diseases. Goldsmith *et al.* (2013) provided evidence of the fact that women engaged in less system justification than men, and this difference partially explained women's greater willingness to acknowledge ecological problems and risks, and to engage in actions that were beneficial to the environment (Goldsmith *et al.* 2013).

In recent years, Jamaican farmers have been hampered by increased production costs, declining state support, and enhanced competition from imports due to trade liberalization (Weis 2004). The impacts climate change on smallholder and subsistence farmers will be compounded by environmental and physical processes affecting production at landscape, watershed and farm levels. Other impacts include those on human health and on non-agricultural livelihoods (Morton 2007), and also on trade and food prices (Anderson *et al.* 2010). O'Brien and Leichenko (2008) proposed a double exposure framework that examines the linkages between the dual processes of environmental change and globalization. Environmental change is typically defined as a set of changes to the earth system that are expected to have major effects on human society and ecosystem services (*ibid.*). Double exposure also describes the ways that the two processes influence exposure and capacity to respond to a wide array of stresses and shocks.

Study area and methodology

Sherwood Content is situated in the northwest of Jamaica, in the parish of Trelawny. About 47 per cent of the Jamaican population lives in rural areas and 16.5 per cent live below the poverty line, of whom, the majority are women (FAO 2013). In the 2002 Jamaica Survey of Living Conditions, Trelawny and two other agriculture-dependent parishes had the highest incidence of poverty, with 30 per cent of residents living in poverty (PIOJ 2007). The Caribbean Catastrophe Risk

Insurance Facility (CCRIF) ranked the parish of Trelawny medium risk with regard to geographical distribution of climate risk in Jamaica (Caribsave 2012).

Sherwood Content was purposively selected due to observations that had been made by farmers and researchers of the drastic changes in the land-use patterns, and based on reports of changes in environmental conditions by farmers. Underlain by Tertiary limestones, the terrain of the area is generally hilly, interspersed with large expanses of flat areas and bordered by the Cockpit Country[1] to the south. The soil conditions in the area vary from place to place, but they are generally thin and range from loam to clayey loam. Farmers generally report that soils are fertile. Farming remains a dominant aspect of livelihood in Sherwood Content changing, since the 2000s, from sugar cane and dairy cattle farming to the present system of small-scale cropping with small livestock. Yam is now widely grown for both subsistence and commercial purposes.

A mapping exercise of the entire community was conducted at the beginning of the research to devise a sampling frame, by assigning a number to each house mapped. The sample was selected using the simple random technique, a form of probability sampling which, according to de Vaus (2002), is the best way of ensuring that the sample is representative, with all people in the population having an equal chance of being included. A household questionnaire survey was then conducted in Sherwood Content to gather data on local social, economic and environmental issues. In addition, interviews and focus group discussions were held with key informants and other local stakeholders.

Socio-economic profile of women

The women in the study constituted 30 per cent of the overall sample. An estimated 20 per cent of women lived with a husband or partner, and the rest were single and heads of their households – which was not unusual but also, was not without social and economic challenges (Crawford 2011). According to the analysis, the average household size was two members, lower than the national average of 3.6 (STATIN 2001).

The number of men in the sample population exceeded women at every level of education. Of those educated to the primary level, 74.3 per cent were male compared to 25.7 per cent female. The difference was less marked at the secondary level where 57.1 per cent were male and 42 per cent female. This was in contrast to the national figures where 74 per cent of females had secondary education at least, compared to 71.1 per cent of males (UNDP 2013). At tertiary level, 100 per cent of respondents in the sample were male. The low representation of women at higher levels of education was, in part, as a result of the prevalence of teenage pregnancy in the community, leading to girls dropping out of school.

Women generally had less access to credit and, according to the statistics, were less likely to tap into credit facilities, explaining why only 14 per cent had received credit compared to 20 per cent of male respondents. Of those sampled, 100 per cent of the women received and relied on remittances from family members who had migrated, compared to 48 per cent of the men. Equal percentages of men and women described their households as 'poor', but more men than women described their households as 'doing well', with 12 per cent men compared to 4.5 per cent women. Forty-eight per cent of the women produced for subsistence purposes only, while the other 52 per cent produced for both home consumption and the domestic market – with the majority selling their produce at the parish market in the capital town, Falmouth. Men were more likely than women to produce primarily for sale (58% of men produced for sale) which was an indication that women might have been more concerned about producing food for home consumption on backyard gardens or smaller plots. Studies have shown that even as men focused on cash-cropping, women maintained responsibility for household food production (FAO 2014).

Perceptions and observations of climate change

Rural people's perceptions of environmental hazards, including those related to extreme climatic events, are important because they represent the first step towards planning a rational coping strategy to reduce such vulnerability (Roy *et al.* 2002). Studies have indicated that although farmers might not understand the science behind climate change, their continual observation of, and interaction with, the surrounding environment, heightens their awareness of even minor deviations from what is perceived to be normal weather and climate conditions (Gamble *et al.* 2010).

Most respondents were of the impression that the conditions observed in the community had remained largely unchanged until the last 10 years. According to respondents, local temperatures and the pattern of rainfall had altered. It was evident from the survey, too, that most respondents held the view that they had experienced an unprecedented number of hurricanes over the past decade. Climate change perceptions are an important indicator and determinant of attitudes to climate change and willingness to adapt. Awareness of climate change amongst women was relatively low, with only 52 per cent of respondents admitting any awareness of such change. However, amongst those women that had observed changes in temperature and rainfall, the large majority (85.7%) expressed fears that climate-change impacts would lead to decreased yields and other negative impacts on agricultural production. Warming trends have already had considerable effects in Jamaica, most significantly in terms of the increased occurrence of drought and the frequency and magnitude of extreme climate events (FAO 2013).

Women's attitudes towards climate change

Women's attitudes are shaped by their perceptions of, and experiences associated with, the impact of climate change. Damage by hurricanes had caused 92 per cent of women in the sample to lose 1–3 crops in the previous 10 years. This had heightened awareness amongst women about climate-change impacts. Their concerns ranged from how it would affect agricultural activities, to how it would affect their children and households as a result of economic repercussions.

Women expressed greater concern than men about how climate change would affect food production. Focus group discussions revealed that women wished to learn more about climate change and to be more integrally involved in decision-making at the local level. In response to questions about the actions being taken by men to diversify and innovate their agricultural practices due to changing conditions, one female informant referred to male farmers in the community as 'dead' (totally inactive).

Responses and adaptation mechanisms

In response to the changes in rainfall patterns and, in particular, increased drought, women were making more strident efforts than men to secure water for irrigation through purchasing or harvesting water. While 99 per cent of male respondents admitted to relying predominantly on rainwater, only 89 per cent of women said the same. More women were using home-made technologies to harvest water, such as building gutters on the roofs of their houses to channel water to large drums or barrels. Other women explained that they sometimes hired truckers to transport water to their farms from a main stand pipe or a pond, river or other catchment area. The cost of transporting water placed an additional financial burden on the women, but respondents argued that they were sometimes left with no alternative, stating that they refused to 'watch their crops die'.

The large majority of respondents described the soils as generally 'good'; but, with the change in weather conditions, farmers reported a higher incidence of pests and decreased fertility in some soils. The findings showed that women were less likely to use chemical fertilizers than their male counterparts: 45 per cent of men used the additive compared to 32 per cent of women. One female interviewee explained that she refused to use a chemical fertilizer as it was bad for human beings and so she opted not to use it due to health concerns. Others argued that the community had a reputation for producing organically grown yam, unlike the intensively cultivated yams of southern Trelawny. Amongst those who used chemical fertilizers, some explained that they used the commodity only sparingly to ensure the crop would 'ketch' (germinate). The high cost of the commodity was a further deterrent in the more extensive use of fertilizers amongst some farmers. Though fewer women than men utilized chemical fertilizers, 52 per cent indicated that the high cost of the product had affected their overall production costs, whereas only 35 per cent of men indicated this. To address the cost factor, some farmers described how they used ash from the burning of wood as a natural fertilizer. Similarly, other women used home-made compost from kitchen refuse to add nutrient value to the soil. The prevalence of chicken-rearing amongst female farmers had provided another source of fertilizer in the form of chicken dung. The sale of chicken dung provided a further income stream for female chicken farmers who sold the natural fertilizer to other farmers in the community. More importantly, their commitment to the venture of chicken-rearing provided a source of protein for the home as well.

Ash was also used to deal with the upsurge in pests that some farmers described. The 'seven star plague', which farmers explained as a time of year when bugs and pests infested their crops, had sparked increased concern. Farmers reported that they applied ash to the crops as a means of killing and deterring the insects. Slugs and snails were particularly susceptible as the ash hindered their movement. Farmers reported that the use of ash in treating insect infestation had been highly successful and cost-effective.

The challenge of tilling soil under drying conditions, and the need for transporting water, led to increased reliance on hired labour. Women made up the majority of those who had been hiring labour to assist with various tasks: 81 per cent of women compared to 44 per cent of men had done so. The cost of hired labour placed further economic burdens on farmers, particularly women. One female farmer explained how an ankle fracture sustained while she 'forked' or tilled the land, using a hand-held fork, had forced her to hire male labourers to help her prepare the land for yam cultivation. In other cases, the labourers had been hired for other aspects of land preparation, such as the application of weedicides, sowing and harvesting.

The reduction in rainfall and resulting lack of water and other changes in the seasons had led some farmers to vary their crops and cropping systems. Both men and women, but especially the women, had shifted to growing cash crops such as lettuce, cabbage and carrot. While these crops demanded more water, the ease of watering by hand and the shorter growing time made them more favoured by women farmers. Shorter growing periods limited the risk of spanning dry seasons, and in order to facilitate the tending of crops and allow for manual irrigation, some farmers had moved their farming activities to plots closer to home.

There were distinct differences in the types of hazards to which men and women felt they were vulnerable. Of the women sampled, 40 per cent indicated that they were most adversely affected by droughts compared to 17 per cent of male respondents. In terms of hurricanes, 48 per cent of women indicated that this was the hazard with the most severe impact, whereas 39 per cent of men said the same. Most (92%) of the female respondents indicated that they had lost crops due to hurricane damage, compared to 85 per cent of males.

Negative impacts of the changing climate and, in particular, agricultural losses due to extreme weather events, meant that as a means of adapting to the changing conditions, farmers diversified their livelihoods by engaging in other occupations in combination with, or as an alternative to, farming. Women were less likely than men to have an additional skill which they could utilize for economic purposes: 44 per cent of the females had an additional skill compared to 64 per cent of males. Men also had more marketable skills such as carpentry and masonry compared to females' dressmaking, which was stated to be generally less profitable. Other occupations that more women were venturing into were informal shop-keeping and cooking food for sale.

Women indicated that they were less adept at predicting the extent of wetness and dryness and, as a consequence, they were not inclined to develop adaptive mechanisms such as to change farming methods or farming schedules. Further, there were fewer women (63%) who said that they were willing to invest more in their farming activities as against more than three-quarters (77%) of male farmers who said they were willing to invest money in measures to improve operations and reduce vulnerability to hazards.

In focus group discussions, women disclosed that a few of them had pooled resources and efforts to retool themselves by starting a craft group. The group had been initially set up in response to the opening of the cruise ship marina in the parish capital, Falmouth. The lead member of the group explained that with her skills in weaving and craft making she had decided, along with another woman who owned a sewing machine, that they would form a group to include other women who showed an interest. She explained that up to that time, the income had not been significant, nevertheless it had allowed them to diversify their revenue streams and served as a source of encouragement to the group members and other women in the community. A few of them, along with other women, also became involved in a green-house farming project in association with a local university to tap into new opportunities. Other women-led initiatives included a horticulture project and pottery making.

Summary of the gender perspective of farmer responses to climate change

It was apparent from the data that there were similarities in the way men and women perceived climate change and in their general attitudes towards the issue. Despite having lower levels of awareness of climate change than their male counterparts, women displayed higher levels of concern about how it would impact their agricultural production and, in turn, food security and income-generation capacity. While the perceptions of men and women did not differ significantly, they varied with respect to observations of temperature change and hurricane frequency, with women more aware of the former.

Women are said to cope with disasters in different ways than men (Dankelman 2002). Although women were more concerned about climate change, they seemed more inclined to adopt 'soft' measures in response to the perceived threats. In part, this explained the higher losses incurred during hurricanes. Men reported responding more actively by digging channels, pruning trees and securing livestock and tools. Also evident in the interviews was that women were less likely than men to be adversely impacted by droughts, an indication that they made greater efforts to secure water from sources other than direct rainfall. The fact that women made greater efforts to secure water may be connected to their greater use of the resource in other household chores such as cooking, washing clothes and for sanitation purposes.

The livelihoods and earning power of both men and women have been eroded by the effects of climate change. Women in the study area were found to be more impacted by the weakening of their economic base. The role of caring for the household remained largely that of the women in the study. They provided care for children, grandchildren and in some cases spouses and parents. The challenge of caring for the household in the community was made harder by the impacts of climate change on agriculture-based income-earning activities. Despite this, women demonstrated less willingness to switch from agriculture than did men. Whereas 17 per cent of men said they would leave agriculture, only 9 per cent of women were likely to do so. Women's desire to remain in agriculture suggested that they were less concerned about the profitability of the farm and more interested in ensuring that there was a supply of food for the home.

The women in the sample were less likely to have additional, highly marketable skills and formal training in these areas. Short-term coping with climate impacts was one thing, but longer-term strategic responses would require resources and support which were so far conspicuously absent. Because of their gender-specific vulnerability, there were strong arguments for directing aid-funded adaptation projects to poor women. But the gender inequalities that made women more vulnerable in general needed to be tackled at the root causes. They included women's relative lack of assets such as financial capital, but also their lower educational levels compared with men, and their exclusion from decision-making at all levels over how assets such as land should be used (Terry 2009).

The attitudes of men and women were shaped by their awareness of climate change, in particular, through their experiences with meteorologically induced disasters. The role of women as caretakers of the total well-being of children and other members of the household made them anxious about how the changes would affect all facets of their lives, including agricultural productivity and sustained food security in the long term.

Gender, as demonstrated in the study, was not the sole determinant of farmers' perceptions and adaptive responses to the effects of climate change. Gender interacted with other power dynamics in the work cultures of the farm communities, environmental organizations and government agencies, in relation to disaster preparedness, evacuation, migration and a host of other critical decisions that families and communities must make in the face of environmental crisis (Enarson 2013). National and regional climate-change strategies will have a much greater potential to ensure efficiency, effectiveness and quality of implementation if they are developed to include a gender component, paying particular attention to the role and contributions of women (Aguilar 2013). Training for both men and women in gender awareness and technical issues, as well as community environmental education, could help overcome the barriers to women's participation (Perkins 2014).

Conclusion

Climate change posed a significant threat to food production and its food security outcomes in the study area of Trelawny, Jamaica through reduced rainfall, increased temperatures and the impact of hurricanes. Women and men had divergent, but also shared, views in their response to climate change, shaped by their common experiences as farmers. The women in the study demonstrated their commitment to meeting the dietary requirements of their households. The impacts of changing climatic conditions were amplified by the variability of the economic situation. Women appeared to be more adversely affected by the worsening economic times, even as men also grappled to meet those challenges. Women appeared to have responded with greater determination, driven by the need to meet the needs of the household. It is important that women be regarded as more than mere victims of the impacts of climate change. Their efforts to respond to the challenges and harness opportunities, as well as their innovative spirit and pioneering drive as demonstrated by the farmers in the study, should be encouraged and channelled into national efforts to address the threats to food security, especially of smallholder farm communities in the face of climate change.

Note

1 The Cockpit Country is an area of karst limestone topography characterized by steep hills and sink holes. The vegetation is wet limestone forest.

References

Agostino, A. and R. Lizarde (2012) 'Gender and Climate Justice', *Society for International Development*, 55, (1): 90–95.

Aguilar, L. (2013) 'A Path to Implementation: Gender-Responsive Climate Change Strategies' in M. Alston and K. Whittenbury (eds.) *Research, Action and Policy: Addressing the Gendered Impacts of Climate Change*, p.149, Dordrecht: Springer Science & Business Media.

Alston, M. (2013) 'Introducing Gender and Climate Change', in M. Alston and K. Whittenbury, (eds.) *Research, Action and Policy: Addressing the Gendered Impacts of Climate Change 3*, Dordrecht: Springer Science & Business Media.

Alston, M. (2014) 'Gender Mainstreaming and Climate Change', *Women's Studies International Forum*, 47, 287–294.

Bee, B., Biermann, M. and Tschakert, P. (2013) 'Gender, Development, and Rights-Based Approaches: Lessons for Climate Change Adaptation and Adaptive Social Protection', in M. Alston and K. Whittenbury (eds.) *Research, Action and Policy: Addressing the Gendered Impacts of Climate Change*, Springer: Netherlands, 95–108.

Caribsave (2012) 'The Caribsave Climate Change Risk Atlas (CCRA): Climate Change Risk Profile for Jamaica'. Available at: http://intasave-caribbean.org.www37.cpt4.host-h.net/wp-content/uploads/2016/06/47-CCCRA-Jamaica-Full-Risk-Profile.pdf.

Dankelman, I. (2002) 'Climate Change: Learning from Gender Analysis and Women's Experiences of Organising for Sustainable Development', *Gender and Development*, 10, No. 2: 21–29.

de Vaus, D. (2002) *Surveys in Social Research* (5th edition), New South Wales: Allen & Unwin.

Denton, F. (2009) 'Gender and Climate Change: Giving the "Latecomer" a Head Start', *IDS Bulletin*, 35 (3): 42–49.

Enarson, E. (2013) 'Two Solitudes, Many Bridges, Big Tent: Women's Leadership in Climate and Disaster Risk Reduction', in M. Alston and K. Whittenbury (eds.) *Research, Action and Policy: Addressing the Gendered Impacts of Climate Change*, Dordrecht: Springer Science & Business Media 63.

FAO (2008) Climate Change and Food Security: A Framework Document, Rome. Available at: www.fao.org/forestry/15538-079b31d45081fe9c3dbc6ff34de4807e4.pdf.

FAO (2010) 'Livelihood Assessment Tool-Kit Training of the Rural Agricultural Development Authority'. Available at: www.fao.org/climatechange/32717-03564d9b6d2ed9f961fbf7e1ed703e328.pdf.

FAO (2013) 'Climate Change and Agriculture in Jamaica: Agriculture Support Analysis'. Available at: www.fao.org/3/a-i3417e.pdf.

FAO (2014) *Statistical Yearbook 2014: Latin America and the Caribbean: Food and Agriculture*, Santiago: FAO.

Gaard, G. (2015) 'Ecofeminism and Climate Change', *Women's Studies International Forum*, No. 49: 20–33.

Gamble, D., Campbell, D., Allen, T., Barker, D., Curtis, S., McGregor, D. and Popke, J (2010) 'Climate Change, Drought and Jamaica: Local Knowledge and the Climate Record'. *Annals of the Association of American Geographers*, 100 (4): 880–893.

Goldsmith, R., Feygina, I. and Jost., J. (2013). 'The Gender Gap in Environmental Attitudes: A System Justification Perspective', in M. Alston and K. Whittenbury (eds.) *Research, Action and Policy: Addressing the Gendered Impacts of Climate Change*, Dordrecht: Springer Science & Business Media, 150.

Gooden, L. (2011) 'The Role of Rural Women in Agricultural Development', *Jamaica Observer*.

IPCC (2014) 'Climate Change 2014: Impacts, Adaptation, and Vulnerability. Part A: Global and Sectoral Aspects', Contribution of Working Group II to the *Fifth Assessment Report of the Intergovernmental Panel on Climate Change*, C. B. Field, V. R. Barros, D. J. Dokken, K. J. Mach, M. D. Mastrandrea, T. E. Bilir, M. Chatterjee, K. L. Ebi, Y. O. Estrada, R. C. Genova, B. Girma, E. S. Kissel, A. N. Levy, S. MacCracken, P.R. Mastrandrea, and L. L. White (eds.), New York: Cambridge University Press.

Israel, A. and Sachs, C. (2013) 'A Climate for Feminist Intervention: Feminist Science Studies and Climate Change', in M. Alston and K. Whittenbury (eds.) *Research, Action and Policy: Addressing the Gendered Impacts of Climate Change*, Dordrecht: Springer Science & Business Media, 3.

Leichenko, R. and O'Brien, K. (2008) *Environmental Change and Globalization: Double Exposures*, New York: Oxford University Press.

Living Economies Forum (1992) 'People's Earth Declaration' Rio, 1992. Available at: http://livingeconomiesforum.org/1992/Declaration.

McKinney, L. and Fulkerson G. (2015) 'Gender Equality and Climate Justice: A Cross-National Analysis' *Social Justice Research*, No. 28: 293–317.

Momsen, J. (2002) 'Gender Differences in Environmental Concern and Perception', *Journal of Geography*, 99 (2): 47–56.

Morton, J. F. (2007) 'The Impact of Climate Change on Smallholder and Subsistence Agriculture', *Proceedings of the National Academy of Sciences*, 104 (50). Available at: www.pnas.org.ezp-prod1.hul.harvard.edu/content/104/50/19680.full.pdf.

Parikh, J. (2007) 'Gender and Climate Change Framework for Analysis, Policy and Action'. Available at: www.undp.org/content/dam/india/docs/gnder_cc.pdf.

Perkins, P. (2014) 'Gender Justice and Climate Justice: Building Women's Economic and Political Agency in Times of Climate Change'. *Gender Justice and Climate Justice*, 17–20.

PIOJ (Planning Institute of Jamaica) (2007) 'The Poverty-Environment Nexus: Establishing an Approach for Determining Special Development Areas in Jamaica'. Available at: http://pioj.gov.jm/Portals/0/Sustainable_Development/Poverty-Environmental%20 Vulnerability%20 Relationship.pdf.

PIOJ (2015) *Economic and Social Survey of Jamaica 2014*, Kingston: Planning Institute of Jamaica.

Roy, B., Mruthyunjaya and Selvarajan S. (2002) 'Vulnerability to Climate Induced Natural Disasters with Special Emphasis on Coping Strategies of the Rural Poor in Coastal Orissa, India'. Available at: http://unfccc.int/cop8/se/se_pres/isdr_pap_cop8.pdf.

Smith, L. (2015) 'World Food Day 2015: Female Farmers Hold the Key to Food Security and Ending Poverty', *International Business Times*. Available at: www.ibtimes.co.uk/world-food-day-2015-female-farmers-hold-key-food-security-ending-poverty-1524167.

STATIN (2001) *Population and Housing Census 2001*, Kingston: STATIN (Statistical Institute of Jamaica).

Terry, G. (ed.) (2009) 'No Climate Justice without Gender Justice: an Overview of the Issues', *Gender & Development*, 17 (1), 5–18. http://doi.org/10.1080/13552070802696839.

UNFCCC (United Nations Framework Convention on Climate Change) (2011) *Fact Sheet: Climate Change Science – the Status of Climate Change Science Today*, New York: United Nations Framework Convention on Climate Change.

9 Flirting with food security

Resilience in the face of conflict, climate change and communicable disease in rural Sierra Leone

Jerram Bateman, Tony Binns and Etienne Nel

Introduction

Nobel Laureate Amartya Sen wrote in his seminal book *Poverty and Famines: An Essay on Entitlement and Deprivation* that 'starvation is the characteristic of some people not having enough food to eat. It is not the characteristic of there being not enough food to eat. While the latter can be a cause of the former, it is but one of many possible causes' (Sen 1983:1). These sentiments touch on the complexity of food security, indicating that access to food, and not simply the availability of food, is the key barrier to obtaining food security. Others have since argued that qualitative dimensions to food security, such as nutritional value and cultural preference, also need to be considered when measuring the extent to which an individual or household is 'food secure' (Maxwell 2001). In order to encapsulate these complexities, the FAO's World Food Summit in 2009 built on its earlier manifestations to define food security as existing 'when all people, at all times, have physical, social and economic access to sufficient, safe and nutritious food to meet their dietary needs and food preferences for an active and healthy life' (FAO, 2009: 1).

The term 'vulnerability' is indubitably linked to this conceptualization of food security. Anderson (1995: 41) asserts that, 'to be vulnerable is to exist with a likelihood that some kind of crisis may occur that will damage one's health, life, or the property and resources upon which health and life depend'. Given that food is one of the key resources upon which health and life depend, crises threatening its availability, accessibility or utilization, perhaps elicit the most critical manifestation of vulnerability, while food insecurity perpetuates and exacerbates vulnerability, in and of itself. Thus, as Lovendal and Knowles (2006) argue, reducing vulnerability is of critical importance when addressing the issue of food security.

Sierra Leone, a small West African nation considered by the United Nations to be among the least developed in the world, has seemingly been stuck in a perpetual cycle of vulnerability over the past 40 years. Political instability, economic devastation and a brutal civil war that lasted from 1991 until 2002 characterized the country during the last quarter of the twentieth century (Binns and Maconachie 2005), while the post-conflict era has been shadowed by threats associated with climate change, incidences of flooding and drought, and outbreaks of disease, such as the recent Ebola epidemic. While the entire population has suffered to some degree over this period, it is the rural poor who have been the most vulnerable (Richards 1996). Amid such crises, however, rural communities in Sierra Leone have shown a remarkable resilience, adapting livelihood strategies in order to mitigate the impact of each challenge as it has occurred, which has generally enabled a reasonably rapid recovery to pre-crises levels of food security. However, field research undertaken in two rural communities, 40 years apart, indicates that food security is also a significant issue in times of relative stability, and that there has been no discernible improvement, and indeed some evidence of regression, in the food security of rural households over that time.

This chapter will explore the links between vulnerability, resilience and food security. After a brief description of the field sites and methodology used, it will draw on broader literature to discuss the major causes of vulnerability in Sierra Leone over the past 40 years. It will then draw on field research undertaken in Panguma and Kayima, two small towns in the Eastern Province of Sierra Leone, to highlight how rural households have adapted their livelihood strategies in light of such vulnerability. Finally, it will unpack the aforementioned FAO (2009) definition of food security, contextualizing each part within Panguma and Kayima over a forty-year period, to argue that food insecurity is as much systemic, and determined by vulnerability to small-scale and localized shocks, as it is a consequence of vulnerability to large-scale shocks and external trends.

Methodology

Panguma and Kayima are two small towns situated in the Eastern Province of Sierra Leone (see Figure 9.1). Panguma, with a population of approximately 8,000 people, is some two hours' travel north of Kenema, the capital of the Eastern Province. Kayima is significantly smaller, with a population of approximately 2,000 people, and is more remote, located some three hours' travel along poor roads north of Koidu, the second largest city in the Eastern Province. This chapter draws on two distinct, yet inter-related, periods of field research undertaken in Panguma and Kayima in 1974 and 2014. The former, undertaken by Binns, explored food-production systems in the rural economy of Sierra Leone, while the latter, undertaken by Bateman, sought to assess continuity and change within those food-production systems in the time since the original study. Both studies were ethnographic in nature, with the principal researcher on each occasion living within the communities and keeping detailed field diaries over extended periods of time. An in-depth, predominantly qualitative, survey of 50 agricultural households was the primary form of data collection used in both periods of field research, and while the latter survey was altered to reflect the different temporal context in which it was administered, care was taken to ensure that the information collected remained of a comparable nature. In addition to the surveys, semi-structured interviews were conducted with a wide cross-section of informants across both communities, and other methods such as focus group discussions, guided field walks, and participant observation were also used. For the purpose of

Figure 9.1 Sierra Leone indicating the sites of field research.

this chapter, respondents to all primary methods of data collection used have been labelled as 'respondents', and assigned a number based on the chronology of the field research.

Vulnerability and food security in Sierra Leone

On a national scale, Sierra Leone has seemingly been stuck in a cycle of vulnerability since it gained independence from Britain in 1961. Following 30 years of often corrupt and dysfunctional governance, the country was torn apart by a brutal civil war from 1991 until 2002 (Richards 2003). The prolonged conflict devastated much of the country and brought vast suffering to its people. Approximately

50,000 were killed, while countless others were subjected to amputation, rape and assault, and over half the population was displaced (Bellows and Miguel 2009). In the process, economic and subsistence activities were severely disrupted, much of the country's infrastructure was destroyed or badly damaged, and poverty became widespread and deeply ingrained (Binns and Maconachie 2005).

Following the culmination of this conflict, Sierra Leone has experienced continuous peace, thanks largely to a successful disarmament, demobilization and reintegration process (Humphreys and Weinstein 2009). In the post-war period, the country has held three democratic presidential and parliamentary elections, indicating relative political stability, and has made progress in economic and infrastructural reconstruction from the low base created by the war (UNDP 2015). But livelihoods, particularly those in rural areas, have remained vulnerable to numerous other stresses and shocks. Variable climatic conditions and climate events, such as drought and flooding, have created uncertainty for the subsistence agriculture practised by some 70 per cent of Sierra Leoneans (Bangura *et al.* 2012). Boko *et al.* (2009), for example, indicate that precipitation trends have significantly decreased across Africa since the 1960s. Chappell and Agnew (2004) situate this point within West Africa, arguing that annual rainfall regimes have changed such that the established climatic cycle upon which agricultural systems are based are slowly being eroded. Endemic diseases, such as malaria and Lassa fever, remain a constant threat to livelihood continuity. The outbreak of Ebola in 2014/15, which consisted of 14,122 declared cases and 3,955 deaths in Sierra Leone (WHO 2015), brought such vulnerability back into sharp focus. While the full extent of the Ebola outbreak on rural livelihoods is yet to be fully assessed, initial indications suggest that the quarantines and other restrictions imposed to prevent the spread of the disease had a dramatic effect on economic activity, while the agricultural sector has suffered significant decline in production and disruptions in the planting cycle that may take many years to recover from (UNDP 2015).

While vulnerability to large-scale stresses and shocks, such as those discussed above, has undoubtedly had a dramatic impact on livelihoods in Sierra Leone, vulnerability to stresses and shocks that are smaller in scale, and more localized in impact, can have equally damaging implications. A World Food Programme (WFP 2011) survey on household food security found that some 85 per cent of rural households in Sierra Leone had recently experienced a 'shock' of some sort that had affected their household production and consumption. Death and illness among household members, which can reduce family labour inputs and can also interrupt daily farming activities, were most frequently mentioned, while the loss of crops due to pests, either when growing in the fields, or when being stored, was also found to have had a significant impact on food availability among Sierra Leone's rural households (WFP 2011). Over 77 per cent of the households surveyed reported that coping with such shocks could affect both their food production and ability to purchase food (WFP 2011). However, for many households, the impact of such shocks reflects the absence of adequate safety nets to cushion households from the effects of such events.

Given such vulnerability, it is unsurprising that food insecurity is such a significant issue in Sierra Leone. Forty-five per cent of Sierra Leone's population is regarded as 'food insecure', and around 6.5 per cent, some 422,500 people, are categorized as 'severely food insecure' (WFP 2011). The widespread prevalence of food insecurity is reflected in the fact that 34 per cent of children aged 6 to 59 months are stunted and 9.5 per cent are 'severely stunted' (WFP 2011). When compared internationally, Sierra Leone has the highest prevalence of food insecurity among 15 West African countries, and is ranked 36th out of 43 African countries (Spencer 2012). The following section will consider some of the ways in which rural households in the study sites have adapted their livelihood strategies in order to strengthen resilience and reduce food insecurity.

Resilience and adaptation in Panguma and Kayima

Walker *et al.* (2006: 2) defined 'resilience' as 'the capacity of a system to experience shocks while retaining essentially the same function, structure, feedbacks', and therefore identified adaptability as 'the capacity of the actors in a system to manage resilience'. While these concepts of resilience and adaptability both emerged from, and are well established within, ecological literature, they have increasingly been applied to interactions between ecological and social systems across various scales (Berkes *et al.* 1998). Scoones (2009) argued that the extension of resilience concepts to 'social-economic-cultural-political systems' is principally concerned with 'sustaining "life support systems", and the capacity of natural systems to provide for livelihoods into the future, given likely stresses and shocks' (*ibid.*: 190). Thus, the integration of resilience and adaptation into understanding livelihoods can contribute a temporal scale to analysis, enabling an informed understanding of the adaptation of livelihood strategies to circumstances that move households towards achieving more resilient livelihood outcomes over time (Sallu *et al.* 2010). In the cases of Panguma and Kayima, the adaptation of livelihood strategies to vulnerability over time can be broadly categorized in two distinct ways, first, agricultural adaptation and diversification, and secondly, livelihood diversification, both of which will now be considered.

Agricultural adaptation and diversification

Upland rice farming has traditionally been the predominant livelihood strategy for rural households in Sierra Leone. The structure of the farming year in Sierra Leone is closely related to rainfall patterns, with land cleared during the dry season (January–March), crops cultivated during the rainy season (April–October), and harvested towards the end of the rainy season (September–November). While based on generations of indigenous knowledge and an intimate understanding of the environment, this farming system is constantly being adapted, and is characterized by a variety of strategies designed to reduce vulnerability to the stresses and shocks described in the previous section. For example, inter-cropping rice with a wide variety of other crops such as yams, sweet potatoes, groundnuts, maize, tomatoes, okra and beans, and planting other vegetables, particularly cassava, on the edge of the farm, spreads the risk of failure, meaning that if a particular crop fails, there will be others to fall back on. After one year's cultivation, farms were traditionally left fallow for 5–12 years, depending on local pressure on land resources, but more and more farmers are using the previous year's farm to cultivate secondary crops such as groundnuts and cassava. There has also been a recent trend among agricultural households to farm geographically distinct plots to insure against loss caused by pests, fire, flooding or theft, and there has been a significant shift since the 1970s from storing harvested crops in barns on the farm, to storing them in the house, for the same reasons.

Beyond the upland rice farm, supplementary forms of agriculture, such as permanent cash crops and swamp farming are practised, which are also generally motivated by a desire to spread risk over a range of agricultural activities in order to decrease vulnerability to stresses and shocks. Swamp farming, in particular, has significantly increased in popularity, especially in Kayima, where Binns (1980) suggested there was no evidence of such in the 1970s. Swamp rice farms require fewer labour inputs to prepare, are more conducive to high-yield rice varieties, are less reliant on climatic patterns, and do not require a fallow period before re-planting. Further, farmers have developed methods of growing additional crops that were traditionally the preserve of the upland farm, in or around the swamp. This shift is largely in response to government concerns about the sustainability of traditional farming practices amid evidence of climate change, and has been facilitated by the dissemination of resources and information by agricultural extension officers in each community. Cash crops, while certainly not a new phenomenon in either Panguma or Kayima, have also been constantly adapted, with households making decisions to intensify or diversify their cash crop portfolio based on market forces.

The war from 1991–2002, as mentioned above, caused the displacement of more than half the population, but such displacement was experienced in different ways in Panguma and Kayima, and thus, livelihood strategies were also adapted in different ways. The majority of respondents to the survey in Panguma fled to the bush for long periods during the war, generally staying on or near their farms while, wherever possible, sending the more vulnerable household members (young children and the elderly) to stay with family in the relative safety of the cities. This enabled them to continue farming, albeit with significantly reduced capacity, as certain practices such as burning, and even cooking, could place them in danger of detection by combatants from both sides in search of resources. Consequently, many focused their attention on swamp farming during this time. In contrast, respondents from Kayima generally went further afield and thus suffered complete dislocation from their farms, forcing them to find alternative means of generating their livelihood. Some were able to find labouring work elsewhere, but many ended up in aid camps in Masingbi, Freetown and even across the Guinea border in Conakry, or worse, were forced to beg for food and lodging as they moved between towns and villages.

In the immediate aftermath of the war, cash crops took on added significance in both Panguma and Kayima, as they were generally perennial crops, and therefore were able to be harvested straight away to some extent, whereas subsistence crops such as rice and cassava generally do not regenerate, and therefore were not immediately available for harvest upon resettlement, and required greater capital input to restart. Although cash crop yields were impacted significantly by the lack of maintenance during the war years, households were able to use the small income derived from their sale to slowly rebuild their capital base, and re-establish their livelihood portfolios, with a particular emphasis on their upland rice farms. Since then, the growing of cash crops has steadily increased in both communities, as NGOs such as the World Food Programme (WFP) have promoted them as a source of income from which food can be purchased at times of shortage (WFP 2008 2011). In addition, as mentioned earlier, more and more farmers are cultivating swamp land as concerns around climate change grow in the post-conflict era (Bangura *et al.* 2013), while households employ various strategies, such as eating less-preferred food, borrowing food and money, and reducing the size and frequency of meals to cope with the smaller-scale shocks outlined in the previous section (WFP 2011).

Livelihood diversification

The adaptations to livelihood strategies discussed thus far have been agricultural in nature, either involving the adaptation of traditional farming practices, or diversification into different forms of agriculture. But, as Owusu (2009) argued, there has been a shift in focus from agricultural diversification to livelihood diversification within contemporary rural development research and policy. This shift is largely due to the growing recognition that agriculture, in itself, is rarely an adequate means of survival in rural areas of developing countries, a point explicated by Amekawa (2011) who argued that income diversification and asset disposal, rather than agricultural diversification, are the predominant forms of coping strategy adopted by rural households within vulnerability contexts. In light of these arguments, this section will explore livelihood diversification, defined as 'the process by which households construct a diverse portfolio of activities and social support capabilities for survival and in order to improve their standard of living' (Ellis 1998: 4), in the context of Panguma and Kayima.

Binns (1980) discussed at length the symbiosis between agriculture and diamond mining in Panguma and Kayima in the 1970s, highlighting that farmers not only benefited from the ability to sell surplus produce at markets in mining areas, but also actively engaged in mining as a form of livelihood diversification. Beyond the farming–mining nexus, Binns (1980) highlighted blacksmithing, carpentry and hunting as other significant forms of livelihood diversification for agricultural households, while handicrafts, such as the weaving of 'country cloth', as well as basket making, mat weaving, and the production of fishing nets, were also common economic activities in both Panguma and Kayima. The 2014 field research found that the relationship between agriculture and mining, while still in existence, had diminished significantly, with far fewer farmers engaging in mining as a form of livelihood diversification, and fewer selling produce in mining areas. Blacksmithing and carpentry remained vital services in both Panguma and Kayima, but the skills and materials required meant that both were only practised by a handful of people across both communities. In terms of other non-farming activities, hunting, while more widely practised than blacksmithing and carpentry, had notably declined in the post-conflict period, as first the disarmament process, and then the regulation of gun-ownership laws, had significantly limited access to guns.

In contrast, the rapid growth of new technologies in the past decade had seen a dramatic shift in non-agricultural livelihood diversification in Panguma and Kayima. In particular, mobile phone ownership had exploded with the construction of mobile phone masts in recent years which, in turn, had created numerous opportunities for livelihood diversification, including phone sales and repairs, battery charging centres and mobile credit agents. The growth in mobile phone ownership also helped facilitate the electronic transfer of money through international agencies such as Western Union and MoneyGram, as well as domestic mobile-to-mobile transactions through Airtel Money. Consequently, the scale of remittances received in each community had significantly increased, which can be considered a form of livelihood diversification in itself, since remittances contributed to the livelihood portfolios of the households receiving them. The other significant change in livelihood diversification in recent years had been the growth in the number of 'Okada' (motorcycle taxis) since the war. Reduced mobility caused by the deterioration and destruction of the country's road networks, the need to address youth unemployment and greater accessibility to less capital intensive vehicles, had combined to create a new industry of commercial transportation. While this growth is commonly framed as a form of 'self-initiated re-integration' of ex-combatants post-conflict (Peters 2007), there was evidence of it also being used as a form of livelihood diversification among entrepreneurial agricultural households in both Panguma and Kayima.

Food security in Panguma and Kayima

To reiterate the definition used in the introduction to this chapter, food security exists 'when all people, at all times, have physical, social and economic access to sufficient, safe and nutritious food to meet their dietary needs and food preferences for an active and healthy life' (FAO 2009: 1). In unpacking this definition, and contextualizing each part within Panguma and Kayima, this section will illustrate that there had been little improvement in overall food security in either community since 1974. Further, it will highlight that, while food insecurity and vulnerability are clearly interwoven, their incidence is also ingrained within the underlying socio-cultural norms and values of the communities.

Intra-household food allocation

Access to food in both Panguma and Kayima varied significantly between households, but the majority of households surveyed in each village expressed experiencing some form of food stress. The first element of the above definition uses the term 'all people' as a condition of achieving food security, thus in a holistic sense, neither Panguma nor Kayima can be considered food secure from the outset. In a more atomistic sense, an exploration of food security within households uncovered further inequalities in access to, and the availability of, food. Pinstrup-Andersen (2009) argued that the allocation of food within each household is not necessarily based on the needs of each individual member. This assertion was reinforced in both Panguma and Kayima, where an intra-household hierarchy of food distribution, in which the needs of men were privileged over those of women and children, was clearly evident during the 2014 fieldwork. These observations were corroborated by numerous participants in this research. A youth leader in Panguma, for example, stated that:

> There is a lot of hard work on the farm and the women do a lot of it. We say that women work harder than men here. They do all the weeding and harvesting; they carry the crops from the farm to the town; they clean [pound] the rice; they prepare and cook the food; but still, they only eat once the men have eaten.
>
> (Respondent, Panguma, 23 February 2014)

Similarly, a former head teacher in Panguma, in discussing a group of school boys seemingly lazing on a veranda, stated:

> For those boys, they only eat once a day, after the rest of their family has eaten, sometimes as late as nine or ten at night. It is no wonder they can't concentrate on their school work when they are always hungry.
>
> (Respondent, Panguma, 20 February 2014)

While it is difficult to compare these observations with the situation in the 1970s, given Binns' (1980) focus on the production of food, rather than its consumption, similar inequalities in the allocation of food can be gleaned from his field diary, in which he described the centrality of women and children to the production, transport and preparation of food in Panguma and Kayima, but their marginalization when it comes to consumption. It appears, therefore, that little has changed in the way food is allocated. Rather, it indicated that the hierarchy of food distribution evident in the latter study is based on traditional socio-cultural notions of gender and age, and was neither reflective of the individual needs of each household member, nor their contribution to household productivity. This, in turn, is consistent with Barrett's (2010) notion that uneven inter and intra-household food distribution is a manifestation of the socio-cultural limits and prevailing values within a community.

Seasonal food insecurity

The FAO (2009) definition emphasized access to food 'at all times' as the second condition of being food secure, distinguishing seasonal food insecurity from permanent or long-term food insecurity (Pinstrup-Andersen 2009). The former is evident in numerous contexts in Sierra Leone, with food shortages occurring throughout the year, for a variety of different reasons. Seasonal food insecurity, however, was most prevalent during July and August, a time commonly referred to as 'the hungry season'. Although not directly asked, 37 of the 50 households surveyed in Panguma, and 39 of the 50 surveyed in Kayima, referred to 'the hungry season' at some point during their survey. This is consistent with the WFP's (2011) national food security survey, which found that food insecurity increased sharply between June and August, with more than 90 per cent of rural households experiencing seasonal hunger during this time. Binns (1980) described a similar pattern during the 1970s, which illustrates that 'the hungry season' is not a new phenomenon, while Richards (1986) highlighted that 'the hungry season' is not exclusive to Panguma and Kayima, nor indeed the Eastern Province, devoting a whole chapter to it in his book *Coping with Hunger,* which explored agricultural practices in Mogbuama, a medium-sized village in central Sierra Leone, in the early 1980s. Thus, it is clear that seasonal food insecurity is both endemic and enduring in Sierra Leone, existing across time and place.

Food accessibility

The third element of the FAO (2009) definition referred to access to food, indicating that concern is not simply with the availability of food in a particular place, but the range of food which is accessible to a person or household, 'given their income, prevailing prices, and formal or informal safety net arrangements through which they can access food' (Barrett 2010: 825). The range of food available seems to have increased since 1974, with a wider array of imported goods now available in both Panguma and Kayima markets. But a comparison of the 1974 and 2014 surveys indicates that expenditure on food had remained static relative to other items of household expenditure across both communities, while in real terms, there had been a marginal increase in the number of households spending a proportion of their income on food in Panguma (from 25 in 1974 to 30 in 2014), and a marginal decrease in Kayima (from 19 in 1974 to 18 in 2014). Further, there was some evidence of a decline in the 'informal safety net arrangements' for food discussed by Barrett (2010), a point described by an elderly resident in Kayima, who stated:

> In the olden days people were farming just for livelihood, not for commercial purposes. They were farming to ensure enough food for their family, and would help others in the community [with food] if they had any to spare. But now people are trying to farm for commercial gain, they see food as profit, and helping others means less profit.
>
> (Respondent 46, Kayima, 11 April 2014)

The point was further exemplified by numerous survey respondents, such as Respondent A from Kayima, who stated:

Last year somebody was burning some land, but the fire went out of control and destroyed most of my cash crops. Only small small [a small amount of] coffee was okay…when my rice ran out, I had no money to buy extra because I had no crops to sell, and there is no other way [to access food].

(Respondent, Kayima, 22 April 2014)

While this comment was made in the context of a discussion on the impact of micro-scale shocks on livelihoods, it also hints at a lack of safety nets, either informal or formal, from which people were able to access food. Thus, for most agricultural households, food security largely remained governed by what they were able to produce, rather than their income and/or formal or informal safety nets.

Food preferences

Finally, the FAO (2009) definition of food security introduces a qualitative dimension, in stating that food should not only be sufficient in quantity, but needs to be nutritious and meet the dietary needs and food preferences for an active and healthy life. Nutritional and dietary quality in Panguma and Kayima is difficult to assess, as data relating to these indicators was not specifically sought. Further, Pinstrup-Andersen (2009: 6) argued that good nutrition 'depends on a set of non-food factors such as sanitary conditions, water quality, infectious diseases and access to primary health care', and thus nutritional quality is difficult to measure solely on the basis that certain foods are consumed over others. That being said, the prevalent diet in both Panguma and Kayima remained largely undistinguishable from Binns' (1980: 223) description of it in the 1970s:

Rice is eaten on most days in Kono and Mende households, and is normally boiled and eaten with a soup or stew, which has a palm oil base and includes variable amounts of meat, fish and vegetables such as cassava and sweet potato leaf, chilli peppers, tomatoes and okra.

The only ostensible difference with the situation in 2014 being that meat was rarely available in either village, save for auspicious occasions. Of the 15 weeks that Bateman spent between Panguma and Kayima in 2014, he was only served red meat on four occasions, and chicken on three, with all but one instance correlating with a major community event. Therefore, if anything, the variety of diet has decreased slightly, which in turn decreases its overall nutritional quality.

The use of the term 'food preferences' implies that equal access to food does not necessarily ensure food security, as different food preferences may limit actual food choices for some. A common idiom in Sierra Leone states that a Sierra Leonean has not eaten for the day until they have eaten rice, which indicates a widespread preference for rice over other crops. Further, a strong preference for local varieties of upland rice, over imported or swamp-grown rice was uncovered in both the historical and present contexts. This means that households could be considered food insecure if they have no local rice, even though they may have access to imported rice. Pinstrup-Anderson (2009) argued, however, that the word 'preferences' should be interpreted to mean foods that are consistent with social, cultural, religious and ethical values, rather than a broader interpretation to mean a preference for caviar over sorghum.

Conclusion

Bringing the different elements of the FAO (2009) definition back together, it could be argued that sufficient, safe and nutritious food that meets dietary needs and food preferences for an active and healthy life is not accessible to all people, at all times, in either Panguma or Kayima. Moreover, the extent to which this situation has improved over the forty-year period of this research appears negligible at best, with some indications that it may have even regressed. While long-term vulnerability has undoubtedly been detrimental to achieving food security, this chapter has shown how rural households have been resilient in adapting their livelihood strategies in order to cope with stresses and shocks, thus highlighting that the causes of food insecurity are as much systemic as they are a consequence of vulnerability. At the crux of this issue is not so much an inability to produce enough food, but rather the social, cultural and economic barriers in place that prevent the food that is produced from being distributed evenly to all people, and at all times. It is therefore imperative that these barriers are broken down to ensure more equitable access to the food that is being produced.

Community education programmes could be the way forward to achieve greater awareness of the existence and significance of intra-household food insecurity, with particular attention given to the nutritional requirements of women and children. The WFP survey estimated that only 77 per cent of girls and 74 percent of boys in rural areas of Sierra Leone attend primary school, and also found that 'households whose head has a low level of education are more prone to food insecurity' (WFP 2011: 45). If these inequalities are to be addressed, it is vital that universal primary attendance is targeted, and that nutritional education is incorporated into the school curricula. School feeding programmes have been implemented in some schools with some success, but as mentioned above, not all children attend school, and those that do are generally less vulnerable to food insecurity. Furthermore, serious attention should be given to raising the nutritional status of pre-school-age children, in light of Sierra Leone's appallingly high under-five mortality rate.

Another key element to this issue is the amount of food that is lost during and after production. Finding ways of minimizing or eliminating damage caused to crops by pests, for example, was one of the key challenges identified in both periods of data collection. Therefore, targeting pest control could significantly improve food security. Similarly, finding more effective ways of storing crops to reduce post-harvest losses through theft, rain or fire damage or pests, and preserving perishable items could also prevent waste, help reduce the impact of the hungry season, and therefore reduce seasonal food insecurity. Community and household food security might be further strengthened through the establishment of community-based cereal banks, particularly for rice, which households could draw upon during the hungry season.

Such a model has proved to be popular in Sahelian countries where support has been received from governments and NGOs (Plan 2015). Institutions such as community banks and agricultural business centres, which are accessible to households in both Panguma and Kayima, have the potential to assist in improving local food security, but thus far they seem to have made little impact.

Farmers in Panguma and Kayima, with some support from the government, have implemented coping strategies to adapt to climate change, most notably the greater cultivation of inland valley swamps, but as with many rural communities in developing countries, they lack the capacity to deal with the impacts effectively (de Haen 2007). Given predictions that the agricultural sector will continue to decline as a result of climate change over the next hundred years (Mendelsohn *et al.* 2000), continued livelihood diversification is imperative if food security is to be achieved and sustained in the long term.

The vulnerability of communities and households in Sierra Leone was clearly highlighted during the recent Ebola epidemic, where poor health-care facilities proved to be woefully inadequate in coping with the crisis, and international intervention was necessary. The full extent of the Ebola outbreak on rural livelihoods is yet to be fully assessed, though initial indications suggest that the quarantines and other restrictions imposed to prevent the spread of the disease have had a significant impact on the production, accessibility, and therefore consumption, of food. There is clearly a need for further research in this area, and an extension of this long-term association with Panguma and Kayima could be useful in assessing the impact of the Ebola epidemic on food security as households strive to rebuild their livelihoods as they did following the civil war. This, in turn, would further strengthen our understanding of the relationship between vulnerability, resilience and food security across time and place.

References

Amekawa, Y. (2011) 'Agroecology and Sustainable Livelihoods: Towards an Integrated Approach to Rural Development', *Journal of Sustainable Agriculture*, 35(2): 118–162.

Anderson, M. B. (1995) 'Vulnerability to Disaster and Sustainable Development: A General Framework for Assessing Vulnerability', in M. Munasinghe and C. Clarke (eds.) *Disaster Prevention for Sustainable Development,* Washington, D.C.: The International Bank for Reconstruction and Development (IDNDR) and the World Bank, pp. 41–60.

Bangura, K. S., Lynch, K. and Binns, T. (2013) Coping with the Impacts of Weather Changes in Rural Sierra Leone, *International Journal of Sustainable Development and World Ecology*, 20 (1): 20–31.

Barrett, C. B. (2010) 'Measuring Food Security', *Science* 327: 825–828.

Bellows, J. and Miguel, E. (2009) 'War and Local Collective Action in Sierra Leone', *Journal of Public Economics* 93(11–12): 1144–1157.

Berkes, F., Folke, C. and Colding, J. (1998) *Social and Ecological Systems: Management Practices and Social Mechanisms for Building Resilience,* Cambridge: Cambridge University Press.

Binns, J. A. (1980) *The Dynamics of Third World Food Production Systems – An Evaluation of Change and Development in the Rural Economy of Sierra Leone.* Unpublished Ph. D Thesis, Centre of West African Studies, University of Birmingham.

Binns, T. and Maconachie, R. (2005) '"Going Home" in Postconflict Sierra Leone: Diamonds, Agriculture and Re-building Rural Livelihoods in the Eastern Province', *Geography* 90(1): 67–78.

Boko, M., Niang, I., Nyong, A., Vogel, C., Githeko, A., Medany, M., Osman-Elasha, B., Tabo, R. and Yanda P. (2007) 'Africa', in M. Parry, O. Canziani, J. Palutikof, P. van der Linden, and C. Hanson (eds.) *Climate Change 2007: Impacts, Adaptation and Vulnerability: Working Group II Contribution to the Fourth Assessment Report of the Intergovernmental Panel on Climate Change*, Cambridge: Cambridge University Press, pp. 433–467.

Chappell, A. and Agnew, C. T. (2004) 'Modelling Climate Change in West African Sahel Rainfall (1931–90) as an Artifact of Changing Station Locations', *International Journal of Climatology* 24(5): 547–554.

de Haen, H. (2007) 'Climate Change and Rural Development', *Entwicklung and Ländlicher Raum* 5: 1–8.

Ellis, F. (1998) 'Household Strategies and Rural Livelihood Diversification', *The Journal of Development Studies* 35(1): 1–38.

FAO (Food and Agriculture Organization) (2009) *World Summit on Food Security*, Rome: Food and Agriculture Organization of the United Nations (FAO).

Humphreys, M. and Weinstein, J. (2009) 'Demobilization and Reintegration in Sierra Leone: Assessing Progress', in R. Muggah (ed.) *Security and Post-Conflict Reconstruction: Dealing with Fighters in the Aftermath of War*, London and New York: Routledge, pp. 47–69.

Lovendal, C. R. and Knowles, M. (2006) *Tomorrow's Hunger: A Framework for Analysing Vulnerability to Food Security*, Helsinki: United Nations University – World Institute for Development Economics Research (UNU-WIDER).

Maxwell, S. (2001) 'The Evolution of Thinking About Food Security', in S. Devereux and S. Maxwell (eds.) *Food Security in Sub-Saharan Africa*, London: ITDG Publishing, pp. 13–31.

Mendelsohn, R., Dinar, A. and Dalfelt, A. (2000) *Climate Change Impacts on African Agriculture*, Washington D.C.: World Bank.

Owusu, F. (2009) 'Livelihoods' in R. Kitchen and N. Thrift (eds.) *International Encyclopedia of Human Geography*, Amsterdam and London: Elsevier Science, pp. 219–224.

Peters, K. (2007) 'From Weapons to Wheels: Young Sierra Leonean Ex-Combatants Become Motorbike Taxi-Riders', *Journal of Peace, Conflict and Development* 10. Available at: www.bradford.ac.uk/social-sciences/peace-conflict-and-development/issue-10/#d.en.86907.

Pinstrup-Andersen, P. (2009) 'Food Security: Definition and Measurement', *Food Security* 1: 5–7.

Plan (2015) Cereal Banks Empower Women in Niger. Available at: www.plan-uk.org/what-we-do/our-global-programme/economic-household-security/cereal-banks-niger.

Richards, P. (1986) *Coping with Hunger*, London: Allen and Unwin.

Richards, P. (1996) *Fighting for the Rainforest: War, Youth and Resources in Sierra Leone*, Oxford: James Currey.

Richards, P. (2003) *The Political Economy of Internal Conflict in Sierra Leone*. Working Paper 21. Netherlands Institute of International Relations 'Clingendael', Conflict Research Unit, August 2003.

Sallu, S. M., Twyman, C. and Stringer, L. C. (2010) 'Resilient or Vulnerable Livelihoods? Assessing Livelihood Dynamics and Trajectories in Rural Botswana', *Ecology and Society* 15(4): 3.

Scoones, I. (2009) 'Livelihoods Perspectives and Rural Development', *Journal of Peasant Studies* 36(1): 171–196.

Sen, A. (1983) *Poverty and Famines: An Essay on Entitlement and Deprivation*, Oxford: Oxford University Press.

Spencer, D. (2012) *Issues in Food Security and Cash Crop Production in Sierra Leone*, Freetown: Enterprise Development Services Ltd.

UNDP (United Nations Development Programme) (2015) *Restoring Livelihoods and Fostering Social and Economic Recovery: UNDP Response to the Ebola Crisis in Sierra Leone*, New York: UNDP.

Walker, B., Gunderson, L., Kinzig, A., Folke, C., Carpenter, S. and Schultz, L. (2006) 'A Handful of Heuristics and Some Propositions for Understanding Resilience in Social-Ecological Systems', *Ecology and Society* 11(1): 13.

WFP (World Food Programme) (2008) *Sierra Leone: Household Food Security Survey in Rural Areas*, Freetown, WFP.

WFP (World Food Programme) (2011) *The State of Food Security and Nutrition in Sierra Leone, 2011*, Freetown: WFP.

WHO (World Health Organization) (2015) 'Ebola Situation Report – 16 December 2015', http://apps.who.int/ebola/current-situation/ebola-situation-report-16-december-2015.

Part III

Urban food systems and governance in the context of climate change

10 Climate change, food and the city

Agency and urban scale food system networks

Gareth Haysom

Introduction

The Food and Agriculture Organization (FAO) 2015 State of Food and Agriculture review reported that in excess of 795 million people are undernourished globally. While this figure has declined in recent years, it masks some very real food security challenges. The decline in undernourishment can be attributed to economic development in certain developing countries, particularly China. Despite this decline, the related, but separate, issues of hunger, malnutrition and undernutrition remain a persistent challenge globally. The 2015 FAO report offered a number of caveats to the successes enabled through economic development, stating that although economic growth is a key success factor for reducing undernourishment, it has to be inclusive and provide opportunities for improving the livelihoods of the poor (FAO 2015a). This point highlights the fact that global inequalities mean that food insecurity is disproportionately experienced. Food insecurity manifests most severely in specific geographies. Despite positive shifts in the state of food security at a global scale, in a regional FAO report, it was stated that, 'the total number of undernourished people [in sub-Saharan Africa] continues to increase, with an estimated 220 million in 2014–16 compared to 175.7 million in 1990–92' (FAO 2015b: 1). Food security is emerging as a key development challenge for Africa. Several considerations cause limited and inappropriate food access, including, but certainly not limited to, the ability to buy food, itself often a symptom of limited or irregular income. Limited, erratic or inappropriate food access and utilization results in reduced nutrition, poor health and other related consequences. These consequences manifest in public health costs, educational challenges and at times, social challenges.

African cities are expanding rapidly and are key centres of growth and development (UN DESA 2012). The same inequalities highlighted in the FAO southern African report (2015b) are evident in the rapidly expanding African cities (Crush and Frayne 2010). In arguing for a greater urban focus in African development, policy and practice, Pieterse *et al* (2015: 14) painted a picture of the current landscape and the importance of innovative and progressive approaches to African development, but most importantly, to African urban development. For Pieterse *et al* (2015), the urban food system and its functioning is something that falls within wider service delivery concerns. While this may be the case, this perpetuates a particular view of food within cities. Required, is a far more deliberate and strategic engagement in the urban food question. Food system challenges are increasingly evident within cities (Crush and Frayne 2010). While most of the world's poor people have traditionally lived in rural areas, the numbers of urban poor, from market towns to megacities, are substantial (Cohen and Garrett 2009). Food access strategies in cities are dependent on the ability to procure food and not the ability to produce food.

Informed by the 1996 FAO food security definition, food security is generally seen as a situation in which all people, at all times, have physical, social and economic access to sufficient, safe and nutritious food which meets their dietary needs and food preferences for an active and healthy life (FAO 1996). The FAO definition suggests that food security involves the intersection of four food system activities, ensuring that sufficient food is produced (availability), that the food produced can be consumed, bought or traded (access) and that the food can be consumed in a manner that is socially appropriate while enabling optimal nutrition and health (utilization). The fourth aspect that plays a key role in ensuring food security in that of a stable food system (stability), one where society can plan food access approaches with certainty, but also one where the necessary systems, structures and policies are in place to ensure that food is available and accessible during times of extreme food scarcity. This framing of food security has recently been expanded to include availability and accessibility, as well as food adequacy, acceptability and agency, referred to as the '5 A's' (Rocha 2008: 1). The question of agency and the knowledge that certain food system actors draw upon is a key theme that will be explored.

The concept of global environmental change is used here to describe the interconnected nature of the food system and how this impacts on the outcomes and activities of the modern urban food system. When these changes intersect with other societal transitions – including the second urban transition, the nutrition transition and food regime changes – the need for different urban food system interventions is compounded further.

Required: a new conceptual frame?

Highlighting the rural dominance in how the food system is understood and how food security interventions are approached, Donald et al. (2010: 172) argue that 'past conceptual frameworks applied to the analysis of [food and] agricultural systems have emphasized producer over consumer actions and have often been aspatial'. Crush and Frayne (2010: 6) question whether this rural production and development dominance was the right 'fix' for food security. Proposing an alternative city-oriented perspective at once raises questions about the role of both city leadership and all other urban food system stakeholders in urban food security.

Concerns about nutrition, food prices and food security are part and parcel of rapid urbanization in the developing world. In 2008, the demographic composition of the global population shifted to being predominantly urban (FAO 2012: 10). This urban growth and the resultant developmental, economic and infrastructural consequences do not follow the trends of the first urban transition (Pieterse 2008). This urbanization trend has been referred to as the second urban transition (*ibid.*). It is characterized by an absence of industrialization, modernization and technology-driven 'informationalism' (Swilling and Annecke 2012: 114), and is occurring amidst unprecedented resource scarcities. Urbanization within this context has direct governance and developmental consequences.

In the same way that urban change has been referred to as the second urban transition, changes taking place in the food system have been referred to as transitions. Transitions are understood to reflect a convergence of multiple challenges and responses, described by Swilling and Annecke (2012: xvi) as 'the reconfiguration of the institutional and organisational structures and systems of society'.

Within this context of converging transition processes, the current food security discourse requires reassessment. Dominant policy, strategy perspectives and formulations are ill equipped to respond appropriately to the transitional processes of rapid urbanization (Swilling and Annecke 2012; Pieterse 2008), food regime change (Friedmann and McMichael 1989), the nutrition transition (Popkin 2002) and the rise of so-called 'big food' (Montiero and Cannon, 2012). These challenges are most evident within developing world cities. One manifestation of such challenges is urban food insecurity, with numerous attendant consequences. Some cities, predominantly in the North, but with a few examples in South America, are responding by developing new governance approaches and new structures that recognize agency and city-scale networks as necessities in the urban food governance project.

There are many 'agents' active in every food system. The food system comprises the activities of commercial and non-commercial actors that grow, process, distribute, acquire and dispose of food (MacRae and Donahue 2013: 2). Activities in the food system encompass production, processing and packaging, distribution and retail and consumption. All these activities simultaneously generate outcomes that impact on food security, environmental security and other societal interests (Ericksen 2008). These activities are legitimized, enabled or regulated through laws, policies, institutions, stakeholder actions, practice, governance and external pressures.

A further transition that has a direct bearing on the functioning of the urban food system is the onset of environmental change. A key driver of this change is climate change (IPCC 2014). The intersection between climate-related environmental change and the resultant undermining of societal resilience, coupled with high levels of urban food security has two consequences. First, while the drivers of these transitions are often the result of global forces, the consequences are felt equally dramatically at the urban scale. Secondly, the urban scale experiences raise critical questions as to the role of urban space, urban agency and urban government in effectively responding to and mitigating the consequences of such change.

Locating climate change within the food debate

A broad view is taken here which frames the impacts of climate change as part of wider global environmental change (GEC) processes (see Ingram 2011; Ingram *et al.* 2012). Ericksen's (2008) work, focusing on global environmental change and food security perspectives, offers valuable insights concerning the position of the food system within the processes of environmental change, and particularly climate change. Of great utility is how Ericksen speaks to food system activities and food system outcomes, echoing the FAO food security definition. In Ericksen's model, a number of global and national drivers impact directly on food system outcomes.

Food system outcomes give rise to associated socio-economic and ecological feedbacks, which, in turn, contribute to the underlying change drivers. As a result of these dynamics, changes within the food system extend beyond the food system itself, driving socio-ecological vulnerability. The challenge is that these food system outcomes are not felt evenly, with the poor experiencing disproportionate levels of risk. Food security is located within the wider processes driving global environmental change. The food system is both affected by and contributes to global environmental change. It is argued that these food system outcomes at the urban scale, principally food availability, food access and food utilization, are informed by, calibrated to respond to, and emerge as a result of, the various food system activities. At the urban scale, while some food production may take place, dominant food system processes reflect the activities associated with food consumption. Food consumption is driven in part by the urban food retail system, which in turn is driven by the processing and distribution system.

Food security and climate change at the urban scale

Focusing on food system actions at the urban scale requires a theoretical approach that enables investigation of how food flows (from Castells 1997). This relates to hierarchies of policy and governance and, via theories of scale, to the specifics of place and the relationships between places.

First, referring to a particular place as urban is itself an enactment of scale and implies a specific boundary to the particular area of analysis. Second, 'geographical scales cannot be understood in isolation from one another, as mutually exclusive or additive containers; rather they constitute deeply intertwined moments and levels of a single worldwide socio-spatial totality' (Brenner 2000: 370, citing Lefebvre 1978: 305). Scale is thus relational. Whereas more traditional hierarchical notions of scale have been challenged (Brenner 2001; Marston *et al.* 2005), it is argued here that policies, specifically those relating to food, reflect a trilogy of 'the global (world-economy), national (theories of the state) and urban scales' (Taylor 1982: 23). Food is embedded within both hierarchical and horizontal scalar interactions. Taylor describes the associated processes aligned to these scales as: global – the scale of reality; national – the scale of ideology; and urban – the scale of experience (from Taylor 1982: 26). Globalization-driven political, economic and structural shifts have ruptured traditional scalar hierarchies. Scale, however, remains relevant. Hubbard recognizes the usefulness of the urban scale. He suggests that the scale debate 'carries some profound implications for the examination of the city, encouraging urban researchers to question where to locate cities within extant hierarchies of scale' (Hubbard 2006: 164). In the context of food, understanding scale is made more complex by the range of scales (temporal, spatial and organizational) that are at play in any particular context (Battersby-Lennard N.D.: 1). The food system is socially constructed and thus, relational (Brenner 2000; 2001), with a variety of social processes and networks present (Lefebvre 1991; Brenner 2000). The food system operates simultaneously at the hierarchical and vertical scale levels, while also manifesting great complexity with multiple feedback loops (Pickett *et al.* 1997) and emergent properties (Marston *et al.* 2005). The food system thus embodies the scale debate, highlighting the hierarchical components, but also reflecting that contingent outcome of the tensions between structural forces and agentic practices.

In practice, the food system exemplifies the scalar tensions evident within the scale debates within the geography discipline. While the third food regime described by Friedmann and McMicheal (1989) reflects the dissolving of food system scales, policies – particularly those in the developing world – reflect distinct hierarchies of scale, with international treaties dictating certain national processes, and national governments then driving the food security agenda through national agricultural and development policies. Both the flat ontology of the dissolved scales and distinct food policy hierarchies result in a policy void at the urban scale: the 'scale of experience'. This void has distinctly negative consequences for urban residents in the developing world, particularly poor urban residents. These consequences were laid bare in the 2008 African Food Security Urban Network (AFSUN) survey (Frayne *et al.* 2010).

The food system reflects the scalar structuration described by Brenner in the scale hypothesis where, 'processes are constituted and continually reworked through everyday social routines and struggles' (Brenner 2001: 604–608). This speaks directly to the food system and the relationship between the city and the associated food system actions. This also raises questions about the actors involved in these constituted routines and struggles, and how they make meaning of the everyday.

As far back as 2000, the urban planner Kami Pothukuchi suggested that the absence of food system planning (at the urban scale) does not have a neutral consequence, but such an absence has negative consequences. These negative consequences are amplified when confronted by the mutually converging transitions described earlier. Following from Harvey's (1989) assertion that, 'urban governance means much more than urban government' (1989: 6), this chapter sees urban food governance as being far more than just city governments appropriating a food governance role from other more traditional spheres of government responsible for food governance – generally national government. In the rural productionist paradigm, food security implied growing enough food, and that cemented national departments of agriculture (or equivalents) as the custodians of the national food system. The question, reverting to the globalized food system described above, is: should national governments play anything other than a regulatory (policy) role in the food system? Lang and Barling (2012) pointed out that the globalized and corporatized nature of the current food system means that most food system decisions are not being made by national governments. They continue to argue that most international bodies still reflect post World War II development intervention approaches. Thu (2009: 14) described the current food system as being subject to processes reflecting 'industrialised food and global de-agriculturalization', a food system that is typified by what has been referred to as 'big food' (Monteiro and Cannon 2012). These shifts have prompted alternative responses, designed to counter the negative outcomes of the nutrition transition (Popkin 2002) and to wrest a modicum of control back to the domain of the consumer, or society at large.

Perhaps one of the most defining aspects of this act of wresting back some control is that, through interactions between society and the state, space has been created for the emergence of a variety of food governance processes. Writing in 2004, Werkele suggested that, 'community agencies and the local state have worked together to create a new political space for food justice issues' (2004: 381).

A theme in the writings of Pieterse (2006; 2008) is the question of participation. Communities have a key role to play in (re)building their own societies. Pieterse suggested that this rebuilding is facilitated through a form of agency that he called 'agonistic politics', or the creation of 'homebru strategies that emerge and flourish in a context of radical democratic politics that stretch across formal–informal, concrete–symbolic and consensual– conflictual binaries' (Pieterse 2006: 300). The contemporary view of urban governance still views the city as an entity run through a 'nucleated and hierarchically nested process of political governance, economic development, social order, and cultural identity' (Soja 2000: 13–14). This notion has been questioned and challenged (Appadurai 2002; Pieterse and Simone 2013), with arguments that such a perspective implies a top-down governance structure that disregards reciprocal networks, agency, phronesis[1] or other forms of deep democracy. While officials may aspire to the hierarchical model of governance, the lived reality is very different. This is evident in parts of the food systems of developing cities. It is even more evident when the impacts of global environmental change intersect with the food system at the urban scale.

Questions of agency have been the subject of much debate within academic literature, where 'variants of action theory, normative theory, and political-institutional analysis have defended, attached, buried, and resuscitated the concept in often contradictory and overlapping ways' (Emirbayer and Mische 1998: 962). In their work, Emirbayer and Mische considered agency from both a philosophical and sociological perspective, challenging a number of theoretical approaches to agency. Central to their argument was that the current perspectives of agency did not provide insight into how agency 'interpenetrates with and impacts upon the temporal relational context of action' (*ibid.*: 1012) – actors live simultaneously in the past, future and present. Agency is inherently social and relational, and consists of three key elements: iteration, projectivity and practical evaluation. This agency is clearly evident in how poor urban residents navigate their food system and make decisions to activate networks to enable food access. The same applies in the adaptation strategies applied by communities responding to climate change. Agency is expressed in the strategies applied to activate networks that enable food access and scale-oriented responses to climate change. These networks, while thick, are subject to notions of fair exchange and reciprocity. An example of this is, that should the ability to reciprocate following one of the many disasters that befall the poor – particularly the urban poor – be unclear, reliance on state or NGO-provided-welfare supersedes community-level options. This is a deliberate strategic choice, made so as to avoid eroding one's own networks (and agency). When investigating individual food security responses post disasters in Cape Town, Duncan (2013) found that individuals chose to rely on welfare rather than erode social networks – the unknown temporal consequence of the disaster meant that the ability for later reciprocity was unknown. The likelihood of an extended period of dependency influenced response strategies, confirming the interaction between projectivity and practical evaluation.

AFSUN research across the eleven southern African cities enquired into the sources of food accessed by the respondents (Frayne *et al.* 2010). While conventional market sources dominated, a significant proportion of food was accessed through what could be described as reciprocal networks. The AFSUN work also tested the frequency of access considering different temporal scales. In the case of Cape Town, 'food shared with neighbours and other households', 'food provided by neighbours and other households' and 'food borrowed from others' reflected the regional trend and constituted over 30 per cent of food access approaches, with the different approaches predominantly activated 'at least once a month' or 'at least once a week' (Battersby 2011).

It is argued that the networks that enable sharing and exchange are, in fact, a form of alternative food network (AFN) (see Goodman and Goodman 2007) and that these are at play in developed countries, but have not been framed as AFNs. The Southern AFNs differ markedly from the AFNs evident in northern cities. The networks activated by the food insecure are a form of AFN. These networks may not be actively engaging with city officials or other networks on the subject of food, but they are networks that enable access and complement food intake. The presence of these networks allows a measure of food stability. These factors all ensure that the food available is then accessed. Ericksen's (2008) depiction of different food system activities intersecting with food system outcomes assists in highlighting the vulnerabilities of the food system. The same reciprocal networks apply to climate-related threats, particularly in terms of the networks activated by poor communities, both in terms of adaptation responses and in the face of climate-change-related disasters.

Conclusion

The alternative food networks of poor urban residents in the developing world, enacted to enable food access, are generally celebrated as acts of self-determination and proactive agency. While true, they are present because the globalized food system does not work for the poor. The poor are required to then negotiate alternative networks. The middle-class angst of the northern AFNs described by

Goodman and Goodman (2007) are perhaps present in the imaginations of policy makers, but the food networks enacted by the food insecure in African cities reflect a very different type of alternative food network.

These networks are a critical, yet poorly understood, part of the food access process. Stress, competition, imposed planning, violence and other lived realities threaten these alternative food networks and increase vulnerability in ways that are unclear. The same can be argued in terms of the ways in which poor urban residents respond to climatic events and threats.

The alternative food networks emerge when required and then disperse when no longer needed. This fluidity makes such processes difficult to engage. These reciprocal network processes are also embedded in community processes and are contextual. Generalizations are problematic. These issues pose challenges for research. Each network (food, climate change and even combined) has its own history, context and vulnerabilities. Due to their nature, such networks are also often unseen. How such networks are researched and documented remains a key question. Nevertheless, these are important food and climate-system functions, and require deeper understanding. Food-related challenges as a result of global environmental change are drivers that stimulate the activation of such networks. This has profound implications when environmental change impacts are felt across society and such networks are unilaterally destroyed.

From a policy perspective, these networks require two foundational paradigm shifts. The first is the recognition of the urban policy responses. Secondly, food security and climate-change-response-programming needs to be delegated to local authorities. While local municipalities are apprehensive about engaging with communities on such issues, agency as a component of urban crisis mitigation requires engagement. Expecting local authorities to engage in food security matters when they have no formal or fiscal mandate will, ultimately, only provoke issues as the engagement will not have the required depth. National governments need to recognize that local government is at the 'coalface' of such challenges, challenges laid bare by the need to engage in such networks. Power, mandates and resources are required to enable local government engagement in such issues. Concerns over local government competence, while real, should not deter actions at the sites where such concerns are most prevalent.

Acknowledgement

The author's work was funded through the Hungry Cities Partnership: Informality, inclusive growth and food security in cities of the Global South, an International Development Research Centre (IDRC) funded project.

Note

1 Pieterse explains phronesis to refer to the skill and reason of practical judgment 'in the moment of action' (Gunder 2003: 253, in Pieterse 2006). Further, 'Aristotle found that every well-functioning organization and society was dependent on the effective

functioning of all three intellectual virtues – *episteme, techne,* and *phronesis*'. At the same time, however, Aristotle emphasized the crucial importance of *phronesis*, 'for the possession of the single virtue of prudence [*phronesis*] will carry with it the possession of them all' (Flyvbjerg, 2004).

References

Appadurai, A. (2002) 'Deep Democracy: Urban Governmentality and the Horizon of Politics', *Public Culture*, Vol. 14(1): 21–47.

Battersby, J. (2011) 'The State of Urban Food Insecurity in Cape Town', *Urban Food Security Series, No. 11*. Queen's University and AFSUN: Kingston and Cape Town.

Battersby-Lennard, J, (N.D.) 'Scales of Biodiversity Management in the City of Cape Town'. Unpublished working document.

Brenner, N. (2000) 'The Urban Question as a Scale Question: Reflections on Henri Lefebvre, Urban Theory and the Politics of Scale', *International Journal of Urban and Regional Research*, Vol. 24 (2): 361–378.

Brenner, N. (2001) 'The Limits to Scale? Methodological Reflections on Scalar Structuration', *Progress in Human Geography*, Vol. 25 (4): 591–614.

Castells, M. (1997) *The Information Age, Volumes 1, 2 and 3*. Oxford: Blackwell.

Cohen, M. and Garrett, J. (2009) 'The Food Price Crisis and Urban Food (In)Security', *Human Settlements Working Paper Series, Urbanization and Emerging Population Issues – 2*. International Institute for Environment and Development (IIED).

Crush, J. and Frayne, B. (2010) 'The Invisible Crisis: Urban Food Security in Southern Africa', *Urban Food Security in Southern Africa, Urban Food Security Series*, No. 1. African Food Security Network (AFSUN). Cape Town, Unity Press.

Donald, B., Gertler, M., Gray, M. and Lobao, L. (2010) 'Re-Regionalizing the Food System?', *Cambridge Journal of Regions, Economy and Society*. Vol. 3: 171–175.

Duncan, S. (2013) *Food Security in Post-Fire Disaster Context: Experiences of Female-Headed Households in an Informal Settlement*. Honours Thesis, Environmental and Geographical Sciences, University of Cape Town.

Emirbayer, M. and Mische, A. (1998) 'What is Agency?', *American Journal of Sociology*, Vol. 103 (4): 962–1023.

Ericksen, P. J. (2008) 'Conceptualizing Food Systems for Global Environmental Change Research', *Global Environmental Change*, Vol. 18 (1): 234–245.

Food and Agriculture Organization (FAO) (1996) *Rome Declaration on World Food Security*, Rome: World Food Summit, 13 November 1996. Available at: www.fao.org/WFS.

Food and Agriculture Organization (FAO) (2012) *FAO Statistical Yearbook – 2012*, Rome: FAO.

Food and Agriculture Organization (FAO) (2015a) *State of Food Security in the World 2015*. Rome: FAO.

Food and Agricultural Organization (FAO) (2015b) *Regional Overview of Food Insecurity Africa, 2015: African Food Security Prospects Brighter Than Ever*, Rome: FAO.

Frayne, B., Pendleton, W. and Crush, J. (2010) 'The State of Urban Food Insecurity in Southern Africa', *Urban Food Security in Southern Africa, Urban Food Security Series, No. 2*, Cape Town: African Food Security Network (AFSUN).

Friedmann, H. and McMichael, P. (1989) 'Agriculture and the State System: The Rise and Decline of National Agricultures, 1870 to Present', *Sociologia Ruralis*. Vol. 29 (2): 93–117.

Goodman, D. and Goodman, M. (2007) 'Alternative Food Networks', Draft entry for the *Encyclopedia of Human Geography*, 2 July 2007.

Gunder, M. (2003) 'Passionate Planning for the Other's Desire: An Agonistic Response to the Dark Side of Planning'. *Progress in Planning*, Vol. 60(3): 235–319.

Harvey, D. (1989) 'From Managerialism to Entrepreneurialism: the Transformation in Urban Governance in Late Capitalism', *Geografiska Annaler: B, Human Geography*, Vol. 71 (1): 3–17.

Hubbard, P. (2006) *City*. Oxford: Taylor and Francis.

Ingram, J. (2011) 'A Food Systems Approach to Researching Food Security and its Interactions with Global Environmental Change', *Food Security*, 3(4): 417–431.

Ingram, J., Ericksen, P. and Liverman, D. (2012) *Food Security and Global Environmental Change*. London: Routledge.

International Panel on Climate Change (IPCC) (2014) *Climate Change 2014 Synthesis Report: Summary for Policymakers*, Fifth Assessment Report (AR5). Available at: https://www.ipcc.ch/pdf/assessment-report/ar5/syr/AR5_SYR_FINAL_SPM.pdf.

Lang, T. and Barling, D. (2012) 'Food Security and Food Sustainability: Reformulating the Debate', *The Geographical Journal*, Vol. 178 (4): 313–326.

Lefebvre, H. (1978) *La Pensée Marxiste et la Ville (Marxist Thinking and the City)* (Vol. 22) Tournai: Casterman.

Lefebvre, H. (1991) *The Production of Space*. Oxford and Cambridge, MA: Blackwell (translated by D. Nicholson-Smith).

MacRae, R. and Donahue, K. (2013) *Municipal Food Policy Entrepreneurs: a Preliminary Analysis of how Canadian Cities and Regional Districts are Involved in Food System Change*, Toronto: Toronto Food Policy Council and Canadian Agri-Food Policy Institute.

Marston, S., Jones II, J. P. and Woodard, K. (2005) 'Human Geography without Scale', *Transactions of the Institute of British Geographers NS*, Vol. 30: 416–432.

Monteiro, C. and Cannon, G. (2012) 'The Impact of Transnational "Big Food" Companies on the South: A View from Brazil', *PLoS Medicine*, Vol. 9 (7): 1–5.

Pickett, S. T., Burch Jr., W. R., Dalton, S. E., Foresman, T. W., Grove, J. M. and Rowntree, R. (1997) A Conceptual Framework for the Study of Human Ecosystems in Urban areas, *Urban Ecosystems*, Vol. 1(4):185–199.

Pieterse, E. (2006). 'Building with Ruins and Dreams: Some Thoughts on Realising Integrated Urban Development in South Africa through Crisis'. *Urban Studies*, Vol. 43(2): pp. 285–304.

Pieterse, E. (2008) *City Futures: Confronting the Crisis of Urban Development*, Cape Town: UCT Press.

Pieterse, E. and Simone, A. (eds.) (2013) *Rogue Urbanism: Emergent African Cities*. Auckland Park: Jacana Media and Cape Town: African Centre for Cities.

Pieterse, E., Parnell, S. and Haysom, G. (2015) *Towards an African Urban Agenda*. Nairobi: UN-Habitat and Economic Commission for Africa.

Popkin, B. (2002) 'The Shift in Stages of the Nutrition Transition in the Developing World Differs from Past Experiences!', *Public Health Nutrition*, Vol. 5 (1A): 205–214.

Pothukuchi, K. (2000) 'Community Food Mapping', Address to Ontario Public Health Association Workshop on Community Food Mapping, Toronto, 11 September, 2000.

Rocha, C. (2008) 'Brazil-Canada Partnership: Building Capacity in Food Security', Toronto: Centre for Studies in Food Security, Ryerson University.

Soja, E. (2000) *Postmetropolis: Critical Studies of City Regions*. Oxford: Blackwell.

Swilling, M. and Annecke, E. (2012) *Just Transitions: Explorations of Sustainability in an Unfair World*, Cape Town: Juta.

Taylor, C. (1992) 'The Politics of Recognition', in A. Gutmann (ed.) *Multiculturalism and 'The Politics of Recognition'*, Princeton: Princeton University Press.

Thu, K. (2009) The Centralization of Food Systems and Political Power. *Culture and Agriculture*, Vol. 31(1):13–18.

UN DESA (2012) *World Urbanization Prospects: The 2011 Revision.*

Wekerle, G. R. (2004) 'Food Justice Movements Policy, Planning and Networks', *Journal of Planning Education and Research*, Vol. 23(4): 378–386.

11 Urban food deserts in Cape Town

Food security, food access and climate change

Mary Caesar and Jonathan Crush

Introduction

Research on the nature and extent of urban food insecurity in British and North American cities has led to the notion of 'urban food deserts' to describe economically and socially-deprived inner-city areas (Besharov *et al.* 2010; Ghosh-Dastidar *et al.* 2014; Gordon *et al.* 2011; Jiao *et al.* 2012; Martin *et al.* 2014; Walker *et al.* 2010; Wrigley 2002). One of the early definitions from this body of work described urban food deserts as 'areas of relative exclusion where people experience physical and economic barriers to accessing healthy food' (Cummins and Macintyre 2002: 436). In practice, the whole idea of the food desert has become integrally connected to the spatial behaviour of the supermarkets that dominate the urban food system in European and North American cities (Apparicio *et al.* 2007; Guy *et al.* 2004; Larsen and Gilliland 2008; Russell and Heidkamp 2011). Where supermarkets are present, it is suggested, consumers are able to make healthier food choices because of the variety and quality of fresh produce. When they are not, as in many low-income and deprived areas of cities, diets tend to be less varied and lead to poor health outcomes.

The Euro-American concept of the 'urban food desert' has gained limited traction in Africa and the Global South more generally (Battersby 2012a; Battersby and Crush 2014; Gartin 2012; Nickanor 2013). In part, this is because the international focus on rural poverty and food security has meant that urban food insecurity is largely invisible to researchers and policy makers (Crush and Frayne 2011). Supermarkets are recent entrants to food retailing in many countries and cities in the South and tend to target middle and high-income consumers (Reardon *et al.* 2003.) However, where they have a longer history and are present in much greater numbers (as in many Latin American countries and in South Africa), the obvious question is whether the conventional supermarket-driven idea of the food desert can be applied to analysis of African cities. And, if not, would it be better to abandon the idea of the food desert or redefine and delink it conceptually and analytically purely from the absence or presence of supermarkets?

Because the conventional definition of urban food deserts only refers to spatial and economic exclusions from the food system, a number of authors have argued for a broader definition. Shaw (2006), for example, suggests that if we use the causes and attributes of such spaces of exclusion to define urban food deserts, a number of different types of food deserts can be identified. She goes on to identify three different categories of food deserts related to access: ability, assets and attitude-related urban food deserts. Firstly, ability-related food deserts are 'anything that physically prevents access to food which a consumer otherwise has the financial resources to purchase and the mental desire to buy' (Shaw 2006: 241). Personal physical disability is one such barrier as it can prevent a person from opening packaging of desired food items or entering a specific store or section of a store in order to purchase desired food items. Local geography such as road crossings or hilly typology may create problems for those who do not own, or have access to, a car to transport their food. A related element is access to public transport during the times when it is needed. Finally, ability can be affected by the weight of the food to be carried home and the terrain across which it has to be carried.

An asset-related food desert involves the absence of financial assets, thus preventing consumption of desirable food that is otherwise available (Shaw 2006). These assets are both monetary and non-monetary; for example, monetary assets include the funds both to pay for transport to and from the store, as well as to purchase the desired food. Non-monetary assets include refrigerated storage space and access to cooking facilities in the dwelling. There is considerable evidence that in the cities of the Global South, access is the key dimension of food insecurity. While there is a much-touted view that urban agriculture can achieve improved food access and security (Poulsen *et al.* 2015), in many Southern African cities and poor neighbourhoods, the prospects for urban agriculture are fairly limited (Crush *et al.* 2011; Frayne *et al.* 2014). In a predominantly cash environment, with high rates of formal unemployment, households are continually vulnerable to food insecurity. Furthermore, with limited cash resources, healthy food choices often take second place to cheaper, energy-dense foods.

Third, there were attitude-related food deserts. Here, Shaw (2006) was referring to 'any state of mind that prevents the consumer from accessing foods they can otherwise physically bring into their home and have the necessary assets to procure'. The range of attitudes that can influence access to healthy foods in the urban food desert include 'culturally based prejudices against certain foods, lack of knowledge as to how to prepare and cook some foods, or unwillingness to find time in a time-poor but cash-rich lifestyle to cook fresh vegetables' (Shaw 2006: 242). What this essentially negative conceptualization leaves out in its focus on prejudices is the issue of preferences. An attitude-related food desert may also exist when people have certain food preferences (cultural or otherwise) which they are unable to meet. Furthermore, prejudices and preferences are not simply a matter of personal choice as the 'nutrition transition' literature makes clear (Popkin *et al.* 2012).

Despite Shaw's efforts to expand the understanding of urban food deserts, much of the research in this area continues to emphasize the importance of supermarkets in the creation and elimination of food deserts. Mead (2008: 335), for example, argued that the 'steady suburbanization of major food retailers is creating food deserts in city centres as these retailers follow people into ever expanding suburbs. The result is that low-income people in the city centres have poor access to vegetables, fruits and other whole foods'. Ghosh-Dastidar *et al.* (2014) measured the relationship between distance to store, food prices and obesity rates of primarily African-American residents in low-income neighbourhoods. The study found that placing a supermarket in a food desert alone would not necessarily improve obesity rates because better prices for healthy food was an equally significant factor. Martin *et al.* (2014) examined the access to quality food items and food prices in a small town of the USA. They hypothesized that fewer large supermarkets and high food prices correlates positively with limited access to healthy food in smaller towns. While all of this research is important in terms of the health outcomes with regard to access to supermarkets and food prices, it does not challenge the central role of the supermarket in the construction of urban food deserts.

Battersby and Crush (2014) suggested that a simple focus on modern retail does not adequately capture the complex realities of the food system and urban food deserts in African cities. They argued that the use of the food deserts concept in Africa requires a sophisticated understanding of the multiple market and non-market food sources, of the spatial mobility and dynamism of the informal food economy, of the changing drivers of household food insecurity and the local conditions that lead to compromised diets, undernutrition and social exclusion. They went on to redefine urban food deserts as 'poor, often informal, urban neighbourhoods characterized by high food insecurity and low dietary diversity, with multiple market and non-market food sources but variable household access to food' (Battersby and Crush 2014: 149).

With the definitions of Shaw (2006) and Battersby and Crush (2014) in mind, this chapter examines the case of Cape Town, South Africa, where supermarkets now command a significant share of food retailing and have been expanding into all areas of the city. After tracing the spatial expansion of supermarkets in the last two decades, the chapter examines the nature of the food interactions between modern retail, the informal food economy and food access in poor urban neighbourhoods from the perspective of consumer households. The chapter shows that supermarkets have had a growing presence in poorer areas of the city and that many poor households sourced food from supermarkets. Yet, levels of food insecurity were also extremely high in these same neighbourhoods. In other words, in contradiction to the food deserts literature, the mere presence or absence of supermarkets was insufficient to say whether a food desert existed or not. This chapter argues, instead, that the concept of urban food deserts needs to be reformulated and redefined to fit African realities since there is very little evidence that the growth of supermarkets across the city and in low-income areas is eliminating urban food deserts.

The chapter also addresses one of the major silences in the food deserts literature; that is, the relationship between climate change and urban food security. There is a growing literature on the impacts of climate change on African cities, but very little of it examines whether and how climate change is impacting on the food security of the urban poor (Frayne *et al.* 2012; Ziervogel and Frayne 2011). According to Battersby (2012b), the challenge is one of scale mismatch, where climate change is likely to impact on processes and relationships only indirectly connected to the urban area, *per se*. The food deserts literature is extremely situational and micro-scale in emphasis, and therefore falls prey to the problem of spatial mismatch, failing to incorporate any consideration of large-scale environmental change. In this section, we describe how the ways in which climate-change-associated events may comprise rural, peri-urban and urban food production, directly affecting the different dimensions of food security (availability, access, stability, utilization) or threaten the assets of the urban poor. We then demonstrate how adverse climate induced changes to the agricultural system affected the food security of Cape Town's urban poor.

We rely here on data from two household surveys in Cape Town conducted by the African Food Security Urban Network (AFSUN) in 2008 and the Hungry Cities Partnership (HCP) in 2013. The 2008 survey was conducted in three low-income areas of the city: Ocean View (N=226), Brown's Farm in Phillipi (Ward 34) (N=389) and Enkanini and Kuyasa in Khayalitsha (Ward 95) (N=394) (Battersby 2011). The HCP survey was conducted in December 2013 when a city-wide representative sample of 2,504 households was surveyed.

Supermarket expansion in Cape Town

The literature on supermarket expansion in the Global South identifies South Africa as a country of 'first wave' expansion in the 1990s (Reardon *et al.* 2003; Dakor 2012). Continued growth has proceeded since the turn of the century. By 2003, the supermarket sector constituted 50–60 per cent of all national food retail and had reached 68 per cent by 2010 (Battersby and Peyton 2014). Research on the expansion of supermarkets in Cape Town illustrates not only that the absolute number of supermarkets has continued to increase, but that physical access is still highly unequal (Battersby and Peyton 2014; Peyton *et al.* 2015). For example, as Figure 11.1 shows, supermarkets are also expanding into lower-income areas, often as 'anchor tenants' in new shopping malls.

Does the greater concentration of supermarkets in Cape Town's middle and higher-income areas mean that low-income households are excluded from geographical access, or is the expansion of supermarkets into low-income areas making them more accessible? In the 2008 AFSUN survey, households in the three poor areas of Cape Town were asked where they normally obtained their food and how often. Supermarkets were easily the most important source, patronized by almost all households, followed by small retail outlets and then the informal food economy (Figure 11.2). Urban agriculture was completely insignificant by comparison. The 2013 HCP survey data confirmed the importance of supermarkets to poor urban households, as well as those in middle and high-income areas. The vast majority of households in all three income terciles sourced food at supermarkets (Figure 11.3).

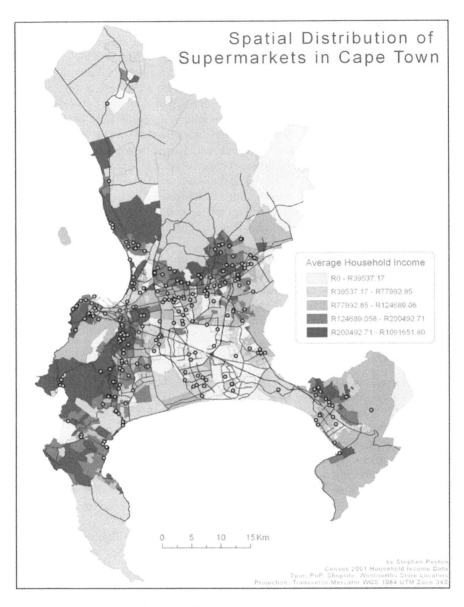

Figure 11.1 Distribution of supermarkets in Cape Town.
Source: Battersby and Peyton 2014: 160, AFSUN.

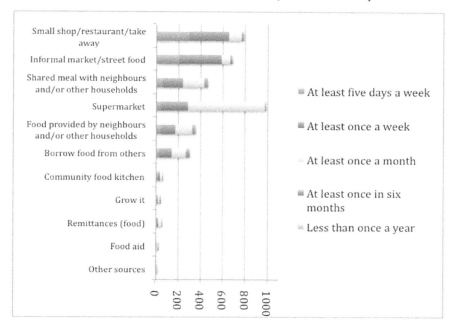

Figure 11.2 Food sources for poor urban households, 2008.
Source: AFSUN.

The other significant finding in both 2008 and 2013 is that poorer households are able to patronize more than one food source, albeit with different frequencies (Figures 11. 4 and 11. 5). Despite the fact that supermarkets are accessible to all households, only 20 per cent of those surveyed in 2008 shopped there at least once a week. On the other hand, around 60 per cent bought food from small retail outlets and informal vendors at least once a week. A similar pattern emerged in the 2013 survey, with lower-income tercile households purchasing food at other outlets, including spaza shops and street vendors (both part of the informal food economy), small stores and, to a lesser extent, fast-food outlets. Patronage frequencies varied with income. Informal food sources were patronized on an almost daily basis by low-income households, while the majority shopped at supermarkets once a month.

The evidence from both the 2008 and 2013 surveys in Cape Town suggests that all households, including low-income ones, can access supermarkets either in their own neighbourhoods, or through use of public and private transport. However, while over 50 per cent of high-income households shop at supermarkets at least once a week, only 20 per cent of low-income households do the same. The question is whether this is a result of differential geographical access or of the availability of alternative, possibly cheaper, food sources in low-income neighbourhoods. The 2013 survey indicates that many poorer households strategically engage with

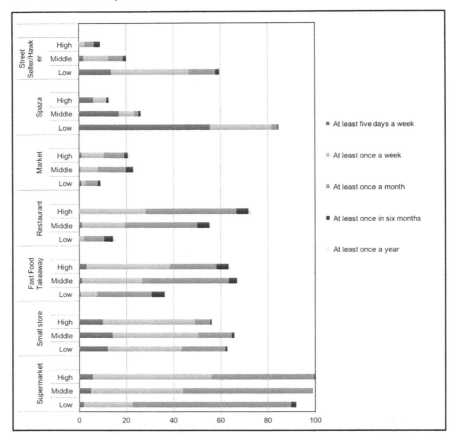

Figure 11.3 Food sources by income tercile, 2014.
Source: Hungry Cities Partnership.

supermarkets by purchasing supplies in bulk on payday and thus lower the average costs they pay for staples, especially mealie meal (maize flour). Their daily food-purchasing needs were largely met from neighbourhood vendors in the formal and informal sectors.

Food insecurity in Cape Town's food deserts

The accessibility of supermarkets and the presence of alternative food sources in Cape Town's low-income areas suggest that there is no shortage of food, and even good-quality food, in the lower-income areas of the city. Does this mean that there are, therefore, 'areas of relative exclusion where people experience physical and economic barriers to accessing healthy food' (Cummins and Macintyre 2002: 436)? The AFSUN and HCP approach to this question is to examine the ability, assets and attitude-related exclusion (Shaw 2006) through a focus on food security outcomes at the household level, where food security is defined as existing when all people, at all times, have physical, social and economic access to sufficient, safe and nutritious food that meets their dietary needs and food preferences for an active and healthy life (FAO 2002).

Both surveys used four common food security measurements designed by the Food and Nutrition Assistance (FANTA) project (Bilinsky and Swindale 2007; Coates *et al.* 2007; Swindale and Bilinsky 2006): (a) the Household Food Security Access Scale (HFIAS) in which households were allocated to categories according to weighted responses to nine questions providing a score between 0 (complete security) and 27 (complete insecurity); (b) the Household Food Insecurity Access Prevalence (HFIAP) Indicator, which groups scores on the HFIAS scale into four main categories, i.e. severely food insecure, moderately food insecure, mildly food insecure and food secure; and (c) the Household Dietary Diversity Scale (HDDS), which asks what foodstuffs household members ate on the previous day. All food items were placed in one of twelve food groups, giving a maximum score of 12 and a minimum of 0.

In 2008, the HFIAS score for the three low-income neighbourhoods combined was a relatively high 10.7 (compared with only 4.9 in similar Johannesburg neighbourhoods, for example) (Frayne *et al.* 2010). In terms of the HFIAP, 68 per cent of households were severely food insecure, while only 15 per cent were totally food secure (Figure 11. 4). The prevalence of food insecurity also varied across the three survey areas (Figure 11.5). Household food insecurity was highest in the informal settlements of Wards 95 (in Khayelitsha) and 34 (in Phillipi), with 80 per cent and 71 per cent of households severely food insecure, respectively.

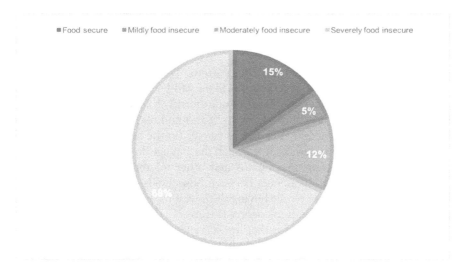

Figure 11.4 Household food security status, 2008.
Source: AFSUN.

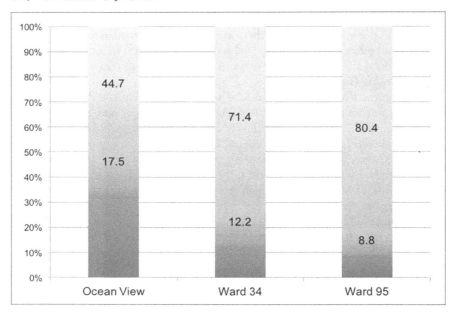

Figure 11.5 Household food security variations, 2008.
Source: AFSUN.

The 2013 HCP survey of the city as a whole confirmed that low-income households were the most food insecure and that very few households in the middle and higher-income terciles were food insecure (Figure 11. 6). More than 50 per cent of households in the lowest income tercile were severely food insecure, compared with less than 20 per cent and 10 per cent, respectively, in the middle and upper-income terciles.

The HDDS scores followed a similar pattern. The mean HDDS score in the three poor neighbourhoods in 2008 was 6.33 out of 12. Of the four most commonly consumed foodstuffs, three were largely non-nutritive: foods made with oils/fats (consumed by 72% of households), sugars (83%) and tea and coffee (88%). The other, consumed by over 90 per cent, was cereals (in the form of mealie meal and wheat in bread). This suggests that although the average diet may have had caloric adequacy, it was deficient in vitamins and other micronutrients. In the HCP survey, there were clear differences between households by income tercile, with those in the lowest income tercile having the lowest mean HDDS and the greatest proportion of households with low scores (Figure 11. 7).

What these findings suggest is that low-income areas in Cape Town qualify as food deserts as defined by Battersby and Crush (2014: 149) and fit the profile of assets-related food deserts elaborated by Shaw (2006). More work is certainly needed on Shaw's attitude-related urban food deserts. In areas of a city like Cape Town, characterized by asset-related urban food deserts, it is hard to disentangle

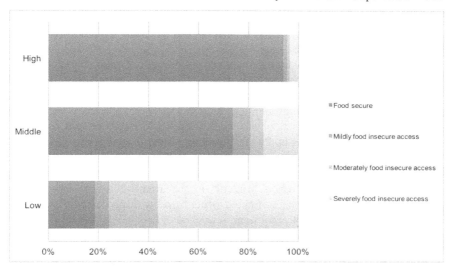

Figure 11.6 Levels of food insecurity by income terciles, 2014.
Source: Hungry Cities Partnership.

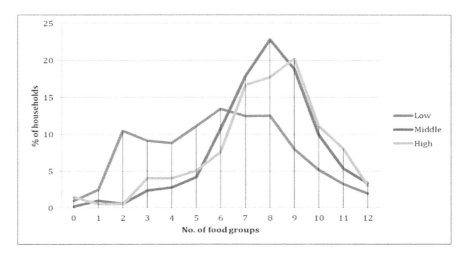

Figure 11.7 Household dietary diversity by income terciles, 2014.
Source: Hungry Cities Partnership.

issues of food affordability from food preference. In other words, is the fact that people cannot afford to eat the foods they prefer purely responsible for unhealthy eating? This is certainly the view of Temple and Steyn (2009; 2011) who saw food prices as the primary barrier to healthy patterns of eating (and by extension to the creation of attitude-related food deserts where people cannot eat what they prefer). Alternatively, are attitudes and preferences themselves actually changing and being reshaped by broader forces such as the so-called 'nutrition transition' towards unhealthy high-fat, energy-dense diets?

Temple et al. (2006) compared the food preferences of high school students from different socio-economic areas of Cape Town and found that food was brought to school by 41–56 per cent of students and that 69 per cent purchased food at, or near, the school. Students from high socio-economic areas were twice as likely to bring food to school although 'unhealthy' foods brought to school outnumbered 'healthy' ones by 2 to 1. Amongst students who purchased food at school, 70 per cent purchased no healthy items at all. Students were aware of what foods were healthy and unhealthy, yet continued to purchase unhealthy foods. A separate study of primary school students in the area found that most of the lunchboxes brought to school contained white bread with processed meat, while the most frequent purchases at, or near, school comprised chips (french fries) and crisps (chips) (Abrahams et al. 2011). These studies are only indicative and focus on only one population group, but they do indicate that preferences for unhealthy foods are strong amongst the young. In other words, in terms of attitude-related food deserts, it is not so much prejudice against healthy foods as preference for unhealthy foods that is characteristic. Steyn and Labadarios (2011) further show that there is a growing preference for fast foods amongst poor South African urban consumers, a phenomenon that Igumbor et al. (2012) attribute to the growing advertising clout of 'big food'.

Changing climates in the food deserts

Understanding the impacts of climate change on urban food security is a conceptual and methodological challenge, 'not least because climate change is a long-term event whereas food security – particularly for poor households – is an immediate and daily concern' (Frayne et al. 2014: 26). There are at least three ways, however, in which this connection can be made: first, a climate-change-induced reduction in agricultural production and productivity may increase food prices and market volatility (which affects food availability, accessibility and stability (Frayne et al. 2014: 28).

Secondly, urban and peri-urban food production losses may result in direct household food supply shocks and local price increases (affecting food availability, accessibility, stability and utilization). Much of Cape Town's fresh vegetable supply, for example, comes from a farming area within the city, the Philippi Horticultural Area (PHA) (Brown-Luthango 2015). The PHA is already under intense pressure from developers wishing to transform the area into housing estates. Longer-term, if the developers are unsuccessful, climate change could well impact on the volume of fresh produce emanating from the area, which would necessitate the import of more expensive substitutes from up-country and overseas.

Thirdly, climate change and associated extreme weather events could mean damage to capital assets that promote food security, affecting accessibility and utilization (Cartwright et al. 2012; Frayne et al. 2014). Cape Town is highly exposed to such extreme events (severe flooding in informal settlements is now a regular winter rainfall occurrence) which can quickly erode capital assets such as shelter, and put even greater pressure on the household food budget of residents of urban food deserts (Battersby 2014; Joubert 2013). Levels of food insecurity were already higher amongst households in informal shacks than formal housing, even in the same area. And it is informal housing that is more likely to be damaged or destroyed during heavy rains.

In the remainder of this section, we examine the first of these three impacts, that is, how climate change affects agricultural systems far removed from the city, which then significantly reduces the food security of residents of Cape Town's food deserts. Southern Africa has seen a warming trend, consistent with global temperature rises, along with a greater frequency of below-normal rainfall years, with a higher number of drought years in the last few decades (Bellprat *et al.* 2015; Ziervogel and Frayne 2011). In 2015 and early 2016, Southern Africa's high-productivity commercial farming areas were ravaged by the most severe drought in decades. Food prices began to rise precipitously. In Cape Town, vegetables cost 21 per cent more and fruit 13 per cent more than they had a year previously. The cost of the staple foods relied on by low-income households was also marching upwards. The cost of potatoes, for example, had more than doubled (Dentlinger 2016). The full impact of the drought on the urban poor will require systematic research, although reports have already begun to emerge of changes in purchasing patterns towards lower-cost, less-healthy processed foods (Dentlinger and Dano 2016), and hungry children (some as young as three) begging in the streets for money to buy chips (McCain 2016).

As a possible clue to impacts, it is worth examining what happened in Cape Town during the last sudden and dramatic round of food price increases in 2007–8. There is now a large body of literature examining the causes and impact of the 2007–8 global food price crisis on Africa (Verpoorten *et al.* 2013). In Cape Town, food inflation between October 2007 and October 2008 reached 17 per cent, almost 5 per cent higher than the general rate of inflation (Battersby 2012b). The AFSUN survey in late 2008 asked households in the three low-income areas of the city about the impact of the food price increases. Seventy-six per cent said that their economic conditions had deteriorated in the previous year and only 11 per cent said that they had improved. Households were also asked if they had gone without food due to food price increases, and how frequently. Eleven per cent had gone without every day, 35 per cent more than once a week and 35 per cent about once a month. Only 28 per cent were unaffected. The other common response to food price increases was to adjust consumption patterns. Dietary diversity declined as households focused on purchase and consumption of energy-dense, high-carbohydrate foodstuffs.

Conclusion

This chapter has argued that, suitably modified and nuanced, the concept of the urban food desert is applicable to Cape Town's low-income areas. While a more detailed mapping of the geography of these food deserts is a task for the future, the three areas of the city surveyed by AFSUN in 2008 certainly fit the standard definition of food deserts, as well as the Africa-centric definition proposed by Battersby and Crush (2014). In addition, there is sufficient evidence from the 2013 HCP survey to suggest that food deserts extend across the low-income areas of the whole city. Where we break from the Euro-American research literature is in decentring the role of supermarkets in defining the absence and presence of food deserts. Most poor households in Cape Town purchase food at supermarkets and this trend will only intensify as supermarkets spread their reach into low-income areas.

However, access to supermarkets certainly does not eliminate food deserts in Cape Town. These are areas of severe food insecurity and low dietary diversity, with heavy dependence on a limited range of foods of high calorific value but low nutritional value. In explaining the reasons for the city's food deserts, the chapter draws on Shaw's (2006) typology of food deserts. Most of Cape Town's food deserts fit the proposed assets-related definition since it is the absence or shortage of assets that forces households into a state of chronic insecurity. However, there is some evidence that a redefined attitudes-related definition also has purchase, particularly if the emphasis is placed on preferences (both for healthy foods that are inaccessible, and accessible but unhealthy foods that are rich in salt and fat) rather than prejudices.

The underlying assumption in much of the Euro-American food deserts literature is that these are dynamic spaces, expanding and contracting with the advent and withdrawal of supermarkets. As we have argued, to tie such dynamism purely to the spatial behaviour of formal food retail outlets is both extremely narrow and inappropriate in the African context. At the same time, it is important not to lose sight of the fact that food deserts as defined here for cities like Cape Town are not static either. It is just that the drivers of change, of the intensification and amelioration of food insecurity are different. This chapter essentially provides a snapshot of the nature of Cape Town's urban food deserts in 2008. However, this provides little insight into one of the major potential drivers of transformation and the entrenching of food deserts, that is, climate change. Extrapolating from data on household responses to food price shocks in 2008, it is abundantly clear that, in the absence of appropriate adaptation strategies, climate change and associated extreme weather events are likely to have an increasingly negative impact on all dimensions of food insecurity in the African city.

Acknowledgements

We wish to acknowledge the support of the Social Sciences and Humanities Research Council (SSHRC) and the International Development Research Centre (IDRC) for their support of the Hungry Cities Partnership research.

References

Abrahams, Z., de Villiers, A., Steyn, N., Fourie, J., Dalais, L., Hill, J., Draper, C., and Lambert, E. (2011) 'What's in the Lunchbox? Dietary Behaviour of Learners from Disadvantaged Schools in the Western Cape, South Africa', *Public Health Nutrition*, 14(10):1752–1758.

Apparicio, P., Cloutier, M. and Sheamur, R. (2007) 'The Case of Montreal's Missing Food Deserts: Evaluation of Accessibility to Food Supermarkets', *International Journal of Health Geographics*, 6:4.

Battersby, J. (2011) *The State of Urban Food Insecurity in Cape Town* Urban Food Security Series No. 11. Cape Town: AFSUN.

Battersby, J. (2012a) 'Beyond the Food Desert: Finding Ways to Speak about Urban Food Security in South Africa', *Geografiska Annaler Series B* 94(2): 141–159.

Battersby, J. (2012b) 'Urban Food Security and Climate Change: A System of Flows' in B. Frayne, C. Moser and G. Ziervogel, (eds.) *Climate Change, Assets and Food Security in Southern African Cities,* London: Earthscan, pp. 35–56.

Battersby, J. and Crush, J. (2014) 'Africa's Urban Food Deserts', *Urban Forum*, 25(2): 143–151.

Battersby, J. and Peyton, S. (2014) 'The Geography of Supermarkets in Cape Town: Supermarket Expansion and Food Access', *Urban Forum*, 25(2): 153–64.

Bellprat, O., Lott, F., Gulizia, C., Parker, H., Pampuch, L., Pinto, I., Ciavarella, A. and Stott, P. (2015) 'Unusual Past Dry and Wet Rainy Seasons over Southern Africa and South America from a Climate Perspective', *Weather and Climate Extremes*, 9: 36–46.

Besharov, D., Bitler, M. and Haider, S. (2010) 'An Economic View of Food Deserts in the United States' *Journal of Policy Analysis and Management*, 30(1):153–176.

Bilinsky, P. and Swindale, A. (2007) *Months of Adequate Household Food Provisioning (MAHFP) for Measurement of Household Food Access: Indicator Guide*. Washington, D.C.: Food and Nutrition Assistance Project, Academy for Education Development.

Brown-Luthango, M. (ed.) (2015) *State/Society Synergy in Philippi, Cape Town*, Cape Town: African Centre for Cities.

Caesar, M. and Crush, J. (2015) 'Cape Town's Urban Food Deserts' Paper presented at Commonwealth Geographical Bureau Workshop, Kingston, Jamaica, 14–16 April 2015.

Cartwright, A., Parnell, S., Oelofse, G. and Ward, S. (eds.) (2012) *Climate Change at the City Scale: Impacts, Mitigation and Adaptation in Cape Town*, London: Routledge.

Coats, J., Swindale, A. and Bilinsky, P. (2007) *Household Food Insecurity Access Scale (HFIAS) for Measurement of Food Access: Indicator Guide (Version 3)*. Washington D.C.: Food and Nutrition Technical Assistance Project, Academy for Educational Development.

Crush, J. and Frayne, B. (2011) 'Urban Food Insecurity and the New International Food Security Agenda', *Development Southern Africa*, 28(4): 527–544.

Crush, J., Hovorka, A. and Tevera, D. (2011) 'Food Security in Southern African Cities: the Place of Urban Agriculture', *Progress in Development Studies*, 11(4): 285–305.

Cummins, S. and McIntyre, S. (2002) 'Food Deserts: Evidence and Assumption in Health Policy-Making', *British Medical Journal*, 325(7361): 436–438.

Dakor, E. (2012) 'Exploring the Fourth Wave of Supermarket Evolution: Concepts of Value and Complexity in Africa', *International Journal of Managing Value and Supply Chains*, 3: 25–37.

Dentlinger, L. and Dano, Z. (2016) 'Mother of Two Forced to Leave Groceries at Till', *Cape Argus* 24 March 2016. Available at: www.iol.co.za/news/south-africa/western-cape/mother-of-two-forced-to-leave-groceries-at-till-2001283.

FAO (2002) *The State of Food Insecurity in the World 2001*, Rome: FAO.

Frayne, B., Battersby-Lennard, J., Fincham, R. and Haysom, G. (2009) 'Urban Food Security in South Africa: Case Study of Cape Town, Msunduzi and Johannesburg', Development Planning Division Working Paper Series No.15. Midrand, South Africa: DBSA.

Frayne, B., Pendleton, W., Crush, J., Acauah, B., Battersby-Lennard, J., Bras, E., Chiweza, A., Dlamini, T., Fincham, R., Kroll, F., Leduka, C., Mosha, A., Mulenga, C., Mvula, P., Pomuti, A., Raimundo, I., Rudolph, M., Ruysenaar, S., Simelane, N., Tevera, D., Tsoka,

M., Taawodzera, G. and Zanamwe, L. (2010) *The State of Urban Food Insecurity in Southern Africa. Urban Food Security Series No. 2.* Cape Town: AFSUN.

Frayne, B., Moser, C. and Ziervogel, G. (eds.) (2012) Climate Change, Assets and Food Security in Southern African Cities, London: Earthscan.

Frayne, B., McCordic, C. and Shilomboleni, H. (2014) 'Growing Out of Poverty: Does Urban Agriculture Contribute to Household Food Security in Southern African Cities?', Urban Forum, 25(2): 177–189.

Gartin, M. (2012) 'Food Deserts and Nutritional Risk in Paraguay', *American Journal of Human Biology*, 24(3): 296–301.

Ghosh-Dastidar, B., Cohen, D., Hunter, G., Zenk, S., Huang, C., Beckman, R. and Dubowitz, T. (2014), 'Distance to Store, Food Prices, and Obesity in Urban Food Deserts', *American Journal of Preventive Medicine* 47(5): 587–595.

Gordon, C., Purciel-Hill, M., Ghai, N., Kaufman, L., Graham, R. and Van Wye, G. (2011) 'Measuring Food Deserts in New York City's Low-Income Neighborhoods', *Health and Place*, 17(2): 696–700.

Guy, C., Clarke, G. and Eyre, H. (2004) 'Food Retail Change and the Growth of Food Deserts: a Case Study of Cardiff', *International Journal of Retail and Distribution Management*, 32(2): 72–88.

Igumbor, E., Sanders, D., Puoane, T., Tsolekile, L., Schwarz, C., Purdy, C., Swart, R., Durao, S. and Hawkes, C. (2012), '"Big Food", the Consumer Food Environment, Health, and the Policy Response in South Africa', *PLoS Medicine*, 9(7): 1–7.

Jiao, J., Moudon, A., Ulmer, J., Hurvitz, P. and Drewnowski, A. (2012) 'How to Identify Food Deserts: Measuring Physical and Economic Access to Supermarkets in King County, Washington', *American Journal of Public Health* 102(10): e32–e39.

Joubert, L. (ed.) (2013) *Rising Waters: Working Together on Cape Town's Flooding*, Cape Town: African Centre for Cities.

Larsen, K. and Gilliland, J. (2008) 'Mapping the Evolution of "Food Deserts" in a Canadian City: Supermarket Accessibility in London, Ontario, 1961–2005', *International Journal of Health Geographics*, 7(1): 16.

McCain, N. (2016) 'Kids Begging Out of Hunger', People's Post 23 February 2016.

Martin, K., Ghosh, D., Page, M., Wolff, M., McMinimee, K. and Zhang, M (2014) 'What Role do Local Grocery Stores Play in Urban Food Environments? A Case Study of Hartford-Connecticut', *PLoS One* 9 (4): e94033.

Mead, M. (2008) 'The Sprawl of Food Deserts', *Environmental Health Perspectives* 116(8): A335.

Nickanor, N. (2013) 'Food Deserts and Household Food Insecurity in the Informal Settlements of Windhoek, Namibia', Ph.D. Thesis, University of Cape Town, Cape Town.

Peyton, S., Moseley, W. and Battersby, J. (2015) 'Implications of Supermarket Expansion on Urban Food Security in Cape Town, South Africa' *African Geographical Review* 34(1): 36–54.

Popkin, B., Adair, L. and Ng, S. (2012) 'Global Nutrition Transition and the Pandemic of Obesity in Developing Countries', *Nutrition Reviews*, 70(1): 3–21.

Poulsen, M., McNab, P., Clayton, M. and Neff, R. (2015) 'A Systematic Review of Urban Agriculture and Food Security Impacts in Low-Income Countries', *Food Policy*, 55: 131–146.

Reardon, T., Timmer, C., Barrett, C. and Berdegue, J. (2003) 'The Rise of Supermarkets in Africa, Asia and Latin America', *American Journal of Agricultural Economics*, 85(5): 1140–1146.

Russell, S. and Heidkamp, C. (2011) 'Food Desertification: The Loss of a Major Supermarket in New Haven, Connecticut', *Applied Geography*, 31(4): 1197–1209.

Shaw, H. (2006) 'Food Deserts: Towards the Development of a Classification', *Geografiska Annaler: Series B*, 88(2): 231–247.

Steyn, N. and Labadarios, D. (2011) 'Street Foods and Fast Foods: How Much do South Africans of Different Ethnic Groups Consume?', *Ethnicity and Disease*, 21(4): 462–466.

Swindale, A. and Bilinsky, P. (2006) 'Development of a Universally Applicable Household Food Insecurity Measurement Tool: Process, Current Status, and Outstanding Issues', *Journal of Nutrition*, 136: 1449S–1452S.

Temple, N. and Steyn, N. (2009) 'Food Prices and Energy Density as Barriers to Healthy Food Patterns in Cape Town, South Africa', *Journal of Hunger & Environmental Nutrition*, 4(2): 203–13.

Temple, N. and Steyn, N. (2011) 'The Cost of a Healthy Diet: A South African Perspective', *Public Health Nutrition*, 14(10): 1752–1758.

Temple, N., Steyn, N., Myburgh N. and Nel, J. (2006) 'Food Items Consumed by Students Attending Schools in Different Socioeconomic Areas in Cape Town, South Africa', *Nutrition* 22 (2006): 252–258.

Verpoorten, M., Arora, A., Stoop. N. and Swinnen, J. (2013) 'Self-Reported Food Insecurity in Africa During the Food Price Crisis', *Food Policy*, 39: 51–63.

Walker, R., Keane, C. and Burke, J. (2010) 'Disparities and Access to Healthy Food in the United States: a Review of Food Deserts Literature', *Health and Place*, 16(5): 876–884.

Wrigley, N. (2002) '"Food Deserts" in British Cities: Policy Context and Research Priorities', *Urban Studies*, 39(11): 2029–2040.

Ziervogel, G. and Frayne, B. (2011) *Climate Change and Food Security in Southern African Cities, Urban Food Security Series No. 8*, Cape Town: AFSUN.

12 Food insecurity in the context of climate change in Maputo City, Mozambique

Challenges and coping strategies

Inês M. Raimundo

Introduction

The impacts of climate change that have been experienced in Maputo in recent decades include more intense weather events, such as droughts and tropical cyclones, resulting in flooding and major coastal erosion. Floods and disease epidemics dominated the last decades of the twentieth century and the early years of the twenty-first century. As a consequence, the country has been in the constant grip of disasters and emerging new climatic cycles. The National Institute of Disaster Management[1] (INGC 2011) stated that historical records of natural disasters show that there were 10 drought events, 20 flood events, 13 tropical cyclones, 1 earthquake and 18 disease epidemics in Mozambique between 1956 and 2008. The significant increase in the number of natural disasters occurred from the 1980s, including three major cyclones in a single year (2000). Amongst the impacts of such events, Maputo now suffers effects on food production and distribution, together resulting in critical conditions associated with water and food scarcity.

Literature on the relationship between climate change and food security emphasizes the risks and challenges to human society. Frayne *et al.* (2012) stated that climate change is one of the major challenges of this era that threatens food security. Together, climatic hazards and food insecurity undermine poverty-reduction programmes and could undo decades of development efforts. What the literature does not emphasize is the strategy that people under threat of disaster employ to ensure their survival. In this regard, Raimundo (2011) stressed the point that natural disasters destroy the assets of the poorest segment of the population, as well as create conditions for itinerant livelihoods based in the informal sector and dependency on food aid. In these circumstances, city dwellers are the most affected as access to land for agriculture is more difficult and the only survival strategy is through engaging in informal trade.

The UN Food and Agricultural Organization (FAO), the International Fund for Agricultural Development (IFAD) and the World Food Programme (WFP) (2014) stated food security to be a state when all people, at all times, have physical, social and economic access to sufficient, safe and nutritious food that meets their dietary needs and food preferences for an active and healthy life. Added to these factors is the important element of cultural preferences, prejudices and beliefs; the availability and accessibility of some specific foods condition whether or not a community perceives themselves to be food secure. Different communities across Mozambique have their own definition of being food secure. For instance, people of Chicualacula district in Gaza province (southern Mozambique) understand food security to be a situation when they can access *chicutsa* (*Combretun molle*) and *cacana* (*Momordica balsamica*); the people of Nampula (northern Mozambique) define food security according to their access to *caracata* (flour made of dried cassava); and Zambézia (Central region) is highly dependent on *mucapata* (a dish made of rice, beans and coconut). For people living in the city of Maputo, the perception of food security depends on access to fish, rice and maize. Against this background, the FAO's definition indicated five elements: availability, accessibility, acceptability and adequacy.

A baseline study conducted in Mozambique in the year 2004 by the Technical Secretariat for Food Security and Nutrition[2] (SETSAN), indicated that 34 per cent of households were suffering from food insecurity and high vulnerability. About 20.3 per cent were classified as highly vulnerable. The causes of food insecurity were related to lack of productive infrastructure, including transport and markets, as well as the isolation of communities (living in remote areas), and low income that limited the purchase – thus access – to food and basic services. The FAO (2010) stated that Mozambique was still a country that suffered from food insecurity. This situation is aggravated by drought in other parts of Africa since Mozambique is highly dependent on food importation from neighbouring countries. This situation impacts food production and, consequently, food availability, with negative food security outcomes. Since agriculture and fishing depend on natural resources, these activities are affected by the occurrence of extreme weather events. Interviews revealed that fish production had decreased and people were driven to eat more processed food brought by cross-border traders. The debate on food security thus highlights the recognition of the differences that exist in concepts and issues surrounding food production, distribution and scarcity.

The various dimensions of climate change and their impact on food security affect the entire country; from coastal zone to hinterland, Mozambicans have been forced to move out of their homesteads and settle in towns or cities, or even in remote locations, seemingly 'in the middle of nowhere'. In the recent past, people were forced to abandon their homes because of the civil war (1977–92) and currently they are being forced to move out due to the worsening meteorological hazards characterized by destructive and violent cyclones, intense floods and long periods of drought. Without denying the impact of the civil war on reducing food production, nevertheless, the evidence is that the country has become more dependent on food aid due to the impact of floods and cyclones, without the local capacity to solve or mitigate the situation.

Despite economic growth, with an annual average Gross Domestic Product (GDP) above 7 per cent, economic inequalities in Mozambique are high in both rural and urban areas (Pires de Carvalho 2015). It is a country where the human development index is ranked the lowest, both in southern Africa and worldwide. The poverty rate is 57 per cent in rural areas and 50 per cent in urban areas. Apart from the recurrent meteorological disasters associated with cyclones, floods and drought, Mozambique has also regularly suffered from a significantly high rate of HIV (14%) together with its related diseases – tuberculosis, malaria and cholera (UNDP, 2014; INGC 2011).

This chapter presents information from a study that explored the extent to which the people of Maputo responded to the worsening conditions associated with climate change, in particular successive drought, cyclones and floods, and characterized by high levels of vulnerability based on poverty, and precarious livelihoods and conditions of life. Emphasis was placed on how they used their limited assets to devise coping strategies to survive by reducing their vulnerability to the risk of hazards related to climate change.

Maputo City

Maputo City is located on the coastal zone of Mozambique, and is exposed to the risk of cyclones and incursions of seawater resulting in flooding. Central and suburban Maputo extends over an area of 300 km², situated on the banks of five rivers – Incomati, Maputo, Tembe, Umbeluzi and Matola, which flow into Maputo Bay. The city is located in an area of maximum-level tides, causing sea water intrusions. The topographical structure thus favours flooding in the rainy season, with some areas remaining flooded for extended periods. Maputo City is a tropical city marked by a wet and a dry season. The wet season usually occurs between October and April and the dry between May and September. The risk of drought is high in many areas of Mozambique, particularly in the central and southern areas, and this affects over 50 per cent of the population (INGC 2011). The vulnerability of the city is intensified by the fact that its population, mainly poor, is concentrated along the banks of the five rivers which converge in the city.

While the city is under pressure from natural disasters, at the same time it is occupied by people who depend on the informal economy (about 70 per cent of the population), urban agriculture and fishing (15%); another 15 per cent is employed by the state, private sector, and domestic and international agencies (INE[3] 2010). The large number of persons depending on the informal sector for all aspects of their livelihood and assets – including urban agriculture and fishing, as well as housing – is of particular concern in light of climate change.

Maputo's population of 1,120,360 in 2010 was estimated to increase by 3.48 per cent by 2015 (Kihato *et al.* 2012). The population is comprised of a variety of nationalities, chiefly Portuguese (22%), other Africans (47%), as well as Indians, Pakistanis and others (31%) (INE 2010: 33). The languages spoken by Maputo's inhabitants thus represent these nationalities. This population mainly consists of inbound migrants who established themselves in informal settlements in the most hazardous of locations (Raimundo and Frayne 2012). Livelihoods mix rural and urban characteristics as people change from rural to urban ways of living upon moving to the city. The migrants move into urban-style informal activities from previous livelihoods based on agriculture in the Infulene Basin and fishing in the vicinity of Maputo Bay, or more distant coastal areas (Kihato *et al.* 2012).

Maputo contributed 20.2 per cent to national GDP in 2010, chiefly based on trade, transport, communication and manufacturing industries (INE 2010). Most of the population of Maputo City live under poor conditions; approximately 70 per cent without proper sanitation, some sited in swamps or on slopes, and these locations, together with poor infrastructure and basic services, expose people to a range of environmental and health risks. Nevertheless, poverty rates went down from 69.4 per cent in 2002–2003 to 54.7 per cent in 2008–2009 (Matusse 2009); MPD-DNE[4] and CAP[5] 2010; van den Boom 2011). This reduction in poverty was principally due to an increase in employment in the formal economy (Raimundo *et al.* 2014). However, 9.8 per cent of the population is illiterate.

Food insecurity in Maputo in the context of climate change

The study sites and method

The sample of households was drawn from the so-called 'reed wards' (where dwellings are constructed from reeds), as distinct from the 'cement wards' of rich households (Mozambique Census of Population 2007). There were seven study areas identified in Maputo, in localities settled by migrants and where the population was categorized as 'poor' and 'poorest' in the 3rd National Poverty Assessment (2008/09). A questionnaire survey was carried out and included 397 households, of which 192 were male-headed and 205 female-headed. The sample was designed to select households by the sex of household head with the objective of assessing gendered differences in household food insecurity. In each study area, between two and five households were interviewed in depth and their life histories recorded. The quantitative data obtained from the survey were complemented by qualitative information from interviews conducted with a selection of households.

The scale of food insecurity

There are different perceptions of food security or insecurity and climate change, and most respondents in the study of Maputo did not connect the changes in climate with food prices, food availability and food accessibility. Interviewees indicated their perceptions of food security or insecurity as: something related to hunger; uncertainty about what and when they will have food or enough food to eat; about the future, and whether they will have food the following day, or following weeks or months; about the status of the stomach, and whether it is full or empty; about access to food [chiefly cost] that they used to eat while young; about where to buy food, whether from the supermarket, informal market, or receiving it from anyone. From the views expressed about people's understanding of food security, the existence of different levels of food security and insecurity was evident.

The 2008 African Food Security Urban Network (AFSUN)[6] survey indicated that people worried most about not eating the kinds of food they preferred because of lack of resources (62.2%), followed by those who said that in the last month they ate a limited variety of foods due to a lack of resources (58.5%), followed by those who said that they had been worried that their household would not have enough food to eat during the previous month (55.8%), had eaten foods they did not want because of a lack of resources to obtain other types of food (51.6%), had eaten smaller meals than they needed because there was not enough food (46.7%) and had eaten fewer meals in a day because there was not enough food (45.0%). Meanwhile, when it came to the question: 'In the last month, did you eat food of any kind because of a lack of resources to obtain food?' the result was surprising since only 20.9% said 'yes'. The question: 'Did you go to sleep hungry because there was not enough food?' resulted in 16.5% answering 'yes'; and to the question, 'Did you go a whole day and night without anything?' (9.6%) said 'yes'.

The cost of food in the context of food insecurity

Based on the responses of persons in the AFSUN survey to which reference was made above, it was found that households spent most of their income on fuel (18.0%), utilities (17.8%), food and groceries (16.1%), education (12.3%), transportation (11.3%) and medical expenses (10.7%). Other expenses incurred were for home-based domestic help (4.1%), savings (1.8%), goods purchased for sale (1.6%), funerals (1.5%), debt service or repayment (1.5%), housing (1.3%), remittances (1.0%) and insurance (0.7%). It was evident that people spent less on food compared with other necessities. Some households received food from relatives living in rural areas, others as remittances from migrants who worked in South Africa. Some persons, especially those located in the Infulene Basin (one of the rivers that lie in Maputo Bay), obtained food, particularly vegetables, from their home gardens.

The main strategies employed for making a living, and which were the means whereby household expenses were met, was chiefly through total dependence on casual labour; self-employment and working from home. Second in frequency was the cultivation of field crops, and other methods included renting space to lodgers, the sale of garden crops, and making and selling crafts. Even though they were poor, no one indicated that they were totally dependent on gifts or begging. However, when it came to secondary means whereby persons made a living, the distribution of activities was slightly different. In this regard, the majority were partially dependent on producing field crops, followed by casual labour, growing garden crops, informal credit, fifth in order was self-employment from home, then keeping livestock, accessing formal credit, selling crafts, and gifts received. Only one person reported being partially dependent on begging, and no one on trading.

Economic conditions and source of food

When asked about their economic conditions compared to the previous year, the majority of respondents (38.0%) said that they were worse off, followed by those who said they had remained the same (29.7%), and others said that they were much worse (11.6%). Meanwhile, there were households in which conditions were reported to have been better (19.1%), and for a few, much better (1.5%).

Additional questions were asked of households in order to assess the sources of food. The majority (34.6%) of respondents purchased food from informal markets, followed by small shops, restaurants or take-away shops (27.4%), supermarkets (8.1%), grew it themselves (7.9%), borrowed food from others (7.0%), and shared meal with neighbours or other households (6.7%). Other responses were that they had received food from neighbours or other households (3.7%), from food aid (0.4%) and a community kitchen (0.1%).

Food prices and access to food

Food prices can be a determining factor in access to food. The severity of the situation is demonstrated by the finding that 31.6 per cent of the sample population purchased food more than once a week, but not as frequently as every day of the week, followed by 22.9 per cent who went without food about once a month, and 3.9 per cent who went without food almost every day. Only 20.6 per cent of households indicated that they never went without food on account of food prices. Those who never went without food because of the price pointed out that, depending on the amount of money that they had (received as gifts, borrowed and earned from an odd job), they could buy anything in informal markets, where all types of food could be obtained at low prices.

Climate change and food insecurity: two faces of the same coin

Changes in the climate have critically affected household food security in various ways, chief amongst which are the meteorological events that have resulted in disasters. For example, tropical cyclones and droughts have resulted in the assets of the poorest segment of the population being destroyed, reducing many people to a state of permanent impoverishment and dependency. Local knowledge of disaster risk reduction, including planting resistant species such as *cacana* (*Momordica balsamica L.*) and cassava, and storing water in jerry cans, were ways of dealing with drought which have been brought by migrants to the city. Moreover, other strategies, including rotating credit systems (*xitique*); burial and church societies, or prayer groups (Mary legions); and land-support cultivating and co-operatives (*N'tsima* and *Xitoco*) helped the poor to reduce their vulnerability.

Turning to the meaning of climate change, interviewed heads of households agreed with the view of one of the respondents that climate change was 'something that changed the weather conditions'. They recalled that going back 30 or 40 years, they could not recall having previously experienced violent cyclones or flooding in the places where they lived, with the exception of Demoina cyclone, which had left major destruction in downtown Maputo. One of the interviewees said that: 'Cyclones and floods used to be occasional phenomena in this city. Recently, recurrent floods have destroyed our hope of living in the city'. Climate change impacts and food production were viewed as being closely interconnected, as reflected in the statement:

Recurrent floods and long periods of drought, such as we have witnessed in these years, have affected the quantity of cabbage as well as the shape of tomatoes. Sometimes there is a lack of rain and other times there is surplus rain. Here in Zona Verde[7] our vegetables are exposed to these weather variations and we cannot have enough to consume and to sell. Our income is really affected. Since we cannot produce, alternatively we should buy in shops. But there is no money.

(Interview respondent)

Coping with food insecurity in Maputo City

Strategies for making a living

The survey (2008) indicated that under various circumstances, city dwellers used different strategies for making a living. The majority (28.0%) of respondents adopted one strategy, followed by those (21.2%) who had adopted two, then three (12.8%) and four or more strategies (11.1%). Meanwhile, 26.7 per cent of respondents declared that they had not employed any new strategy to make a living. These data were supported by interviews where respondents demonstrated which adaptive methods were used to cope with food insecurity. These were urban agriculture, street vending, remittances, informal credit and suburban tourism.

A small number of households lived from urban agriculture carried out in Zona Verde, or on land some distance away, such as in Gaza and Inhambane provinces, both located more than 200 km. from Maputo. On small plots of land, they cultivated onions, tomatoes, cabbages, spinach, spring greens, lettuce and other vegetables. Most of these households farmed as a survival strategy. One of the interviewees said that the challenge they had in Zona Verde was the unavailability of land. There was the additional issue of land tenure as they were given their plots of land during the civil war, or when people had been displaced by the floods in 2000. With population growth, most formerly vacant lands had been used for house construction. Some households, particularly the poorest, did not have land in the city on which to carry out any urban agriculture; therefore, they had to rely either on remittances or informal businesses. Street vending was an important part of the informal economy. Children were sent out by their parents to sell various items including sweets, knick-knacks, boiled eggs and soup so that the family could obtain food to survive.

Many urban households maintained relationships with relatives living in rural areas, from whom they received food. Women survived by being members of the rotating credit association commonly known by *xitique*. This helped them to participate in marketing activities, thereby saving some money to buy food for their households. Some families had taken advantage of living in so-called historical wards such as Mafalala and Xipamanine, where a number of famous persons had grown up. In general, Mafala is settled by poor people who lack several basic services, including sewage disposal and formal housing. It is a neighbourhood settled by Makuwa people from Nampula, a northern Mozambique province where women are known for the *Tufo* dance – a dance performed by women, usually during Islamic festival seasons and holidays. Some families open their houses to tourists who are interested in the local history and enjoy eating local dishes, such as *badjias* (a spiced Indian snack), or participate in the *Tufo* dance.

Conclusion

The study indicated that climate change and, in particular, extreme oscillations in the rainfall over the past three decades, had impacted many aspects of the lives of the people of Maputo, including their food security. The interviews conducted in the AFSUN survey on which the data for this analysis was based, drew attention to people's perceptions of their food status, whether secure or insecure. It was evident that the way in which food security had been affected had more to do with culturally conditioned food preferences than the accessibility of food which would meet their essential dietary needs *per se*.

The food security status of households was also affected by their state of migrancy, conditioned by their relationship with place of origin, the extent to which they received remittances, and exposure to processed food that was brought by cross-border traders and sold in informal markets and on the street. Urban agriculture in Maputo had also been impacted by cyclones and floods. Poor households were pushed to buy food on a daily basis because they did not have enough cash to buy more food than immediately required. Although food was very important, nevertheless, on average, households spent more of their total income on fuel (18.0%) than on food (16.1%). With the increase in food prices, and constant floods or long periods of drought, people were forced to adjust their diet to deal with the new reality. Although they used to eat *cacana* (that grows locally) or fish caught locally, they were more and more driven to eat imported and processed food.

Food security and climatic changes have been demonstrated to be closely interrelated in Maputo. Access to food was dependent on food prices, food availability and some urban food production. In the face of climate variability, the entire food production system was impacted. To avoid hunger or even starvation, the residents of Maputo had adopted several strategies to cope with their vulnerability in terms of food insecurity, especially in terms of their access to food due to price increases. This had included increased reliance on urban agriculture (in the Zonas Verdes), street vending, remittances and urban tourism. However, the level of vulnerability was great and coping strategies are only just maintaining the situation to prevent acute hunger, suggesting that in the face of ongoing climate change, Maputo City dwellers may not even be able to find *cacana*. On reaching that stage, they will definitely regard themselves as being absolutely 'food insecure'.

Notes

1 Instituto Nacional de Gestão das Calmidades (INGC) - National Institute for National Disaster Management.
2 Secretariado Técnico de Segurança Alimentar e Nutricional (SETSAN) Technical Secretariat for Food Security and Nutrition.

3 Instituto Nacional de Estatitisca (INE) National Statistics Institute.
4 Ministerio da Planificação e Desenvolvimento – Direcção Nacional de Economia (NPD) Ministry of Planning and Development – National Directorate of Economy.
5 Centro de Análise de Políticas (CAP) Cente for Policy Analysis.
6 This study results from African Food Security Urban Network (AFSUN) household survey and interviews with heads of households (2008).
7 Zona Verde (Green Zones) is a farm belt where families grow vegetables. Historically, these areas were reserved as a green belt to the west of Maputo City, to supply Maputo with vegetables. With the worsening civil war, this agricultural area was used for construction of houses.

References

FAO (2010) Global Forest Resources Assessment 2010, Main Report, Rome: FAO.
FAO, IFAD and WFP (2014) The State of Food Insecurity in the World: Strengthening the Enabling Environment for Food security and Nutrition, Rome: FAO.
Frayne, B., Moser, C. and Ziervogel, G (2012) 'Understanding the Terrain: The Climate Change, Assets and Food Security Nexus in Southern African Cities', in B. Frayne, C. Moser and G. Ziervogel (eds.) Climate Change, Assets and Food Security in Southern African Cities, New York: Earthscan, pp. 1–34.
INE (Instituto Nacional de Estatitisca/National Statistics Institute) (2010) III Recenseamento Geral da População e Habitação 2007 – Indicadores Sócio-demográficos (III General Census of Population and Housing 2007 – Socio-Demographic Indicators), Maputo: INE.
INGC (Instituto Nacional de Gestão das Calamidades) (2011) Atlas for Disaster Preparedness and Response in the Zambezi Basin, USAID/FEWS NET, Anaconda Press.
Kihato, C., Royston, L., Raimundo, J. and Raimundo, I. (2012) 'Multiple Land Regimes: Rethinking Land Governance in Maputo's Peri-Urban Spaces', Urban Forum, Volume 24 (1).
Matusse, C. (2009) Políticas Públicas de Redução da Pobreza. Ministério da Planificação e Desenvolvimento – Direcção Nacionald de Planificação (Public Policies for Poverty Reduction. Ministry of Planning and Development – National Directorate of Planning). Unpublished report, Maputo: Ministry of Finance and Planning.
Pires de Carvalho, A. (2015) Accelerating Economic Growth and Job Creation to Harness the Demographic Dividend in Mozambique. Unpublished technical report, Maputo: Ministry of Planning and Development.
Raimundo, I. (2011) Population Mobility, Natural Disaster Management in Southern Mozambique and Strategies for Reducing Poverty and Dependency (working paper), Maputo: Department of Geography of the Faculty of Arts and Social Sciences of Eduardo Mondlane University.
Raimundo, I. and Frayne, B. (2012) 'Impacts of Climate Change on Migration and Food Security in Maputo, Mozambique', in B. Frayne, C. Moser and G. Ziervogel', Climate Change, Assets and Food Security in Southern African Cities, New York: Earthscan, pp 96–109.
Raimundo, I. Crush, J. and Pendleton, W. (2014) The State of Food Insecurity in Maputo, Mozambique, Cape Town: Urban Food Security Series No 20.
UNDP (2014) 'Sustaining Human Progress: Reducing Vulnerabilities and Building Resilience', The 2014 Human Development Report, New York: UNDP.

Part IV

Strengthening resilience for enhancing food security in the context of climate change

13 Global biomass rush

Land grabbing, food security and socio-political stability of sub-Saharan Africa

Akunne Okoli

Introduction

The past decade has seen manifold increases in the rate of material resource extraction and consumption. Agriculture biomass – an essential material resource for the global food and energy system – was reported to have accounted for over one-third of global material consumption in 2010 (Krausmann *et al.* 2008; Nonhebel and Kastner 2011). The demand for biomass, which has currently outpaced production, is projected to further double – considering the dramatic changes that have occurred in global socio-economic structures, marked by rapid human population growth, thriving middle classes from emerging economies and the unabated consumerism lifestyle of a global minority (von Braun and Meinzen-Dick 2009; GRAIN *et al.* 2014). Under the current global food and energy scenario characterized by volatile food prices, diet 'meatification', and biofuel imperatives due to climate change, biomass material has come under pressure from intense competing end uses, hence putting commercial pressure on productive lands (Cotula, Dyer, and Vermeulen 2008; Anseeuw *et al.* 2012; GRAIN *et al.* 2014). According to Antonelli *et al.* (2015: 98) 'By 2030, an additional 47 million ha of land will be needed for food and animal feed production, 42–48 million ha for large-scale afforestation and 18–44 million ha for producing biofuel feedstock'.

The global biomass rush is facilitating the expansion of land market liberalization in developing countries where there is a relative abundance of productive arable lands (McMichael 2012; Zoomers 2010). Consequently, investors from industrialized and emerging economies are racing to acquire large tracts of land for the purpose of corporate-led agricultural and industrial plantations with the implicit or written consent of their host governments. The sub-Saharan Africa region has seen the greatest share of lands involved in these acquisitions, with 34.3 million hectares sold or leased since 2000 (Anseeuw *et al.* 2012; GRAIN 2008). This current trend of 'resource extraction by dispossession' is depriving poor rural communities of their right to land and water resources, as well as denying them access to other land-based livelihood strategies such as wood collection, grazing and hunting, upon which their subsistence hinges (Anseeuw *et al.*, 2012; Cotula, Dyer, and Vermeulen 2008; GRAIN *et al.* 2014).

The region of sub-Saharan Africa is no newcomer to land appropriation and forcible dispossession of ordinary people's assets (Alden Wily 2012). The historical antecedents of the Euro-American imperial-style economic scramble of the colonial and post-colonial era are still visible in rural economic development and land relations in Africa. However, the recent race for global farmland is unprecedented in our present time. The extent, character and modalities of occurrence differ quite significantly from what happened in the past. Contemporary land grabbing is now occurring in an era of neoliberal globalization and it is driven by biomass investment projects, with a visible element of state–private interactions, facilitated by a boom in foreign direct investment/FDI (GRAIN et al. 2014; McMichael 2013; Nally 2014b). Most distinctively, the configuration of actors and sectors involved in today's land grab, which is comprised of corporate private sector investors of both foreign and domestic origins, and also inter-regional and intra-regional government actors (Borras et al. 2012; GRAIN et al. 2014), has shifted the traditional bipolarized North–South resource-appropriation relations towards what Margulis et al. referred to as a more polycentric configuration of power and production (2013: 82), with the emergence of BRICS nations as new economic nerve centres of global capital, thus producing a North–South–South dimension to resource exploitation and control.

It is important to note that not all investments in large-scale land acquisitions are regarded as land grabs. For the sake of clarity, the International Land Coalition (ILC) report identifies certain key distinctive features that differentiate ordinary land acquisition from land grabbing (Anseeuw et al. 2012: 11). While there is no standard analytical definition of what land grab is, due to the complexity and fluidity of the phenomenon, this paper adopts what is here considered a broader conceptual definition offered by Borras et al., which refers to land grabbing as:

> the capturing of control of relatively vast tracts of land and other natural resources through a variety of mechanisms and forms involving large-scale capitals that often shifts resource use to that of extraction, whether for international or domestic purposes, as capital's response to the convergence of food, energy and financial crisis, climate change mitigation imperatives and demands for resources from newer hubs of global capital.

(2012: 851)

Given the opacity and intricate modalities of these deals, it is quite difficult to ascertain the exact amount, in hectares, of land that has been acquired in sub-Saharan Africa (Odhiambo 2011). With limited access to reliable data, estimations vary from one report account to another. A regional report on the African perspective by Odhiambo (2011) claimed that as of 2009, there were already transactions of over 20 million hectares of land in 15 countries across Africa. The ILC report in 2012 stated that of the 71 million hectares of land successfully verified as concluded transfer deals between 2000 and 2010, 66 per cent of them were in sub-Saharan Africa (Anseeuw et al. 2012). The World Bank report claims that approximately 56.6 million hectares in 464 projects were announced before the end of 2009, with two-thirds of deals in sub-Saharan Africa (Deininger and Byerlee 2011). Despite variations in the number of hectares involved, the estimates from various land grab reports underscore the reality of the pace and scale of this disturbing trend.

An emerging body of literature attributes the land grab phenomenon to the concatenation of various factors. The prevailing narrative centres on the global food, energy and financial crisis of 2008 (Anseeuw *et al.* 2012; Cotula 2009; GRAIN *et al.* 2014; GRAIN 2008; von Braun and Meinzen-Dick 2009; Deininger and Byerlee 2011). However, recent literature has explored the phenomenon from a broader dynamism of political, economic and social change using various paradigmatic approaches (Fairbairn 2015; GRAIN *et al.* 2014; Margulis, McKeon and Borras Jr. 2013; Nally 2014a; McMichael 2013; Lavers 2012; Robertson and Pinstrup-Andersen 2010; Zoomers 2010; Borras Jr. *et al.* 2011). The expansion of land grabbing in sub-Saharan Africa has evoked controversial debates amongst policy makers, mainstream development actors, economists, civil society organizations and environmental and social movements, with critics calling it a recolonization of Africa. Arguments from policy makers and mainstream international development actors centre on the food security discourse, which of course presents a social reality in sub-Saharan Africa within which the discursive elements of land grab operations are circumscribed, and the phenomenon somewhat justified. Within this context, land grabbing is framed as 'corporate land investment' seen to offer an economic opportunity that will forge development and solve Africa's hunger crisis and ensure global food security (Deininger and Byerlee 2011; UNCTAD 2009). Also central to mainstream thinking on the land grab debate is the emphasis on transitioning to a bio-based economy as a sustainable alternative to the current fossil-run global economy in the face of climate change threat – a vision that is driving today's global biomass rush.

On the other side of the land grab debate, transnational agrarian movements (La via Campesina, civil society groups), NGOs, social and environmental justice movements, as well as other critics of land grab, have raised legitimate concerns regarding the socio-economic and environmental cost of this phenomenon. Their argument stems from the point of livelihood sustenance, food sovereignty, social justice and environmental sustainability (Ambalam 2014; Cotula, Dyer and Vermeulen 2008; GRAIN *et al.* 2014). According to the Ejolt report no. 10, '… evidence shows clearly that land grabs are undermining local food security and land rights, while displacing thousands of families from their homes and livelihoods' (GRAIN *et al.* 201411). The vast majority of the rural communities are smallholder farmers who cultivate these lands for their livelihood and sustenance. Contrary to the optimistic and often unrealized promise of fair compensation, employment and productivity gains presumed to ensure food security, testimonials of victims from various case studies suggest that these land investments are impacting negatively on their well-being as tales of expulsion, dispossession and evictions have been recorded (see GRAIN *et al.* 2014 and Anseeuw *et al.* 2012).

Against this backdrop, this chapter builds on the synthesis of existing literature to examine the nexus between the expansion of land grab, food security and socio-political stability in sub-Saharan Africa. A brief discussion of land grabbing as an aspect of a broader neoliberal agrarian restructuring drive is presented. Further, the legitimacy of the development objective underlying propositions of large-scale agricultural investment as the gateway to poverty reduction, rural development and realization of food security and nutritional goals, is brought under scrutiny. This chapter argues that the promotion of corporate, export-led agricultural production that is based on intensification and mono-cropping, exacerbates global food inequality and hence undermines regional food security in sub-Saharan Africa. In the absence of clearly defined land tenure rights, good governance, rule of law, or strong legal and institutional frameworks to enforce existing regulations, the current mode of large-scale acquisitions of agricultural lands in sub-Saharan Africa poses a direct threat to the sustainable livelihoods of rural communities. This will further deepen social inequities and trigger social conflicts which are inimical to rural development and will have an adverse impact on the overall stability of sub-Saharan Africa.

Framing the global land grab as an element of neoliberal agrarian reform

The ongoing contemporary land grab is beyond the food-crisis-centred narrative that has often dominated the discourse as it has a combined element of market-led resource control, capital accumulation drive and expansion of capitalist agro-industrial production (Borras and Franco 2010; Zoomers 2010). The neoliberal market-led economic policies characterized by capitalist hegemonic socio-political property and power relations offers an epistemological insight into the politics of the ongoing contemporary land grabbing in sub-Saharan Africa. Within the prevailing model of neoliberal economic growth and development strategy, trade liberalization and foreign direct investments are strongly propagated as a means to stimulate economic growth and forge rural development in the southern hemisphere (Borras and Franco 2010; Nally 2014b; McMichael 2012).

For this purpose, the World Bank, under its agriculture and rural development assistance programme, is vigorously promoting the market-led agrarian reform (MLAR) policy framework as part of a broader neoliberal agrarian restructuring drive towards modernizing the agricultural sector of developing economies (Lahiff, Borras Jr, and Kay 2007; Akram-Lodhi 2007; Deininger 2003). The MLAR – an offshoot of the failed 1980s–1990s IMF/World Bank structural adjustment programme – is predicated on what Akram-Lodhi (2007: 438) describes as a 'willing buyer, willing seller model in which market-facilitated and price-mediated transactions are undertaken to generate improvements in economic efficiency and social welfare'. The overarching aim rests on the assumption that the liberalization of food and agricultural markets will inevitably lead to a more efficient and productive use of land resources, thereby achieving the much-needed industrialization of the traditional agricultural system of developing countries, alleviate rural poverty and lead to rural development (Deininger 2003; Wolford 2007).

Consequently, institutional restructuring of the agricultural sector in developing countries towards neoliberal ascendancy has become a major mainstream development policy agenda (Akram-Lodhi 2007). This has seen rapid integration of land as a commodity into the cash market economy under the legal frameworks regulating international trade and FDI (Zoomers 2010; McMichael 2013). In line with this economic imperative, and to create a conducive investment atmosphere that will advance global capitalist agricultural production, sub-Saharan African governments, particularly those saddled with the burden of foreign debt, have adopted a developmental state that entails the privatization and commercialization of their rural economy to attract both private and foreign investors (Robertson and Pinstrup-Andersen 2010).

By treating land resources as purely a factor of production, the neoliberal market-oriented-driven land investments are insensitive to the dynamic socio-cultural relations embedded in land transfers (Akram-Lodhi 2007); hence, it undermines the historical underpinnings of customary land ownerships. Much of sub-Saharan Africa's land is under customary tenure arrangements, with only about 2–10 per cent in formal tenure, while some is held collectively as commons or as free holdings (Cotula and Chauveau 2007). The failure to legally legitimize customary tenure and confer statutory right status to communal lands leaves the vast majority of rural farmers in the region at the mercy of community chiefs and the state. They can reallocate or dispose of communal lands at will (usually for profit), without free prior and informed consent; hence, predisposing the locals to economic and social risk. Further, the uncontrolled and unregulated appropriation of poor people's land promotes monopoly of land and associated resources by regional and national elites, domestic corporate investors, local chiefs and agribusinesses. This has created what Akram-Lodhi (2007: 1448-49) refers to as a 'bifurcated agrarian structure that has resulted in the emergence of an export-oriented capitalist sub-sector more closely integrated into the global agro-food system than ever before and more important to the internationalized circuit of capital', while furthering the decline of the subsistence-producing farm sector. Therefore, while the liberalization of the land market under the neoliberal MLAR policy framework has opened up space for global capitalist agricultural production to thrive, it has failed to provide maximum economic security for these vulnerable rural farmers, leaving them disadvantaged. It is within this systemic structure of neoliberal agrarian change, which promotes the commodification of land that grants unhindered access to those with purchasing power, while marginalizing poor rural farmers who work the land, that the ongoing global land rush is subsumed.

The food–security nexus

As various scholars have documented, food security concern is the central focus of the recent surge in agricultural land investments (Cotula and Vermeulen 2009; Anseeuw *et al.* 2012; GRAIN *et al.* 2014). Securing the sustainability of global food systems in the face of a growing human population has become a major challenge. The Food and Agricultural Organization (FAO), in its 2012 *State of Food and Agriculture Report*, stressed the urgent need for capital investments in farm lands as a pragmatic strategy to boost productivity yield towards sustainable food security. To meet the task of feeding over 9 billion people on the planet by 2050, a 50 per cent annual increase in agricultural investment to the tune of US$ 209 billion must come from the private sector (FAO 2012). It is important to note that half of the projected population growth will occur in sub-Saharan Africa (Angola, Burundi, Democratic Republic of Congo, Malawi, Mali, Niger, Somalia, Uganda, United Republic of Tanzania and Zambia) and some of these countries are currently dependent on food aid (UN 2015). With shortfalls in developmental aid, governments of these food-insecure nations are rapidly leasing out, granting concessions, or selling off substantial portions of their productive lands to foreign investors in the hope that it will bring rural development and ensure national food security (Lavers 2012; Robertson and Pinstrup-Andersen 2010). These investments are adjudged necessary by claiming that the lands are 'idle, marginally exploited or underutilized' (Deininger and Byerlee 2011). In actuality, these lands are inhabited, farmed, used for livestock grazing, or held under collective rights as commons by rural dwellers and indigenous communities, who exploit the resources for their livelihood. According to Hall (2011), much of the land is utilized by Africa's eighty million small-scale farmers, who supply most of Africa's food needs and produce 30 per cent of its GDP. Therefore, as mainstream development policy makers, national governments, local elites, and industrial food corporations embark on a 'de-peasantization' drive and rural dislocation, under the rhetoric that development of the rural agricultural sector through commercialization holds the solution to global food insecurity, one cannot but question the legitimacy of this development objective. Whose access to food is being secured? Whose interest matters and whose reality counts?

Food security for all or food security for the few?

It has been argued that the imperative of doubling food production through large-scale agriculture as a solution to the global food security threat rests on a faulty premise (Ambalam 2014; Lavers 2012). Food security is dependent upon food accessibility and equitable distribution, not solely availability (Pretty et al. 2003). The world produces enough food to feed everyone, amounting to 17 per cent more food per person than it did 30 years ago (Pingali 2002). Sub-Saharan Africa has remained vulnerable to the threat of food insecurity. In 2014, the region recorded the highest global hunger index (GHI), with a GHI score of 18.2, representing a marginal decrease from the 2013 score of 19.2. Yet, still bedevilled by the socio-economic malaise of poverty, hunger and malnutrition, sub-Saharan Africa has been the region with the highest number of large-scale farmland deals (Odhiambo 2011).

The control of vast tracts of land by global commodity food chains, industrial agribusinesses and financial corporations has birthed a new corporate food and energy regime. This is fast redrawing the agricultural farming map in sub-Saharan Africa and putting regional food security at risk. Data from Land Matrix (2014) indicates that out of the 29 million hectares of land deals in July 2014, only 11 per cent were exclusively used for food crops and these were mostly destined for the export market. The greater proportion was committed to commercially viable agricultural production: non-food crops (35%), followed by flex-crops used for biofuels and animal feed (21%), and cash crops (43%). While these investments may have recorded a boost in agricultural productivity, they failed to ensure an equitable distribution and access to food for the poor and vulnerable groups. According to the ILC report: 'The land and resource rights and livelihoods of rural communities are being put in jeopardy by the prevailing model of large-scale land acquisition' (Anseeuw *et al.* 2012: 1). Agrarian and environmental justice movements, as well as some academic contributors on the food security debate, contend that the promotion of an agricultural model which advances a public-peasant investment partnership will better ensure food sovereignty – which is critical to food security – while also protecting the ecosystem (Tscharntke *et al.* 2012). Similarly, agro-ecological food production by small-scale farmers remains the agricultural model best suited to meeting future food needs (Rosset and Martinez-Torres 2013). The export-oriented capitalist agro-food production practice that characterizes the ongoing global land grab exacerbates global food inequality and is making access to food in sub-Saharan Africa a privilege rather than a right.

Food security or bio-energy security?

Climate change policy intervention and energy security is driving demand and pushing support for increased biofuel and agrofuel production. The United States renewable fuel standard, established in its Energy Policy Act, requires that a 3.5-billion-gallon increase in annual ethanol consumption be reached by 2022, the Kyoto protocol agreement demands a 30 per cent cut in greenhouse gas emissions (GHGs) from developed nations by 2020. Meanwhile, the EU energy policy mandate requires that 10 per cent of its transport energy needs be met from renewable sources, both biofuel and agrofuel, by 2020 (Bailey 2008). These obligations establish a clear market for bio-energy crops which, given the constricted spatial distribution of arable land, would be inevitably met from imports. According to the International Food and Policy Research Institute (IFPRI), China secured 2.8 million hectares of land in the Democratic Republic of the Congo for biofuel-oil palm plantation in July 2007 (Von Braun and Meinzen-Dick 2009). In Mozambique, out of over 2.5 million hectares of land concessions granted to investors between 2004 and 2009, 13 per cent were designated for agrofuels (mainly from the Jatropha plant) and sugar production. An approximate amount of US\$ 513 million was to be invested in 30,000 hectares of land for the cultivation of ethano-producing sugarcane plant in a ProCana project (GRAIN *et al.* 2014). This was a project that threatened to dislocate the local communities in the District of Chókwé south of the Gaza province, had it not been for the stiff confrontational resistance by the community, backed by international NGOs.

A financial paradigm of the food and agricultural sector has shifted production to favour economically viable and profit-maximizing crops as financial interest in agrofuel and biofuel-producing crops has risen. According to Borras *et al.* (2015: 3)

... reconceptualization of agriculture as a source of biomass for a future bioeconomy pushes an agenda that seeks extra flexibilities from mainly non-food biomass in global value chain... biomass denotes renewable raw materials which can be readily decomposed and recomposed in more profitable ways... this places agriculture as oil wells of the 21st century.

The growing competition for land by commercial biofuel and agrofuel biomass feedstock against edible food crops poses great danger to food security in sub-Saharan Africa. Cotula *et al.* (2008: 2) opined that:

> ... rapid spread of commercial biofuel production may result – and is resulting – in poorer groups losing access to the land on which they depend. In this context, the spread of commercial biofuel crop cultivation can have major negative effects on local food security and on the economic, social and cultural dimensions of land use.

It is expected that biofuel production will continue to expand in coming years. This scenario makes land grabbing more of an economic need for profit than a moral imperative obligation for food security (GRAIN *et al.* 2014).

Socio-political stability nexus: looming regional agrarian uprising?

Resource extractivism (oil, minerals and ore, timber and so on) is a major cause of lingering violent conflicts around the globe. Land struggles are rooted in unjust resource-appropriation and inequitable resource-distribution (Wehrmann 2008). The character of the ongoing contemporary land grabbing in sub-Saharan Africa is altering the local economic structures, which for centuries have been ingrained in agrarian practices. Much of the land grabs occur in politically volatile states with weak governance systems, rooted in corruption and a near non-functioning judicial system, where citizens' rights are infringed and their interests hugely underrepresented (Goetz 2015). These unethical land deals are breeding social exclusion, deprivation and marginalization with far-reaching implications for regional socio-political stability. Mabikke (2011) echoes this sentiment, and opined that, considering the crucial role of land for livelihood strategies and poverty reduction, the escalating land grabbing would eventually become the centre of major conflicts and disputes. Similarly, the narrative language of victims of land grab underscores a looming agrarian war. An elder in Omar village, Tana delta, Kenya, was quoted as saying 'everything is in danger. People thought they owned the land. We have been here for hundreds of years. Now we will fight; we are ready to die, for what else is there?' (GRAIN *et al.* 2014).

In addition to the land deals, water sources are appropriated as well, thus exacerbating water scarcity in these rural communities. Communities are responding through various forms of opposition (covert and confrontational resistance, litigation and so forth) against investors and the state, though most of these measures have not been successful (GRAIN *et al.* 2014). Much of the localized opposition is met with the use of brutal force by the state. There have been cases of violent clashes between locals and police and military used by the state to guard leased/sold lands at the request of investors. In the absence of formal tenure rights, litigations are null and void, and hence often turn out to be an exercise in futility. Displacement of rural populations poses a threat to urban security and stability because of conflicts resulting from population movements from rural to urban areas (GRAIN *et al.* 2014). Further, the violent domestic unrest and socio-political instability that rocked North Africa and the Middle East region over the 2008 food crisis (Daniel and Mittal 2009), and the infamous South Korean Daewoo logistics deal that caused the overthrow of a sitting government in Madagascar (Barrett 2013), are reminders of how vulnerable socio-political structures are in situations of exploitation and oppression. Unless a feasible solution is devised and deployed to deal with the growing local and state food insecurity in the face of land grabbing, a new era of perpetual civic unrest in the sub-Saharan African region looms.

Conclusion

There is no gainsaying the fact that the growing population and competing end uses for biomass material will continue to put pressure on land. While investment in agriculture holds the potential to resuscitate sub-Saharan Africa's comatose rural economy, the trajectory and structure of large-scale land investments, as grounded in neoliberal market-led agrarian reform, threatens the food and agricultural system sustainability of rural populations, and hence, their existence. 'Depeasantization' of global food systems in favour of industrial agricultural intensification poses more risks than benefits – the biggest risk being the increase in greenhouse gas emissions from such developments, with major implications for climate change. For centuries, agricultural production systems in developing countries have been built on indigenous knowledge and traditional farming practices, producing generations of skilled smallholder farmers with a wealth of traditional agro-ecosystem knowledge needed to adapt to climate variability (Ambalam 2014). The loss of genetically and biologically diverse indigenous farming knowledge would be a huge loss to the sustainability of the global food system. With the prevalence of poverty, income inequality and weak tenure rights, rural communities will continue to remain powerless and vulnerable with respect to food insecurity. Therefore, any policy intervention targeted at ensuring productive uses of lands must focus on rural farmers in an engaging and participatory manner. Although many case studies have been carried out on the land grab phenomenon, there is a need for a well-developed framework of analysis in order to fully assess, understand, and contest the many dimensions of this phenomenon so as to steer policy in the direction of a sustainable future.

References

Akram-Lodhi, A. H. (2007) 'Land, Markets and Neoliberal Enclosure: An Agrarian Political Economy Perspective', *Third World Quarterly* 28 (8): 1437–1456.

Alden Wily, L. (2012) 'Looking Back to See Forward: The Legal Niceties of Land Theft in Land Rushes', *Journal of Peasant Studies* 39 (3–4): 751–775.

Ambalam, K. (2014) 'Food Sovereignty in the Era of Land Grabbing: An African Perspective', *Journal of Sustainable Development* 7 (2): 121–132.

Anseeuw, W., Alden Wily, L., Cotula, L. and Taylor, M. (2012) *Land Rights and the Rush for Land: Findings of the Global Commercial Pressures on Land Research Projects*. Rome: International Land Coalition.

Antonelli, M., Siciliano, G., Turvani, M. E. and Rulli, M. C. (2015) 'Global Investments in Agricultural Land and the Role of the EU: Drivers, Scope and Potential Impacts', *Land Use Policy* 47: 98–111.

Bailey, R. (2008) 'Another Inconvenient Truth: How Biofuel Policies are Deepening Poverty and Accelerating Climate Change', *Oxfam Policy and Practice: Climate Change and Resilience* 4 (2): 1–58.

Barrett, C. B. (2013) *Food or Consequences: Food Security and its Implications for Global Sociopolitical Stability*, Oxford: Oxford University Press.

Borras, S. M. and Franco, J. (2010) 'Towards a Broader View of the Politics of Global Land Grab: Rethinking Land Issues, Reframing Resistance', Initiatives in Critical Agrarian Studies Working Paper Series 1. Available at: https://www.tni.org/files/Borras%20Franco%20Politics%20of%20Land%20Grab%20v3.pdf.

Borras, S. M., Hall, R., Scoones, I., White, B. and Wolford, W. (2011) 'Towards a Better Understanding of Global Land Grabbing: An Editorial Introduction', *Journal of Peasant Studies* 38 (2): 209–216.

Borras, S. M., Franco, J. C. Gómez, S., Kay, C. and Spoor, M. (2012) 'Land Grabbing in Latin America and the Caribbean', Journal of Peasant Studies 39 (3–4): 845–872.

Cotula, L. (2009) *Land Grab or Development Opportunity?: Agricultural Investment and International Land Deals in Africa.* Publication of International Institute for Environment and Development (ISBN 978-1-84369-741-1).

Cotula, L. and Chauveau, J-P. (2007) *Changes in Customary Land Tenure Systems in Africa.* Publication of International Institute for Environment and Development (ISBN: 978-1-84369-657–5).

Cotula, L. and Vermeulen, S. (2009). 'Deal or No Deal: the Outlook for Agricultural Land Investment in Africa', *International Affairs* 85 (6): 1233–1247+viii.

Cotula, L., Dyer, N. and Vermeulen, S. (2008) *Fueling Exclusion?: the Biofuels Boom and Poor People's Access to Land.* Publication of International Institute for Environment and Development (ISBN: 978-1-84369-702-2).

Daniel, S. and Mittal A. (2009) *The Great Land Grab: Rush for World's Farmland Threatens Food Security for the Poor.* Berkeley, CA: Oakland Institute.

Deininger, K. (2003) 'Land Markets in Developing and Transition Economies: Impact of Liberalization and Implications for Future Reform', *American Journal of Agricultural Economics* 85 (5): 1217–1222.

Deininger, K. W. and Byerlee, D. (2011) *Rising Global Interest in Farmland: Can it Yield Sustainable and Equitable Benefits?* The World Bank, Washington D.C.

Fairbairn, M. (2015) 'Foreignization, Financialization and Land Grab Regulation', *Journal of Agrarian Change* 15 (4): 581–591.

FAO (2012) *The State of Food and Agriculture: Investing for a Better Future.* Available at: www.fao.org/docrep/017/i3028e/i3028e.pdf.

Goetz, A. (2015) 'Pushing the Limits: International Land Acquisitions in Comparative Perspective', Theses and Dissertations (Comprehensive). Paper 1716.

GRAIN (2008) 'Seized! the 2008 Land Grab for Food and Financial Security'. Available at: https://www.grain.org/article/entries/93-seized-the-2008-landgrab-for-food-and-financial-security.

GRAIN, Temper, L., Munguti, S., Matiku, P., Ferreira, H., Soares, W., Firpo Porto, M., Douguet, V., Haas, W. and Mayer, A. (2014) 'The Many Faces of Land Grabbing', *Cases from Africa and Latin America* (No.10) EJOLT Report.

Krausmann, F., Erb, K-H., Gingrich, S., Lauk, C. and Haberl, H. (2008) 'Global Patterns of Socioeconomic Biomass Flows in the Year 2000: a Comprehensive Assessment of Supply, Consumption and Constraints', *Ecological Economics* 65 (3): 471–487.

Lahiff, E., Borras, S. M. Jr, and Kay, K. (2007) 'Market-Led Agrarian Reform: Policies, Performance and Prospects', *Third World Quarterly* 28 (8): 1417–1436.

Land Matrix (2014) 'The Online Public Database on Land Deals'. Available at: www.landmatrix.org/en/.

Lavers, T. (2012) 'Land Grab as Development Strategy? The Political Economy of Agricultural Investment in Ethiopia', *Journal of Peasant Studies* 39 (1): 105–132.

Mabikke, S. B. (2011) 'Escalating Land Grabbing in Post-Conflict Regions of Northern Uganda: a Need for Strengthening Good Land Governance in Acholi Region'. International Conference on Land Grabbing, pp. 6–8.

Margulis, M. E., McKeon, N. and Borras S.M. Jr. (2013) 'Land Grabbing and Global Governance: Critical Perspectives', *Globalizations* 10 (1): 1–23.

McMichael, P. (2012) 'The Land Grab and Corporate Food Regime Restructuring', *Journal of Peasant Studies* 39 (3–4): 681–701.

McMichael, P. (2013) 'Land Grabbing as Security Mercantilism in International Relations', *Globalizations* 10 (1): 47–64.

Margulis, M. E. and Porter, T. (2013) 'Governing the Global Land Grab: Multipolarity, Ideas, and Complexity in Transnational Governance', *Globalizations* 10 (1): 65–86.

Nally, D. (2014a) 'Governing Precarious Lives: Land Grabs, Geopolitics, and "Food Security"', *The Geographical Journal*, 181(4), 340–349.

Nally, D. (2014b) 'Governing Precarious Lives: Land Grabs, Geopolitics, and "Food Security"', *Geographical Journal*.

Nonhebel, S. and Kastner, T. (2011) 'Changing Demand for Food, Livestock Feed and Biofuels in the Past and in the Near Future', *Livestock Science* 139 (1): 3–10.

Odhiambo, M. O. (2011) 'Commercial Pressures on Land in Africa: a Regional Overview of Opportunities, Challenges, and Impacts', *RECONCILE Contribution to International Land Coalition Collaborative Research Project on Commercial Pressures on Land*, Rome.

Pingali, P. (2002) 'Reducing Poverty and Hunger: the Critical Role of Financing for Rural Development, Food & Agriculture'. International Conference on Financing for Development, Monterrey, Mexico. Available at: ftp://ftp.fao.org/docrep/fao/003/y6265e/y6265e.pdf.

Pretty, J., James, N., Morison, I. L., Hine, R. E. (2003) 'Reducing Food Poverty by Increasing Agricultural Sustainability in Developing Countries', *Agriculture, Ecosystems & Environment* 95 (1): 217–234.

Robertson, B. and Pinstrup-Andersen, P. (2010) 'Global Land Acquisition: Neo-Colonialism or Development Opportunity?' *Food Security* 2 (3): 271–283.

Rosset, P. and Martinez-Torres, M. E. (2013) 'La Via Campesina and Agroecology', *La Via Campesina's Open Book: Celebrating 20 Years of Struggle and Hope*. Available at: http://viacampesina.org/downloads/pdf/openbooks/EN-12.pdf.

Tscharntke, T., Clough, Y., Wanger, T. C., Jackson, L., Motzke, I., Perfecto, I., Vandermeer, J., and Whitbread, A. (2012) 'Global Food Security, Biodiversity Conservation and the Future of Agricultural Intensification', *Biological Conservation* 151 (1): 53–59.

UNCTAD (2009) 'World Investment Report 2009: Transnational Corporations, Agricultural Production and Development', Switzerland, Geneva.

United Nations (2105) 'World Population Projected to Reach 9.7 billion by 2050'. Available at: www.un.org/en/development/desa/news/population/2015-report.html.

von Braun, J. and Meinzen-Dick, R. S. (2009) *Land Grabbing by Foreign Investors in Developing Countries: Risks and Opportunities* International Food Policy Research Institute Washington, D.C.

Wehrmann, B. (2008) *Land Conflicts: A Practical Guide to Dealing with Land Disputes* Technische Zusammenarbeit (GTZ) GmbH Eschboen, Germany. Available at: https://www.giz.de/fachexpertise/downloads/Fachexpertise/giz2008-en-land-conflicts.pdf.

Wolford, W. (2007) 'Land Reform in the Time of Neoliberalism: A Many-Splendored Thing', *Antipode* 39 (3): 550–570.

Zoomers, A. (2010) 'Globalisation and the Foreignisation of Space: Seven Processes Driving the Current Global Land Grab', *The Journal of Peasant Studies* 37 (2): 429–447.

14 Ecosystem-based Adaptation (EbA) as a climate change adaptation strategy in Burkina Faso and Mali

Kennedy Muthee, Cheikh Mbow, Geoffrey Macharia and Walter Leal Filho

Introduction

One of the major threats to sustainable development is climate change (SDSN 2014). The world climate is still changing fast, posing serious challenges to sustainable livelihood and socio-economic development, particularly in developing countries. Climate change effects are evident in different sectors, such as environment, health, education, food security, energy, and so on (WWF 2009; Andrade *et al.* 2010) and they are a major risk to poor communities, which lack the financial, institutional and technical capacity to adapt (Munang *et al.* 2014). Notably, a temperature rise beyond 2°C can have devastating effects on crop production, water access, health and economic development (UNFCCC 2011a). This calls for different players such as governments, communities, institutions and individuals to recognize the urgency of addressing the social, environmental and economic effects of climate change.

The United Nations Framework Convention on Climate Change (UNFCCC) has recognized that the Least Developed Countries (LDCs) are the most vulnerable to climate change effects, and has guided them in establishing the National Adaptation Programmes of Action (NAPA) (Pramova *et al.* 2012). NAPAs is a political instrument that helps countries to identify and prioritize their most urgent adaptation needs, whose further delay can imply increased vulnerability and high costs later (UNFCCC 2010). Further, they provide an ideal starting point for country-specific adaptation initiatives through adaptation projects. Most recently, the UNFCCC parties have adopted the Intended Nationally Determined Contributions (INDCs) as part of their National Adaptation Plan (NAP), which seeks to establish the medium to long-term adaptation plans for each country. The INDCs highlight countries' priority actions for contributing voluntarily to mitigation efforts and support adaptation needs in developing countries (UNFCCC 2014).

Over the years, different adaptation approaches that can play a vital role in enhancing the NAPA's ability in promoting adaptation and sustainable development have emerged. One of them is through ecosystem-based adaptation (EbA), which seeks to promote societal resilience via ecosystems-management and conservation (Colls *et al.* 2009). This approach recognizes the centrality of ecosystems in the adaptation process (Munang *et al.* 2014). Ecosystems, amongst others, maintain, strengthen and enrich different elements of life and livelihood on the planet (Capistrano 2005). They support life on earth through provision of ecosystem services (BirdLife International 2010), which are defined as the benefits that natural ecosystems provide to society (Boyd and Banhzaf 2007; Prato 2008). These benefits are classified into four broad categories – supporting, provisioning, regulating and cultural (MEA 2005). The capacity of the ecosystem to deliver ecosystem services depends on its condition (healthy state), as well as the ability of society to access it (Pramova *et al.* 2012).

The current study sought to (a) analyse the dimensions of climate-change adaptation strategies, (b) Explore how ecosystem-based adaptation initiatives are incorporated in NAPA projects, and (c) draw lessons on EbA as a sustainable development strategy using Mali and Burkina Faso as case studies. It further made recommendations on how to improve the projects to harness ecosystem services, reduce negative impacts on ecosystems and promote social well-being.

The concept of ecosystem-based adaptation

EbA is the process of sustainably managing, conserving and restoring different ecosystems with the aim of providing environmental services that allow people to adapt to the effects of climate change (Colls 2009; IUCN 2015). These strategies utilize ecosystem services and biodiversity as part of community adaptation strategies to climate change effects (Gupta and Nair 2012; Munang *et al.* 2013a). The approach considers those adaptation projects that have both an 'ecosystem face' and a 'human face'. EbA recognizes the fundamental role played by ecosystem services in the reduction of people's vulnerability to the effects of climate change (Vignola *et al.* 2009; UNFCCC 2011a).

Benefits of EbA

EbA strategies provide an array of institutional, socio-cultural, ecological and economic benefits. The approach promotes restoration and protection of ecosystems, thus promoting healthy ecosystems (McGray *et al.* 2007), which in turn act as natural barriers to extreme weather conditions such as droughts, landslides, flooding, and extreme temperatures, amongst others (Andrade *et al.* 2010). A healthy ecosystem is resilient to the effects of climate change and ensures that communities continue to enjoy the ecosystem services that they provide (Falkenburg *et al.* 2010). Livelihood support contributes towards poverty alleviation in communities. The EbA approach leads to protection, restoration and management of ecosystems (Locatelli *et al.* 2008), which in turn promotes the conservation of biodiversity in addition to building the capacity of people to adapt to climate change variability (Mercer *et al.* 2007), ultimately leading to sustainable development. According to Munang *et al.* (2013c), EbA also provides applicable alternatives in the development of food systems using flexible and cheaper options. This approach not only promotes food security, but also reduces climate change risks in the agricultural sector.

Principles of EbA

Several principles guide EbA strategies. These include the promotion of a multi-sectoral approach in the ecosystems management of different landscapes (Speranza *et al.* 2010). The EbA approach promotes collaboration and coordination of various sectors, communities and players that utilize ecosystem services (Richardson 2010; Delica-Willison and Gaillard 2011). The EbA functions at multiple spatial scales and landscapes such as local, sub-national, national and regional (Cadag and Gaillard 2012). It is important to consider the complexity of ecosystems such as drivers of vulnerability, the geopolitics involved in ecosystems management, and the trans-boundary nature of an ecosystem (McConney and Mahon 2005; Orlove *et al.* 2010). Finally, it promotes participation, cultural appropriateness, accountability and embracing diversity in project design and execution (Munang *et al.* 2013b).

Applications of EbA

The role and application of ecosystems in adaptation is recognized at the international level under the United Nations Framework Convention on Climate Change (UNFCCC), the Convention on Biological Diversity (CBD) and the United Nations Convention to Combat Desertification (UNCCD) (IUCN 2015). When one considers a global change context, it is widely known that climate change has a wide range of implications and impacts which are beyond those affecting ecosystems (Leal Filho 2001). One special feature in EbA is the fact that, apart from the use of ecosystem services for people's adaptation, they can provide a concrete contribution towards increasing the resilience of these ecosystems to climate change (Locatelli and Pramova 2015). EbA can be used in areas as varied as: (a) agriculture, (b) water resource management, (c) forest management interventions and (d) biodiversity conservation and management.

In outlining the applications of EbA, we should not overlook the fact that we need new and enhanced adaptation approaches, so as to cope with the many problems and pressures posed by climate change at different levels. One of them should be the engagement of decision makers in the process, since the active participation of ecologists or environmentalists alone does not suffice (Vignola *et al.* 2009). Thus, there is a pressing need to engage various sectors in the planning and allocation of resources for adaptation action.

Materials and methods

The study followed a survey approach. Two NAPAs (Gouvernement du Burkina Faso 2007; Gouvernement du Mali 2007) with a total of 31 projects were studied, after which, a summary was created in the form of a database for further analysis to reveal the adaptation patterns, extent of incorporation of EbA strategies, lessons learnt and prospects for EbA. The criteria for project inclusion and exclusion for analysis is summarized in Table 14.1.

Table 14.1 Criteria for project selection

No.	Type of project	Description
1	Projects without ecosystems management	These are projects that do not mention any ecosystem management practice
2	Projects with ecosystem management for the environment	These are projects geared towards conserving the ecosystem without mentioning human benefits and well-being
3	Projects with ecosystem management for both ecosystem resilience and human adaptation	These projects link ecosystem management and ecosystem services to human-adaptation strategies and social well-being. They are defined as EbA projects in the study

Results and discussion

Analysis of adaptation projects in the study areas

Thirty-one projects were examined from the two countries' NAPAs (61% in Mali and 39% in Burkina Faso). They were categorized into different thematic (sectors) areas that dictated the EbA approach they took. Most of the project studies (49%) fell into the agricultural sector, with Mali recording 53 per cent and Burkina Faso 42 per cent of the total projects. These results were consistent with studies by Richardson (2010), Pramova *et al.* (2012) and McGray *et al.* (2007) that singled out agriculture as the main area of focus in climate change adaptation due to historical food insecurity in Africa. The water resources sector, energy sector and forestry sector also recorded a significant percentage of adaptation projects as summarized in Figure 14.1.

The adaptation projects each took a different geographic scope and scale of execution. Three broad categories were established – local, sub-national and national scales. Most of the projects (61%) fell under the sub-national category, which referred to the projects that cut across two or more geographical locations (districts or regions), as well as projects that targeted ecosystems cutting across several geographical areas. Burkina Faso had most of these projects at 75 per cent, as summarized in Table 14.2.

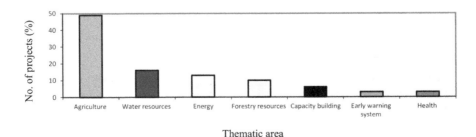

Figure 14.1 Percentage number of projects per thematic area.

Table 14.2 Percentage of projects per geographical scope and scale

	Local	*Sub-national*	*National*
% of projects	13	61	26

The adaptation projects also varied with the implementation duration (in years). The study established five categories based on the project's duration, ranging from less than one year to over five years; 68 per cent of the projects studied were scheduled to be implemented within three years and 23 per cent within two years. It is notable that 100 per cent of the projects in Burkina Faso had three-year implementation schedules.

Ten ecosystem services were established from the study and were categorized based on the MEA (2005) report – provisioning, support, regulatory and cultural services. The study established that 58 per cent of the projects sought to provide provisioning services, while regulatory services were provided by 21 per cent of the total projects studied. Among the provisioning services, food and fodder topped the list at 50 per cent and 29 per cent, respectively. The dominant support service was soil formation and fertility to support the provision of food and fodder, while the principal regulatory service was soil erosion/siltation control at 50 per cent. These results were consistent with those of Pramova (2012), which established that provisioning and regulatory services are dominant within the adaptation projects. Notably, there is also a clear pattern of the high priority of the number of projects within the agricultural sector and the service they seek to provide, that is food and fodder provision (Table 14.3).

The projects also varied with their budgetary considerations. The study defined five categories of budget between US$ 1 and over US$ 4 million. Most of the projects (64%) had a low budgetary consideration of less than US$ 1 million (92% and 47% in Burkina Faso and Mali, respectively). Only 16 per cent of the projects recorded the highest budgetary consideration of over US$ 4 million. The results concur with those of UNFCCC (2011b) and Wamunyima and Miga (2014) who point out budgetary and financial constraints as the major challenge facing the implementation of adaptation projects. The results are summarized in Figure 14. 2.

Table 14.3 Summary of ecosystem services identified

Provisioning services	*Regulatory services*	*Support Services*
Food	Erosion / siltation / sedimentation control	Soil formation / fertility / productivity
Fodder	Disease control	
Habitats	Bushfire prevention	
Non-timber products	Pollution control	
Water services		

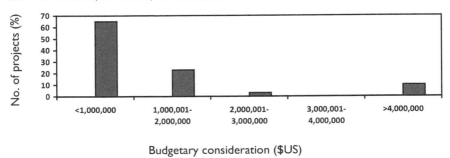

Budgetary consideration ($US)

Figure 14.2 Percentage number of projects per budgetary consideration.

EbA Approaches identified in the projects

The EbA approach was largely dependent on the thematic area of the adaptation. Sixteen per cent of the total projects studied mentioned a different way of employing an EbA approach in their implementation activities and outputs, as summarized in Table 14. 4.

Lessons, prospects and recommendations of EbA in adaptation projects

This study reveals several key lessons, prospects and recommendations on EbA and climate change adaptation strategies as reflected in the National Adaptation Programmes of Actions (NAPA) of the two countries.

The adaptation strategies are not uniform: they vary in terms of scope, duration, thematic area, ecosystem services provided and the EbA approach put in place. The key determinant is the thematic area (sector). A common pattern of the adaptation projects was drawn from the current study. The majority fell within the agricultural sector (49%) with low budgetary allocation (US$ 1–1 million), conducted within sub-national geographical and ecological coverage (61%). They had a medium implementation duration (68% within three years), and the majority sought to enhance provisioning ecosystem services (58%). This variability informed the diverse EbA approach taken by these projects. The 'one size suits all' adaptation strategy may not be appropriate for current and future EbA projects.

The EbA strategies should integrate indigenous and contemporary knowledge. These include sustainable agricultural practices using indigenous knowledge and crops (such as sorghum and millet) to ensure food security and promote soil productivity. Basing the EbA approaches on the community's experience is likely to yield more participation and success. Studies such as Walmsley (2006), Mercer *et al.* (2010), and Speranza *et al.* (2010) all point out the need for community knowledge and participation integration in the adaptation processes.

There is a need for project contextualization based on the previous social, economic and environmental experiences within the project areas. Indeed, the whole NAPA process is based on the country-specific environmental changes that

Table 14.4 EbA approaches established in different sectors

No	Sector	Adaptation approach	Examples of activities established	Case studies
1	Agricultural sector	Integrated/sustainable agricultural practices to enhance food security and enhance ecosystem functioning	Rehabilitation of rangeland and agro-forestry practices, and planting drought tolerant food crops	• The extension of improved varieties adapted to climatic conditions in major food crops (millet, sorghum, maize and rice) in Mali • Securing pastoral areas in the Sahel and East Burkina Faso
2	Water sector	Integrated watershed management to address food insecurity, reduce poverty, enhance watershed functionality and improve people's living conditions	Runoff control, restoration of watersheds and water points, rehabilitation of watersheds, reducing watershed degradation and reforesting catchment areas	• Catchment runoff, creation and restoration of water points in Mali • Development and management of the pond Oursi in Burkina Faso
3	Cross-cutting sectors	Multi-sectored ecosystems management to reduce people's vulnerability to climate change effects	Improving soil productivity and fertility, controlling soil and water erosion, rehabilitation of degraded lands, natural resources conservation and reforestation exercises	• Development action CES/DRS for agriculture, forestry and pastoralism projects in Mali
4	Forestry sector	Integrated forestry management	Promotion of non-timber products, promotion of reforestation, creation of new plantations, natural tree regeneration and biodiversity conservation	• Planning, management of natural formations and development of non-timber forest products (NTFPs) in Eastern Burkina Faso
5	Wildlife sector	Sustainable wildlife management	Species monitoring, ecological/eco-zones conservation, wildlife management, sustainable harvesting and co-management plans	• Towards promotion of management of wildlife and its habitat by local communities in the Mouhoun in Burkina Faso

have affected the region's social and economic development. This approach aids in the prioritizing of the activities that are aimed at promoting ecosystem resiliency, promoting human well-being and reduction of vulnerability, supporting ecosystem services and ultimately enhancing sustainable development.

The need for research and development of EbA cannot be understated. Research involves testing, refining and upscaling the EbA approach based on the local context. The project designers should employ tried and tested EbA approaches that seek to enhance both ecosystems and human well-being. There is also the need to document such initiatives for replication in other areas with similar geographical and ecosystems characteristics.

The incorporation of EbA and non-EbA activities in a project is also fundamental. This includes the development of infrastructures to support the ecosystem services provided by these projects. To illustrate, the planning, management of natural formation, and development of the non-timber forest products project would require non-EbA approaches, such as development of roads, to ensure that the communities make a living from their conservation and wise resource-use exercises.

Adaptation activities should seek to integrate multi-sectoral and multi-stakeholder approaches to meet the broad EbA objectives and principles. The designing and execution of these projects should incorporate social, economic, and ecological dynamics to yield multiple benefits. To realize this, the project designers and implementers should understand, and try to achieve a balance between the benefits and trade-offs related to the execution of such projects.

Conclusions

The NAPAs provide an ideal entry point to country-specific adaptation strategies. The focus is currently shifting from NAPA to INDCs, creating the need to incorporate more EbA strategies in adaptation projects to meet both human and ecosystem needs; thus promoting sustainable development. The study shows a clear adaptation pattern, with more projects classified under agricultural sector, low budgetary consideration, medium implementation duration, and mainly seeking to provide provisioning and regulatory ecosystem services. The EbA strategies are considered in 16 per cent of the studied projects and depend largely on the project's thematic area. Some of the strategies were based on agricultural practices, integrated watershed management, multi-sectored ecosystem management, integrated forestry management and sustainable wildlife management. The analysis of the two NAPA projects also yielded several key lessons and recommendations on EbA. The community participation and local (indigenous) knowledge should be central in the design and implementation of NAPA projects. External knowledge, research, monitoring and evaluation are essential aspects of EbA, and should be incorporated in future adaptation projects. Finally, adaptation projects should be contextualized according to the communities and ecosystems around them. The study concludes that incorporation of the diverse ecosystem-based approaches in different thematic areas can promote sustainable development. Notably, inclusion of EbA approaches in the agricultural sector can provide a flexible and cheaper option in the developing of food systems, thus promoting food production and minimizing climate change effects in this sector.

Acknowledgement

The authors are very grateful to the BIODEV project funded by the Finland Government and the CGIAR Research Programs (CRP) 6.3 and 6.4.

References

Andrade, A., Herrera, B., Cazzolla, R. (2010) *Building Resilience to Climate Change: Ecosystem Based Adaptation and Lessons from the Field*, Gland, Switzerland: IUCN.

BirdLife International (2010) *Partners with Nature: How Healthy Ecosystems are Helping the World's Most Vulnerable Adapt to Climate Change*, Zeist, Netherlands: BirdLife International.

Cadag, J. and Gaillard, J. (2012) 'Integrating Knowledge and Actions in Disaster Risk Reduction: The Contribution of Participatory Mapping', *Area*, 44:100–109.

Colls, A., Ash, N., Ikkala, N. (2009) *Ecosystem-Based Adaptation: A Natural Response to Climate Change*, Gland, Switzerland: IUCN.

Delica-Willison Z., Gaillard, J. (2011) 'Community Action and Disaster', in Wisner, B., Gaillard, J.C., Kelman, I. (eds.) *The Routledge Handbook of Hazards and Disaster Risk Reduction*, London: Routledge.

Falkenburg, J., Burnell, W., Connell, D., Russell, B. (2010) 'Sustainability in Near-Shore Marine Systems: Promoting Natural Resilience', *Sustainability*, 2, 2593–2600.

Gouvernement du Burkina Faso (2007) Programme d'Action National d'Adaptation a la Variabilite et aux Changements Climatiques (National Adaptation Programme of Action on Variability and Climate Change) (PANA Du Burkina Faso). Available at: http://unfccc.int/resource/docs/napa/bfa01f.pdf.

Gouvernement du Mali (2007) Programme d'Action National d'Adaptation aux Changements Climatiques (National Action Programme of Adaptation to Climatic Changes). Available at: www.undp-alm.org/sites/default/files/downloads/mali_napa.pdf.

Gupta, K., Nair, S. (2012) *Ecosystem Approach to Disaster Risk Reduction*, New Delhi: National Institute of Disaster Management. Available at: http://unfccc.int/focus/indc_portal/items/8766.php.

IUCN (2015) Ecosystem-Based Adaptation. Available at: https://www.iucn.org/about/work/programmes/ecosystem_management/climate_change/eba/.

Leal Filho, W. (ed.) (2001) *The Economic, Social and Political Aspects of Climate Change*, Berlin: Springer.

Locatelli, B., Kanninen, M., Brockhaus, C., Murdiyarso, D. and Santoso, H. (2008) 'Facing an Uncertain Future: How Forests and People Can Adapt to Climate Change', CIFOR (Center for International Forestry Research), *Forest Perspectives*, No. 5: 1–86.

Locatelli, B. and Pramova, E. (2015) *Ecosystem-Based Adaptation*, Indonesia: École Thématique.

McConney, P. and Mahon, R. (2005) 'Size Matters: Scaling Management and Capacity to Achieve Sustainability in SIDS', *FAO Fish Report*, Vol. 782, 293–306.

McGray, H., Hammill, A. and Bradley, R. (2007) *Weathering the Storm: Options for Framing Adaptation and Development*, Washington, D.C.: World Resources Institute (WRI)

Mercer, J., Dominey-Howes, D., Kelman, I. and Lloyd, K. (2007) 'The Potential for Combining Indigenous and Western Knowledge in Reducing Vulnerability to Environmental Hazards in Small Island Developing States', *Environ. Hazards*, Vol. 7, 245–256.

Mercer, J., Kelman, I., Taranis, L. and Suchet-Pearson, S. (2010). 'Framework for Integrating Indigenous and Scientific Knowledge for Disaster Risk Reduction'. *Disasters*, Vol. 34, 214–239.

MEA (Millennium Ecosystem Assessment) (2005) *Ecosystems and Human Well-Being: Synthesis*, Washington, D.C.: Island Press.

Munang, R., Thiaw, I., Alverson, K., Mumba, M., Liu, J. and Rivington, M. (2013a) 'Climate Change and Ecosystem-Based Adaptation: A New Pragmatic Approach to Buffering Climate Change Impacts'. *Current Opinion in Environmental Sustainability*, Vol. 5, 1–5.

Munang, R., Thiaw, I. and Rivington, M. (2013b) Ecosystem Management: Tomorrow's Approach to Enhancing Food Security under a Changing Climate, *Sustainability*, Vol. 3, 937–954.

Munang, R., Thiaw, I. and Alverson, K. (2013c) 'Using Ecosystem-Based Adaptation Actions to Tackle Food Insecurity Environment', *Science and Policy for Sustainable Development*, 55 (1): 29–35.

Munang, R., Andrews J., Alverson, K. and Mebratu, D. (2014) 'Harnessing Ecosystem-Based Adaptation to Address the Social Dimensions of Climate Change', *Environment* (56), 1, 18–24.

Orlove, B., Roncoli, C., Kabugo, M. and Majugu, A. (2010) 'Indigenous Climate Knowledge in Southern Uganda: the Multiple Components of a Dynamic Regional System', *Climatic Change* Vol. 100, 243–265.

Pramova, E., Locatelli, B., Brockhaus, M. and Fohlmeister, S. (2012) 'Ecosystem Services in the National Adaptation Programmes of Action', *Climate Policy*, Vol. 12 (4), 393–409.

Richardson, R. (2010) 'Ecosystem Services and Food Security: Economic Perspectives on Environmental Sustainability', *Sustainability*, Vol. 2: 3520–3548.

SDSN (2014) *Solutions for Sustainable Agriculture and Food Systems*. NY: The Sustainable Development Solutions Network.

Speranza, C., Kiteme, B., Ambenje, P., Wiesmann, U. and Makali, S. (2010) 'Indigenous Knowledge Related to Climate Variability and Change: Insights from Droughts in Semi-Arid Areas of Former Makueni District, Kenya', *Climatic Change*, Vol. 100: 295–315.

United Nations Framework Convention on Climate Change (UNFCCC) (2010) National Adaptation Programmes of Action (NAPA). Available at: http://unfccc.int/national_reports/napa/items/2719.php

United Nations Framework Convention on Climate Change (UNFCCC) (2011a) *Ecosystem-Based Approaches to Adaptation: Compilation of Information*, Bonn, Germany: UNFCCC

United Nations Framework Convention on Climate Change (UNFCCC) (2011b) *Assessing the Costs and Benefits of Adaptation Options: An Overview of Approaches*, Bonn, Germany: UNFCCC.

United Nations Framework Convention on Climate Change (UNFCCC) (2014) Intended Nationally Determined Contributions (INDCs). Available at: http://unfccc.int/focus/indc_portal/items/8766.php.

Vignola, R., Locatelli, B., Martinez, C. and Imbach, P. (2009) 'Ecosystems-Based Adaptation to Climate Change: What Role for Policy-Makers, Society and Scientists?' *Mitigation and Adaptation Strategies for Global Change*, 14 (8): 691–696.

Walmsley, J. (2006) 'The Nature of Community: Putting Community in Place', *Dialogue*, Vol. 25, 5–12.

Wamunyima, M. and Miga, W. (2014) Assessment of Adaptation Financial Flows in Zambia. Consultancy report prepared for AFAI in Zambia, unpublished.

WWF (2009) *WWF Adaptation Case Studies for Responding to Climate Change Impacts*. Buenos Aires, Argentina: WWF Publication.

15 Micro-insurance in disaster risk reduction

A strategy for enhancing domestic food security in CARICOM countries

Balfour Spence

Introduction

Agriculture continues to be a critically important sector in the economies of countries of the Caribbean Community (CARICOM) in spite of its declining contributions to GDP. In the case of Jamaica, primary agriculture (agriculture, forestry and fishery) as a share of GDP has declined from 6.14 per cent in 1999–2003 to 4.83 per cent in 2010. Likewise, expanded agriculture (primary agriculture plus agro-processing) declined from 5.18 to 4.69 per cent over the same period (IICA 2010). In spite of declining contributions to GDP, agriculture continues to feature prominently in the livelihood profile of Caribbean states, particularly because it remains a major employer of labour and the pillar of domestic food production and, by extension, domestic food security for these states. In that context, direct employment in agriculture averages about 16.2 per cent of the labour force among CARICOM states (FAO 2014).

The food production systems are dualistic, characterized by large farms occupying prime arable lands and with an export orientation, and small farms on marginal agricultural lands and producing primarily for the domestic market (Williams and Smith 2008). It is in that context that Jamaica, for example, records one of the highest levels of land concentration in Latin America and the Caribbean with a Gini Coefficient of Land Holding of 0.81 (USAID 2010). This value indicates that a large number of small farms occupy a small proportion of arable lands, while a few large farms account for the bulk of arable lands. It is the specific vulnerability of the agricultural sector in general and small-scale farming in particular, to impacts of hydro-meteorological hazards such as hurricanes, floods and droughts, that pose some of the greatest risks to domestic food security in the region. For instance, Hurricane Gilbert in 1988 cost US$ 4 billion in damage to the agriculture sector in Jamaica and wiped out over 40 per cent of crop production (FAO 2008). This vulnerability is aggravated by the virtual absence of catastrophic insurance coverage amongst small-scale producers, including fishers. In the absence of insurance mechanisms to aid recovery, these producers are forced to initiate their own recovery, or become reliant on governments as a *de facto* insurer. In either case, the recovery process is slow and often incomplete, thus eroding domestic food security in the aftermath of hazard impact events. Food and nutritional insecurity not only directly undermine social well-being but also accentuate vulnerability to the impact of other hazards.

This chapter explores the role that specifically tailored micro-insurance interventions could have in reducing vulnerability among small-scale agricultural producers (including fishers), and thereby in contributing to continuity and sustainability in domestic food production systems and food security in Caribbean economies. The chapter proposes a parametric micro-insurance intervention that would provide affordable coverage for small-scale farmers and fishers in CARICOM states and allow timely 'bounce-back' from the impact of hydro-meteorological hazards and enhance domestic food security.

The food security debate

Food security is said to exist when 'all people, at all times have physical and economic access to sufficient, safe and nutritious food that meets their dietary needs and food preferences for an active and healthy life' (World Food Summit 1996). Within the context of this definition, as indicated previously, four dimensions of food security are evident: food availability, food access, food utilization, and stability of food availability, access and utilization.

As discussed in a previous chapter, food availability addresses the supply side of food security of production and trade. Food access is considered to be the fundamental pillar of food security and in the absence of food aid, legal access to food is a function of capacities to produce or procure food, and as such is defined by access to land as a basis for food production and income for food procurement. Food utilization defines the nutritional context of food security as this relates to sufficiency of energy and nutrient intake that contribute to the good nutritional status of individuals (FAO 2008).

The two broad pathways to food security are namely: a) food self-sufficiency, and b) food self-reliance. Since food self-sufficiency emphasizes production by domestic producers, it rules out food import as a major source of food for satisfying local demands (Chandra and Lontoh 2010). Small-scale enterprises, such as those comprising the domestic food production sector of CARICOM countries, are usually the pillar of this food security strategy. The notion of food sovereignty over food supplies is an underpinning philosophy of this pathway (FAO 2013a; 2013b). Food self-reliance, on the other hand, emphasizes food availability and as such, considers food import as an integral part of the food security strategy. Trade liberalization from the perspective of comparative advantage is a key component of this strategy.

Chandra and Lontoh (2010) pointed to the shortcomings of both the food self-sufficiency and food self-reliance strategies. Critics of the food self-sufficiency approach posit that this strategy cannot make economic sense for countries that incur a high opportunity cost in food production when compared with other domestic products, and in relation to the opportunity cost of food production in countries with excess capacity to produce food. Such countries, based on their comparative advantage, would garner greater economic benefits by focusing their resources on those economic sectors in which they have a comparative advantage, in order to generate foreign exchange for the purchase of food to satisfy domestic demand. Likewise, critics of the self-reliance strategy argue that the gains from trade liberalization can neither be ascertained nor guaranteed and, as such, its effect in enhancing the food security of vulnerable groups is questionable (FAO 2003).

CARICOM states strongly advocate a food self-sufficiency approach to food security. It is in that context that the Caribbean Food and Nutrition Security Policy (2010) stresses enhancement of the comparative advantage of member states in the production of food as a key component of food security in the region.

Food security profile of CARICOM states

Understanding of the food security profile of CARICOM provides a platform for assessing vulnerabilities in the food production sector and, by extension, the rationale for risk management/transfer initiatives. The food security profile of CARICOM states can be summarized in terms of the social and economic importance of agriculture, level of dependence on food import and trends in food trade.

Figure 15.1 summarizes the social and economic importance of agriculture among CARICOM states.

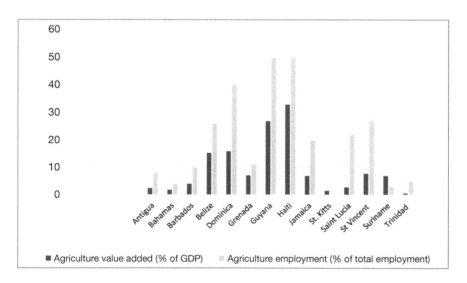

Figure 15.1 Comparative percentage contribution of agriculture to GDP and employment in the Caribbean.

Note: Antigua refers to Antigua and Barbuda; St. Vincent refers to St. Vincent and the Grenadines; and Trinidad refers to Trinidad and Tobago.

Source: Compiled from World Bank-LAC 2012, World Bank Group, 2016.

Except for the island states of Haiti and Dominica and the mainland states of Guyana and Belize, agriculture accounts for less than 10 per cent of GDP in CARICOM states and, as such, is not considered a prominent economic earner. However, among productive sectors, agriculture features prominently in the livelihood profile of all CARICOM states, accounting for levels in excess of 20 per cent of the labour force for more than half of the states. Therefore, in the context of the livelihood contribution of agriculture to the social well-being of CARICOM states, as well as its relevance to food security, continuity and sustainability of this sector in relation to impact – especially from hydro-meteorological hazards – is of paramount importance.

While food security advocacy amongst most individual CARICOM states tends towards a food self-sufficiency approach, the food security profile of the region reflects a self-reliance strategy characterized by extreme dependence on imported food to satisfy demand, as reflected in an ever-increasing food import bill (Figure 15.2).

This situation is paradoxical and reflects an element of food and nutrition insecurity resulting from a lack of food sovereignty. Liberalization of food trade resulting in the availability of cheap imported food in CARICOM markets between the 1980s and 2006 stymied and, in some cases, stifled the domestic food production sector. This led to soaring food prices in 2007 and 2008, spurred by the global financial meltdown, which served to expose vulnerabilities associated with dependence on the global food market to satisfy domestic demands. It is with

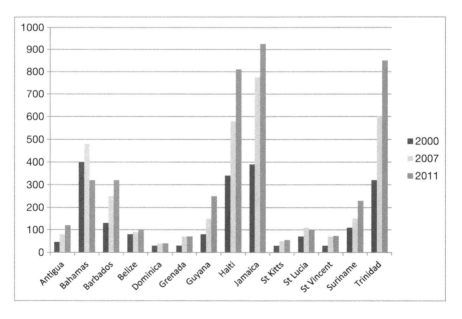

Figure 15.2 CARICOM Food Import Bill – US$ millions – for years 2000, 2007, 2011.
Note: Antigua refers to Antigua and Barbuda; St. Vincent refers to St. Vincent and the Grenadines; and Trinidad refers to Trinidad and Tobago.
Source: Generated from FAO (2013) Statistics.

reference to these vulnerabilities and the advocacy for a self-sufficiency approach to food security in CARICOM states, that the President of Guyana posited in his contribution to the World Food Summits (WFS), 2009 that:

> ...the region was seduced by the importation of cheap food and paid less attention to food security... The soaring food and agricultural commodity prices in 2007/08 and financial crisis of the last few years caught the Region unprepared and put food security at the forefront of the Regional agenda.
>
> (CARICOM 2010)

In spite of recognition of the adverse implications of dependence on food import to satisfy domestic demands, a negative balance in CARICOM regional agricultural trade persists and the gap between agricultural exports and imports widens (World Bank-LAC 2012).

Small-scale agriculture and domestic food security

Implicit in the self-sufficiency approach to food security that is advocated by CARICOM states is the notion of the continuity and sustainability of small-scale agriculture, especially as these relate to resourcing and capacity building to recover from the impacts of hazards in the shortest possible time. Small-scale agriculture constitutes the domestic food production sector, but the specific vulnerability of this sector is underscored by low levels of resourcing and absence of economies of scale that result from low levels of capitalization. For instance, while small-scale farms (farms less than 5 hectares) account for 98 per cent of all farms in Jamaica, they occupy a mere 41 per cent of the farmed area (Table 15.1). Yet, from a livelihood perspective, these farms feature prominently, accounting for 18 per cent of total livelihood activities, and providing the foundation of the domestic food production on which the advocated food self-sufficiency – to facilitate domestic food security – is hinged.

Table 15.1 Area in farms by size groups

Size group of farms	Number of farms		Area in farms	
	Total	*Percent of total*	*Total (hectares)*	*Percent of total*
Under 1 ha.	151,929	75.73	47,712	14.64
1 to under 5 ha.	43,731	21.80	86,011	26.40
5 to under 50 ha.	4,543	2.27	50,783	15.59
50 to under 200 ha.	270	0.13	25,449	7.81
200 ha. and over	140	0.07	115,854	35.56
All farms	200,613	100.00	325,810	100.00

Source: Statistical Institute of Jamaica, 2007.

Besides the low level of resourcing and capitalization that contribute to the hazard vulnerability of the domestic food production sector, there is a virtual absence of any form of emergency insurance. In the absence of this type of emergency risk transfer mechanism, national governments within CARICOM are the *de facto* insurers of small-scale agriculture, placing immense pressure on already overstretched public coffers and aggravating food insecurity in the aftermath of hazard impacts.

Micro-insurance as disaster risk reduction tool for enhancing food security in CARICOM

Micro-insurance is an extension of the emergent micro-financing strategy aimed at alleviating poverty in low-income households and micro-enterprises through transfer of risk in return for payment of specially designed low-cost premiums. Specifically, micro-insurance for disaster risk reduction is aimed at protecting low-income families, communities and production groups against livelihood erosion, hardships and enhancing the ability to bounce back from losses incurred from the impact of hazards. This protection is provided in exchange for payments of premiums that are proportionate to the likelihood and cost of assessed risks. Within the context of CARICOM food security, a micro-insurance intervention that is designed for small-scale farmers could ensure continuity and sustainability of farming systems in the aftermath of impacts, especially from hydro-meteorological hazards. As such, the benefits of micro-insurance as a food security enhancement measure are several and include poverty alleviation, promotion of productive investment, incentives for disaster risk mitigation through rewards built into insurance portfolios, and promotion of a dignified way of the poor coping.

Viability of micro-insurance for the CARICOM domestic food production sector

Viability considerations are critical to the effective design and implementation of any micro-insurance intervention for disaster risk reduction and food security enhancement in CARICOM states. While viability has social and spatial implications, four overarching considerations are identifiable.

Contribution of intervention to CARICOM food security enhancement

There are two salient questions in this regard. First, can or will the intervention contribute to sustainable disaster risk reduction in the domestic food production sector by reducing vulnerability? Second, does intervention promote and encourage risk reduction measures that will influence immediate disaster losses among small-scale farmers and fishers? These questions are pertinent because it can be argued that insurance premiums divert funds which could otherwise be used for preventive engagements (Spence 2013).

Financial robustness

It is more difficult to assure financial robustness of micro-insurance interventions that cover covariant losses, for example, those that affect a large number of persons at the same time, than those covering independent losses. Covariant losses are typical of the small-scale farming and domestic food production sector of CARICOM states, as a single hydro-meteorological event can completely devastate the food production sector of island states. Covariant risk insurance therefore presents the insurer with the possibility of large payouts and even insolvency for high impact events. In that regard, the financial robustness of the scheme must be a key consideration of the design criteria (Spence 2013).

Affordability

The provision of services to people who do not have access to regular insurance is central to the design of micro-insurance interventions. Therefore, affordability of premiums is a key consideration in product design. Given the added cost of risk transfer, the dilemma faced in the provision of low-cost micro-insurance to the low-income domestic food producers is, whether covariant disaster insurance that typifies the risk profile needs of the CARICOM states, can be offered at an affordable price. Possible options include:

- Lowering of transaction costs by offering simple products to client groups (such as a farming or fishing association), relying on group pressure for timely payments, enlisting the services of non-profit organizations that do not charge high commissions, and streamlining through integration with existing infrastructure. Index-based (parametric) insurance mechanisms in which payouts are triggered by a quantitative index, such as an environmental trigger (e.g. a hurricane of a specified magnitude), reduce the cost of premiums through elimination of costs associated with risk and loss assessments, which then can be an effective affordability tool owing to low transaction costs.
- A second option for effecting affordability in the provision of micro-insurance for disaster risk reduction in the domestic food production sector of CARICOM states, is the provision of capital reserves for re-insurance. This would be effected through the intervention of national government, international donors and local private sector stakeholders whose businesses depend on inputs from the domestic food production sector. The multi-donor arrangement spearheaded by the Caribbean Development Bank (CDB) in 2011 and which involves a donor partnership with the UK Government and the Government of Ireland, is typical of this type of arrangement. The CDB, along with its donor partners, makes cash allocations to a Micro-Insurance Catastrophic Risk Organization (MiCRO-Haiti) Fund for provision of index-based disaster risk insurance to Haiti's poor (MiCRO 2011). The Fund is integrated into the operations of an existing micro-finance agency – Fonkoze (International Financial Consulting 2014).

- Affordability can also be effected through direct subsidy to disaster claims settlement or premiums for domestic food producers from national government or donor agency. Alternatively, support for micro-insurance cost reduction can come through technical support for conducting feasibility studies and undertaking risk assessments, which can contribute to the cost of premiums.

Governance

The risk reduction capacity, financial robustness and affordability of micro-insurance interventions for disaster risk reduction are a function of the effectiveness of governance. Good governance implies legitimacy and credibility of social institutions and procedures responsible for development, implementation and regulation of insurance schemes. Relevant social institutions include government agencies, NGOs, private sector, national and international financial and donor institutions, public or social-group based organizations.

Design framework for micro-insurance intervention in the domestic food production sector of CARICOM states

The design framework has two components: the scope of micro-insurance intervention for domestic food produced and a conceptual model of the intervention.

Scope of intervention

While commonalities abound in the domestic food production sectors and food security issues of CARICOM states, unique differences occur. In that regard, micro-insurance interventions must accommodate this uniqueness through a phased approach. An initial phase should be limited in scope in order to facilitate an evaluation of viability. Results of this evaluation will inform a more expanded intervention. The proposed scope of the initial intervention is defined in terms of players in the provision of coverage, hazards focus of coverage, domestic food production subsectors to be targeted and the type of coverage to be provided.

Players in provision of coverage

CARICOM governments will continue to play a central role in any disaster risk reduction intervention for the domestic food production sector, but instead of remaining the *de facto* insurer of small farmers and fishers, they will engage in risk transfer through subsidized micro-insurance premiums. Other players will include international donor and aid agencies which can contribute to the offset of premium cost, instead of engaging in post-impact recovery assistance for the small-scale agricultural sector. Local food processors and agricultural exporters that rely on inputs from small farmers for continuity of business can also be engaged in the offsetting of premiums to ensure affordability.

Hazards focus of coverage

The domestic food production sector of CARICOM states is a multi-hazard environment. It is proposed that the initial phase of a micro-insurance intervention focus on the most recurrent hydrological hazards that impact most severely on the domestic food production sector. This focus can vary among CARICOM states for most would include hurricanes (wind damage) and floods. Narrowing the hazard focus of coverage in this initial stage will facilitate manageability and provide opportunities for application of lessons learned during more comprehensive coverage. Future evaluation and lessons learned would inform a broadening of the scope of hazard coverage (Spence 2013).

Domestic food production sector to be targeted

The proposed micro-insurance intervention is intended to facilitate quick and sustainable bounce-back of the domestic food production sector of CARICOM states as a strategy for overall enhancement of food security. In that regard, the intervention should focus on small-scale farmers and near-shore fishers, as defined by the individual states. It is recognized that the domestic food security sector entails livelihood activities other than small-scale farming and fishing. Nevertheless, by limiting the scope of activities, administrative and implementation complexities will be minimized in support of more effective evaluation and incorporation of lessons learned for an expanded intervention.

Type of coverage

Traditional insurance coverage is indemnity-based, that is, compensation is based on assessed losses. This type of coverage allows for discriminatory compensation, but requires the engagement of claim adjusters to undertake assessment in the aftermath of a hazard event. The cost of these adjusters is often reflected in premiums. More recently, index-based schemes for slow-onset events such as hurricanes and floods have emerged, and these are especially relevant in the design of micro-insurance interventions for the domestic food production sector of CARICOM states.

Index-based insurance schemes are distinguished from indemnity-based schemes in that compensation is contracted against a physical trigger (parametric insurance) such as a specific quantity of rainfall at a specific location or region, or a hurricane of a specified magnitude. In the case of weather derivatives, the insured would receive a payout once that trigger is reached, irrespective of loss. Since payouts are not coupled with individual loss experiences, the insured have an incentive to undertake disaster loss-reduction measures, given the possibility that if they can keep loss to a minimum, their benefits from payouts could exceed actual loss. Since the claim is a prefixed amount per unit of protection, the transaction is simplified and related costs lowered, making an index-based insurance attractive in micro-insurance-demand environments.

This type of insurance intervention is transparent since the payout is fixed in advance. The main potential drawback relates to the possibility that the established trigger might be insufficiently correlated with loss experience, in which case there might be no payout. Additionally, the trigger-contracted-payout might not cover actual loss for a particular event, essentially constituting under-insurance. However, the benefits of this type of intervention have to be weighed cumulatively, and not in relation to single events.

The specific type of coverage proposed for the domestic food production sector of CARICOM states is a parametric micro-insurance intervention for farmers and fishers, involving triggers for cyclones (tropical storms and hurricanes) and floods. Additionally, CARICOM states, especially those in the northern Caribbean might want to consider the establishment of a trigger for 'ground seas' (sea swells) associated with the passage of cold fronts over the northern Caribbean, which can incur significant damages to fishing traps. The architecture of the design framework which follows is not intended to be prescriptive but, rather, to provide guidance on how a micro-insurance intervention to enhance domestic food security in CARICOM states can be configured.

Conceptual model of the intervention

Figure 15.3 represents a conceptual model of a micro-insurance intervention for the domestic food production sector of CARICOM states.

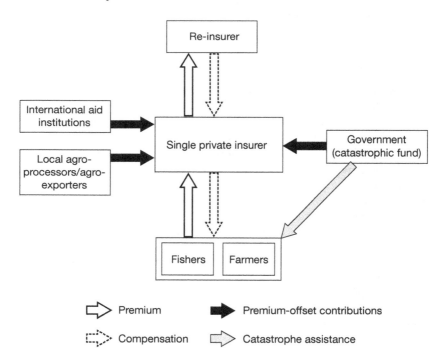

Figure 15.3 Conceptual framework of micro-insurance intervention.

The model assumes the following:

a) The private sector, government and international donors in CARICOM states form an alliance in support of a micro-insurance intervention for the domestic food production sector.
b) A parametric micro-insurance mechanism is appropriate for disaster risk reduction in CARICOM states.
c) Micro-insurance target groups (fishers, farmers) lack capacity to underwrite the full cost of micro-insurance for disaster reduction.
d) Government, international donors and local private sector interest groups will subsidize premiums through offset contributions and provide 'catastrophic assistance' when impact-cost far exceeds compensation, or where significant loss is incurred without activation of the environmental trigger.

Conceptualization of the model is premised upon partnership amongst governments, donor and aid agencies, private sector stakeholders and private insurance agencies in CARICOM states in the provision of micro-insurance coverage to small-scale farmers through a process of re-insurance.

An explicit definition of each group of insured is required for operational purposes of the micro-insurance intervention. Tentatively, definition of the micro-insurance target groups could be informed by the level of reliance on the particular activity as a source of livelihood. It is proposed that in order to qualify for participation in the scheme, the insured should have good standing in a membership organization that provides collective facilitation of the liaison between insured and insurer. Individual liaison would increase operational expenses and is likely to be reflected in higher levels of premium. Premiums can be incorporated into membership fees as a specified proportion, or form a dedicated contribution, and could be paid to the local insurer through the membership organization. The insurer will facilitate coverage as deemed appropriate, including the use of re-insurers.

Given that low income is considered to be the main obstacle to insurance access by small-scale farmers, fishers and other low-income groups, it is anticipated that targeted groups for micro-insurance might not be in a position to make a sufficient premium contribution towards requisite coverage. Therefore, it is proposed that shortfalls in premiums be offset through contributions from a government catastrophic fund and/or through donor contribution. A third option of contributions is local ago-processors, whose inputs and continuity of business are linked to productivity of the domestic food production sector. Any of these approaches would be cost-effective with respect to the no-insurance alternative.

Within the context of parametric coverage in this initial phase, an environmental 'trigger' for the activation of compensation must be determined for each of the hazard types proposed. For tropical cyclones, the proposed trigger is the impact of a tropical storm, while compensation for flooding could be triggered by rainfall intensity and duration. In instances where compensation related to the environmental trigger fall short of impact-cost, or where loss to the insured is incurred without a trigger, government should be prepared to provide catastrophic assistance to facilitate livelihood continuity and sustainability, and to enhance food security.

Conclusion

The importance of small-scale farmers and fishers in the domestic food security of CARICOM states, and the specific vulnerabilities of those sectors – especially to hydro-meteorological hazard impacts – is underscored. Recovery of the domestic food production sector in the aftermath of hazard impacts is hinged on the capacity of governments, as *de facto* insurers of the poor, and international and national aid organizations, to provide assistance to domestic food producers. Where shortfalls exist in such capacities, recovery of the domestic food production sector and related livelihood activities is prolonged or irrevocably jeopardized. Micro-insurance mechanisms provide options for effective risk transfer to promote loss-reduction in the domestic food production sector of CARICOM states, and to establish a path towards sustainable food security and livelihood continuity.

References

CARICOM (2010) *Regional Food and Nutrition Security Policy*, Caribbean Community 2010.
Chandra, A. and Lontoh, L. (2010) *Regional Food Security and Trade Policy in South-East Asia*, Winnipeg: International Institute for Sustainable Development (IISD).
FAO (2003) Trade Reforms and Food Security: Conceptualizing the Linkages. Rome: FAO.
FAO (2008) An Introduction to the Basic Concept of Food Security, Food Security Information for Action: Practical Guides. Rome: EC-FAO Food Security Programme, 2008.
FAO (2010) Country Report on State of Plant Genetic Resources for Food and Agriculture, FAO: Rome.
FAO (2013a) CARICOM *Food Import Bill, Food Security and Nutrition*, Barbados: Sub-regional Office for the Caribbean, October 2013.
FAO (2013b) *Food Security and Sovereignty*, Rome: FAO.
FAO (2014) FAO Statistical Yearbook 2014: *Latin America and the Caribbean: Food and Agriculture*, Santiago: FAO.
International Financial Consulting/Caribbean Development Bank (2014) 'Mid-term Evaluation of Performance of the Operations of MiCRO in Haiti'. Unpublished Report.
Micro Insurance Catastrophe Risk Organization (MiCRO) (2011) *News Release*, Barbados: MiCRO and CDB Sign Grant Agreement Supporting Innovative Micro-Insurance Facility.
Segura, J. A. (2010) Contribution of Agriculture to Sustainable Development in Jamaica, San José, Costa Rica: IICA.
Statistical Institute of Jamaica (2007) *Agricultural Census, 2007*, Kingston: Government of Jamaica.
USAID (2010) *USAID Country Profile: Property Rights and Resource Governance, Jamaica*. Washington D.C.: USAID.
Williams, T. & Smith, R. (2008) 'Rethinking Agricultural Development: The Caribbean Challenge'. Paper presented at 40th Annual Monetary Studies Conference, St. Kitts, 2008.
World Bank-LAC, (2012) 'Agricultural Risk Management in the Caribbean: Lessons and Experiences, 2009–2012', Washington D.C.
World Food Summit (1996) *Rome Declaration on World Food Security*, Rome: FAO.

Index

 Taylor & Francis eBooks

Helping you to choose the right eBooks for your Library

Add Routledge titles to your library's digital collection today. Taylor and Francis ebooks contains over 50,000 titles in the Humanities, Social Sciences, Behavioural Sciences, Built Environment and Law.

Choose from a range of subject packages or create your own!

Benefits for you

>> Free MARC records
>> COUNTER-compliant usage statistics
>> Flexible purchase and pricing options
>> All titles DRM-free.

Benefits for your user

>> Off-site, anytime access via Athens or referring URL
>> Print or copy pages or chapters
>> Full content search
>> Bookmark, highlight and annotate text
>> Access to thousands of pages of quality research at the click of a button.

 Free Trials Available
We offer free trials to qualifying academic, corporate and government customers.

eCollections – Choose from over 30 subject eCollections, including:

Archaeology	Language Learning
Architecture	Law
Asian Studies	Literature
Business & Management	Media & Communication
Classical Studies	Middle East Studies
Construction	Music
Creative & Media Arts	Philosophy
Criminology & Criminal Justice	Planning
Economics	Politics
Education	Psychology & Mental Health
Energy	Religion
Engineering	Security
English Language & Linguistics	Social Work
Environment & Sustainability	Sociology
Geography	Sport
Health Studies	Theatre & Performance
History	Tourism, Hospitality & Events

For more information, pricing enquiries or to order a free trial, please contact your local sales team: **www.tandfebooks.com/page/sales**